CW00460403

Scepticism and Reliable Belief

For my friends
Jonathan & Sabine

# Scepticism and Reliable Belief

José L. Zalabardo

OXFORD
UNIVERSITY PRESS

## OXFORD
### UNIVERSITY PRESS

Great Clarendon Street, Oxford, OX2 6DP,
United Kingdom

Oxford University Press is a department of the University of Oxford.
It furthers the University's objective of excellence in research, scholarship,
and education by publishing worldwide. Oxford is a registered trade mark of
Oxford University Press in the UK and in certain other countries

First Edition published in 2012

Impression: 1

British Library Cataloguing in Publication Data

Data available

Library of Congress Cataloging in Publication Data

Data available

ISBN 978–0–19–965607–3

Printed in Great Britain by
MPG Books Group, Bodmin and King's Lynn

# Contents

# Preface

We take ourselves to know many things. These knowledge self-ascriptions are, of course, not infallible. We accept that we might actually not know some of the things we take ourselves to know. However, we see some of our knowledge claims as more secure than others, and we regard some of them as so secure that if it was shown that our philosophical outlook refutes them we would count this result as strong evidence against our philosophical outlook. Sceptical arguments challenge some of our most unshakable knowledge claims. Hence, if they are sound, they cast serious doubt on our philosophical outlook. This is the reason why many of us have taken sceptical arguments to be philosophically important. Crispin Wright expresses this attitude well when he writes that some sceptical arguments 'signal genuine collisions between features of our thinking which go deep. Their solution has therefore to consist in fundamental change, in taking up conceptual options which may have been overlooked' (Wright 1985: 429–30).

But in order to do this job, sceptical arguments have to be sound—they have to derive their conclusions from true premises by valid inferential steps (according to our deep-seated ways of thinking). And there is a growing consensus among epistemologists that the sceptical arguments on offer do not meet this requirement. This assessment of scepticism is eloquently expressed by Alex Byrne: 'The sceptic is just another guy with a bad argument' (Byrne 2004: 299).

I was always among those who assumed that scepticism could teach us important lessons, and 11 years ago I decided to try to articulate in detail the vague ideas that had convinced me that our philosophical outlook was incompatible with some of our most cherished knowledge claims. I thought this would be a quick, one-paper job. I've done little else since then.

The main obstacle to a cogent sceptical argument seemed to be the reliabilist approach to the analysis of knowledge. Sceptical arguments appeared to rest on assumptions that would be illegitimate if reliabilism were correct. I thought that this obstacle would be easily removed, with a refutation of reliabilism. But my attempts to produce this refutation convinced me that reliabilism was actually correct—that it provided the right account of the basic nature of knowledge. Sceptical arguments could survive only if they could be made compatible with reliabilism.

I tried to save scepticism from this outcome by giving up on the attempt to show that knowledge is impossible, and aiming to show instead that some other epistemic goal is unattainable. However, I failed to identify an epistemic goal that would do the job. Every candidate seemed to exhibit one of two fatal shortcomings: either a plausible reliabilist construal of the goal rendered it feasible, after all, or the conclusion that it was unattainable didn't seem particularly disturbing.[1]

The main goal of this book is to determine whether the threat of scepticism can survive the adoption of the (reliabilist) account of knowledge that I regard as correct. I argue that there is a form of scepticism that passes this test. The basic idea of this sceptical argument is fairly simple. We might have considerable success in the enterprise of forming true beliefs and, if this is so, we have knowledge of the world. However, we can't know that we are successful, even if we are. Beliefs to this effect can't be knowledge—on the reliabilist account of knowledge that I advocate.

Although I came to the analysis of knowledge from the problem of scepticism, I believe that our verdict on a theory of knowledge should be largely independent of how it affects the prospects of sceptical arguments. Hence in the five chapters of the book that are devoted to developing and defending a theory of knowledge, the problem of scepticism doesn't play a prominent role.

The account of knowledge that I put forward uses the theory of probability as its main analytical tool. Knowledge, I argue, is largely a matter of probabilistic links between what we believe and our evidence for it, and between our beliefs (the mental states) and the states of affairs that determine their truth value. However, the book presupposes no prior knowledge of the theory of probability. The material is developed from the ground up, with detailed proofs of the results that I invoke collected in an appendix.

If there is, as I argue, a sound sceptical argument against some unrenounceable knowledge claims, we have evidence, after all, of 'genuine collisions between features of our thinking which go deep'. The next step we need to take is to identify the nature of the problem and the changes that are needed to make it go away. This is work for the future, but in the final chapter I have outlined the direction in which I think the answers to these questions might lie.

The book is organized as follows:

*Chapter 1* introduces the problem of scepticism and provides a preliminary overview of the resources that reliabilism can deploy against the three main lines of sceptical reasoning: the regress argument, arguments based on sceptical hypotheses, and the problem of the criterion. I argue that all these arguments rest on the assumption that knowledge requires adequate evidence, but this assumption would be false if reliabilism were correct.

The fact that reliabilism makes it possible to know in the absence of evidence is seen by many as a reason for abandoning reliabilism. Laurence BonJour has provided important arguments in support of this point. In *Chapter 2* I take issue with BonJour's arguments. I argue that BonJour has failed to show that there is anything wrong in

---

[1] For this approach, and the obstacles it faces, see the exchange between Barry Stroud and Ernest Sosa (Stroud 1989; Sosa 1994; Stroud 1994). See also (Bergmann 2000).

principle with theories of knowledge that make it possible to know in the absence of evidence.

The main ideas of the theory of knowledge that I defend in this book originate with Robert Nozick's tracking account. In *Chapter 3* I argue that there are three main respects in which Nozick's ideas need to be revised. First, a plausible theory of knowledge must attach much more importance to sensitivity (Nozick's clause 3) than to adherence (Nozick's clause 4). Second, truth tracking should not be relativized to the method employed in forming the belief. And third, truth tracking has to be restricted to non-inferential knowledge. Inferential knowledge has to be possible in cases in which the subject's belief doesn't track the truth.

In Chapters 4–6 I present a theory of knowledge based on truth-tracking ideas, modified as required by the conclusions of Chapter 3. In *Chapter 4* I provide an account of how a proposition E has to be related to a proposition H in order to make it possible for someone to know H inferentially on the basis of the evidence provided by E. I argue that the relationship between E and H that does the job is an objective, contingent probabilistic relation.

In *Chapter 5* I address the following question: assuming that E provides adequate support for H, as explicated in Chapter 4, how would a subject have to be related to E and to the relationship between E and H, in order to have inferential knowledge of H based on the evidence provided by E? My preliminary answer to the question is that the subject needs to know E and that E supports H. The bulk of the chapter is devoted to dealing with two problems arising from treating these as sufficient conditions for knowledge. The first is a version of the Gettier problem. The second is the fact that this view would force us to treat Moorean inferences and bootstrapping arguments as cases of inferential knowledge. I introduce two additional conditions on inferential knowledge to deal with these issues.

In *Chapter 6* I present an account of non-inferential knowledge. I argue that non-inferential knowledge can take two forms. The first is truth tracking, construed in terms of conditional probabilities. I consider how the theory can handle the standard counterexamples to tracking accounts. The second form that non-inferential knowledge can take is knowledge by default. I argue that for standing beliefs, those that don't result from the operation of cognitive mechanisms, truth is a sufficient condition for knowledge.

In *Chapter 7* I apply the theory of knowledge developed in Chapters 4–6 to the assessment of sceptical arguments. I show how the theory deals with the regress argument, arguments based on sceptical possibilities, and the problem of the criterion. I then present a form of sceptical reasoning that my theory of knowledge can't block. It concerns, as I suggested above, the epistemic status of my reflective beliefs about the truth value of my first-order beliefs. I argue that if my account of knowledge is correct, these reflective beliefs can't be knowledge.

In *Chapter 8* I explore the possibility that the sceptical problem presented in Chapter 7 can be blamed on a realist conception of cognition as an activity with truth as its goal, with truth construed as independent of human attitudes. I consider first anti-realist attempts to solve the problem by replacing realist truth with a more accessible belief property as the goal of cognition (e.g. warranted assertibility, consensual agreement . . . ). I argue that these construals of cognition face very important difficulties and that they don't really solve the sceptical problem. Then I provide a brief sketch of a 'middle position' between realism and anti-realism that might provide an attractive construal of cognition as well as having the resources for blocking the sceptical argument.

The book ends with an appendix containing proofs of all the results in probability theory invoked in the main text. It can be used as a self-contained introduction to the basic results in the area for readers who are not familiar with it. The proofs presuppose only basic logical and arithmetical knowledge.

In developing these ideas I have profited from conversations or correspondence with Keith DeRose, Miguel Angel Fernández, Sebastian Gardner, Donald Gillies, Bob Hale, Manuel Hernández Iglesias, Carl Hoefer, Franz Huber, Valeriano Iranzo, Mark Kalderon, Jesper Kallestrup, Mike Martin, Sarah Richmond, Gianfranco Soldati, Ernest Sosa, Scott Sturgeon, Andri Toendury, and Crispin Wright. I am especially grateful to Marcus Giaquinto and Dorothy Edgington, for looking at some of the more technical passages of the book and saving me from a few mistakes. Those that remain are of course my own. I have benefitted from the comments of two readers for Oxford University Press: James Beebe and one who remains anonymous. I am also grateful to Peter Momtchiloff, for making the publication process so painless.

I have presented these ideas, at various stages of development, at the University of Murcia, the University of Valencia, the Universidad Nacional Autónoma de México, Trinity College Dublin, Cambridge University, the University of Sheffield, the University of Barcelona, the University of Navarra, a Sequitur conference held at the University of Bern, the University of Manchester, Edinburgh University, the University of Durham, and two Basic Knowledge workshops, one hosted by the Arché Centre at St Andrews University and another hosted by the Northern Institute of Philosophy at the University of Aberdeen. I am grateful to these audiences. In 2010 I gave a series of three seminars at the Northern Institute of Philosophy presenting the central ideas of the book. The book was substantially improved thanks to the feedback I received during those sessions. I have also presented these ideas in my postgraduate seminars at UCL. Discussion during these seminars has led to important improvements. Some passages of the book draw on previously published material. These are: Chapter 2 (Zalabardo 2006), used with kind permission from Springer Science + Business Media; Section 4.2 (Zalabardo 2009a), used with kind permission from Oxford University Press and the Analysis Trust; and Section 8.5 (Zalabardo forthcoming-a), used with kind permission from the Continuum International Publishing Company.

I conducted research that ultimately resulted in this book during periods of leave funded by the Arts and Humanities Research Board, the Arts and Humanities Research Council, and the Mind Association. I am grateful to these institutions for their support.

After a long, frustrating exploratory period, the actual writing of the book was surprisingly quick—less than two years during which I was carrying a full teaching and administrative load at UCL. Achieving this efficiency required a substantial measure of detachment from the outside world, and my outside world is mainly my family: my wife Inma and my children Clara, Alicia, and Damian. The book is dedicated to them, in gratitude for their forbearance.

# 1

# The Problem of Scepticism

## 1.1 Sceptical arguments

We have a sophisticated array of devices that provide us with information about the world. Their operation produces representations of our environment that can inform our behaviour. We generally behave in ways that would satisfy our goals if these representations were true. We time our jaywalking in such a way that if our representation of the traffic were correct we wouldn't get run over. We make presents that would please the recipients if our representation of their tastes were accurate.

These representations are accompanied by varying degrees of awareness. At one extreme we have the distracted driver, whose attention is entirely focused on a conversation but still manages to drive her car in ways that are informed by representations of the relevant factors. At the other extreme we have the person who is deliberately trying to remember a phone number when a number that seems to her to be the right one suddenly pops into her head.

Somewhere in this conglomerate of cognitive activity belongs the concept of belief. Perhaps not all our sub-personal representations of our environment should be counted as beliefs, but it doesn't seem right either to insist on full conscious access for any representation to which we are prepared to extend this treatment. We believe propositions at times at which we are not entertaining them in consciousness. It also seems natural sometimes to ascribe belief in propositions that the subject has never entertained in consciousness. And the phenomenon of self-deception would seem to require occasionally ascribing beliefs that are in conflict with what the subject feels consciously convinced of. So, even though the precise boundaries of the concept are open to debate, the rough area that it occupies is sufficiently clear: beliefs are representations of the world that inform our behaviour for which our conscious feelings of conviction provide incomplete and possibly imperfect but nevertheless generally accurate evidence.

We have a common-sense, pre-theoretical conception of the adequacy of our cognitive devices for the task of producing accurate representations of the world and, in particular, true belief. We think, on the one hand, that there are important limitations to what we can achieve in this area. There are vast regions of reality on which we are unable to gather information, and in many cases there is nothing we can do to improve the situation. We also realize that, even in those regions of reality that generally lie within the scope of our cognitive devices, some of our representations are incorrect. Even in those areas where we take them to work best, we don't regard our cognitive devices as infallible. Furthermore, sometimes non-cognitive factors interfere in the production of these representations. Whether or not you believe that your neighbour is responsible for the litter outside your house may well be affected by how much you like him.

However, in spite of the limitations that we recognize, we ascribe to our cognitive devices a substantial measure of success in the task of forming accurate representations of the world. Our senses, we think, furnish us with very accurate representations of our immediate surroundings, and our faculty of reasoning enables us to infer, from these, generally accurate representations of less immediate matters. In general, we think that there are large areas of reality for which our cognitive devices can produce fairly accurate representations. I am going to use the term *epistemic optimism* to refer to this positive aspect of our pre-theoretical assessment of the adequacy of our cognitive devices for the task of producing accurate representations of the world.

The subject matter of this book is a cluster of phenomena that many have seen as undermining epistemic optimism. These phenomena are simple and familiar. Three will be the main focus of our attention. We will discuss them in great detail later on. Here I only want to offer the briefest characterization.

The first is the claim that there are possible states of the world with the following two features: on the one hand, we are not equipped to detect their obtaining; on the other hand, if they obtained, most of our beliefs would be false and most of our information-gathering devices would be ineffective. The second is the observation that any chain of evidence, or reasons, in which each link is offered in support of the previous one, has to have one of three shapes: either it will have a final link for which no support is offered, or it will continue indefinitely, or it will form a loop, with a link being supported by an item that has appeared earlier in the chain. The third is the thought that if we try to identify evidence in support of the reliability of our basic cognitive devices we can't seem to avoid appealing to information supplied by these devices.

These phenomena have been noticed since the beginning of Western philosophy. They were championed by a philosophical movement in the Hellenistic period whose members referred to themselves as *sceptics*.[1] The challenge to epistemic optimism posed by these phenomena is known as the problem of scepticism. The problem of scepticism is the subject matter of this book.

Epistemic optimism is often expressed in the form of knowledge claims: our cognitive devices have the power to furnish us with knowledge of the world, and many of our beliefs have the status of knowledge as a result. Consequently, challenges to epistemic optimism usually target these knowledge claims, with arguments purporting

---

[1] Our main source for ancient scepticism is (Sextus Empiricus 1990). On the original sceptics see (Hankinson 1995), and the essays collected in (Burnyeat and Frede 1997).

to establish that we don't actually know many of the things that we take ourselves to know. We shall refer to them as *sceptical arguments*.

Sceptical arguments played a very important role in the development of modern philosophy.[2] Their importance resided to a large extent in the perception that they put pressure on the view that the reality that our beliefs purport to represent is fundamentally independent of the procedures that we employ for forming and testing our beliefs. I am going to use the label *realism* to refer to a conception of reality along these lines. It has seemed to many that, if realism were correct, sceptical arguments would force us to abandon epistemic optimism. The point can also be put by saying that sceptical arguments force us to choose between realism and epistemic optimism. Given the intuitive appeal of epistemic optimism, sceptical arguments were often treated as arguments against realism. On this conception, sceptical arguments show that realism has to be abandoned, as this is the only way to preserve epistemic optimism. I am going to refer to this conception of the problem of scepticism as the *anti-realist conception*.[3]

Clearly, showing that epistemic optimism would need to be abandoned if realism were correct doesn't amount to showing that abandoning realism would enable us to save epistemic optimism. It might be that epistemic optimism is simply wrong. Showing that it can be saved by abandoning realism would require articulating a plausible alternative to realism that doesn't fall prey to sceptical arguments, and this project faces formidable obstacles.

The anti-realist conception of the sceptical problem is not as influential nowadays as it once was. This is due in large part to developments in epistemology over the last few decades. The second half of the twentieth century saw the emergence of a family of accounts of knowledge for which I am going to use the label *reliabilism*.[4] Reliabilists see belief as a natural phenomenon—as something that happens to some creatures under certain circumstances. Belief is then part of the natural order, and belief states will be connected by causal/nomological links to other states of affairs. In particular, the state of affairs of S believing that p will be connected in various ways to p, the state of affairs whose obtaining or otherwise determines the truth value of the belief. According to reliabilist accounts of knowledge, whether a true belief has the status of knowledge depends on how S's belief that p is connected with p by the natural order.[5]

The two main extant versions of reliabilism are process reliabilism and tracking accounts. According to process reliabilism, the aspect of the connection between S's belief that p and p that determines whether S knows p is the reliability of the

---

[2] For a fascinating account of this influence, see (Popkin 2003).

[3] The thought that realism has to be abandoned in order to save epistemic optimism is a source of Protagoras's relativism. See (Plato 1963: 152a–b). Other milestones in the development of this idea include Berkeley and Kant. For Berkeley see (Popkin 1951–2). For Kant (Forster 2008).

[4] Seminal sources for reliabilism, and its bearing on sceptical arguments, include (Armstrong 1973; Dretske 1970; Nozick 1981; Goldman 1986).

[5] This approach is directly applicable only to cases in which the state of affairs that p represents is itself part of the natural order. I shall leave this complication aside.

belief-forming method that produced (or sustains) S's belief that p. Very roughly, S's belief that p will have the status of knowledge just in case it was formed with a reliable method (Goldman 1986: 309; 1988). Tracking accounts, by contrast, do not focus in the first instance on the method with which S's belief that p was formed, but on a direct comparison between the circumstances in which p would be true and the circumstances in which S would believe that p. If p is true, and S believes p, S will know p if and only if the circumstances in which S would believe p track in a specific way the circumstances in which p would be true (Nozick 1981).

We will soon scrutinize some versions of reliabilism in considerable detail. However, all that matters at this point is to understand how reliabilism can be claimed to sustain a strategy for dealing with sceptical arguments. An argument against our knowledge claims can be expected to be grounded in the contention that some necessary condition for knowledge is not satisfied. Hence the argument will be cogent only if the condition that plays this role is indeed necessary for knowledge—if knowledge is impossible in its absence. The anti-sceptical power of reliabilism is based on the contention that if reliabilism is correct, then knowledge is possible in circumstances that violate conditions that the sceptical arguments need to treat as necessary for knowledge. Hence reliabilism deprives sceptical arguments of essential premises and defuses the challenge to epistemic optimism.

If sceptical arguments can be refuted in this way, the anti-realist conception of the problem of scepticism rests on a mistake. Even if realism is assumed, sceptical arguments fail to put pressure on epistemic optimism. Sceptical arguments cannot be used to motivate the adoption of alternative metaphysical pictures. Reliabilism can be seen, in this way, as saving realism from the threat of scepticism.

I believe that this assessment of the problem of scepticism is in many respects incontestable. If we consider the versions of reliabilism on offer and the arguments that have been levelled against our knowledge claims, we find that none of the arguments survive the adoption of any of the versions of reliabilism. If one of these versions of reliabilism provided the right account of knowledge, and no other sceptical arguments were available, we would have to conclude that the problem of scepticism has finally been solved—that it was a consequence of our failure to understand the true nature of knowledge.

Now, I think that a version of reliabilism does provide the best account of the concept of knowledge, but the version of reliabilism that I favour is importantly different from those currently on offer. These differences have consequences for the problem of scepticism. The extant sceptical arguments can be defused by my version of reliabilism as well as by any other. However, there is a neglected way of articulating sceptical phenomena as an argument against our knowledge claims that my version of reliabilism cannot refute. If my version of reliabilism is correct, there is a sceptical argument that puts epistemic optimism under genuine pressure.

In the rest of this chapter I want to provide an overview of how reliabilism affects the prospects of the main extant lines of sceptical reasoning. There is a wide range of principles that can be invoked to good effect in arguments against our knowledge claims which would have to be rejected if knowledge were construed along reliabilist lines. They are principles treating certain conditions as necessary for knowledge. If reliabilism were correct, knowledge would be possible in cases in which these conditions are not satisfied.

This situation is exemplified by the principle that in order to know something you need to know that you know it, usually referred to as the KK principle. The KK principle would sustain a compelling line of reasoning against the possibility of knowledge, but if reliabilism is true, the principle is false: it is possible to know something although you don't know that you know it. Another principle in this situation is the claim that knowledge requires that you have some kind of cognitive access to the factors that confer on your belief the status of knowledge. Once again, the principle opens up a range of strategies for refuting our knowledge claims, but reliabilism also invalidates this principle. If reliabilism is true, then a belief can obtain the status of knowledge from factors to which the subject has no cognitive access.

One of the epistemic principles that reliabilism would refute is particularly central to sceptical reasoning. It is the principle that knowing p requires having adequate evidence in support of p. I shall refer to it as the *evidential constraint*. The evidential constraint is clearly incompatible with reliabilism, on any plausible account of when someone counts as having adequate evidence for a proposition. If reliabilism is true, you can know propositions for which you have no adequate evidence. And the evidential constraint plays a fundamental role in all the main lines of sceptical reasoning. My next goal is to show this. I am going to argue that the rejection of the evidential constraint would open major gaps in all the standard lines of reasoning against our knowledge claims. I am going to defend this claim for the lines of argument generated by each of the three sceptical phenomena that I mentioned above. My discussion of these lines of reasoning in the present chapter will rest on assumptions concerning the nature of evidence that strike me as plausible, although they are not by any means universally endorsed. These assumptions will be defended in Chapter 4, where I articulate an account of evidential support.

## 1.2 The epistemic regress argument

I want to consider first the line of reasoning against the possibility of knowledge that can be extracted from the observation that a chain of reasons or evidence can only have one of three shapes. Let p be a proposition that I claim to know. The evidential constraint entails that my claim to knowledge will be correct only if I have adequate evidence in support of p. In subsequent chapters we shall discuss in some detail the conditions under which someone counts as having adequate evidence for a proposition. Here we are only concerned with the features of the concept of evidence that are necessary for generating an argument against the possibility of knowledge.

Adequate evidence for p will consist in a collection of facts suitably related to the state of affairs that would make p true.[6] But being suitably related to p won't suffice for turning these facts into *your* evidence for p. This requires, in addition, that you are suitably related to these facts. One obvious way of satisfying this requirement is to know that these facts obtain—to believe propositions that represent these facts, with your beliefs having the status of knowledge. Let me refer to evidence that requires knowing propositions that represent your evidence as *inferential evidence*.

Notice that knowing your evidence does not require having identified it in consciousness. Believing a proposition, as we've seen, doesn't require entertaining it in consciousness. And beliefs without conscious manifestation could in principle have the status of knowledge. You could count as knowing q even if you haven't entertained in consciousness the proposition that q.

Now, if your evidence for p is inferential, applying the evidential constraint to your knowledge of the evidence will generate a demand for evidence for it. This evidence, in turn, might be inferential, which would generate a fresh demand for evidence. In this way, inferential evidence will generate a structure connecting p with a set of propositions that we know, each proposition in this set for which you have inferential evidence with another set, and so on. Call this your *inferential evidence* (IE) *structure* for p. Let's say that an *evidential chain* for p is a sequence of propositions starting with p, with each subsequent term being a proposition in the set (if any) that your IE structure for p connects with the previous term. Thus an evidential chain for p will contain p, possibly followed by one of the propositions in your evidence for p, possibly followed by one of the propositions in your evidence for this proposition, and so on.

It is an uncontroversial logical fact that an evidential chain for p can only have one of three shapes: either it ends with a proposition that is not connected with a set of propositions by your IE structure for p (call these *terminating chains*), or it closes a loop, with one of its terms followed by a proposition that has already appeared in the chain (call these *circular chains*), or it is infinitely long (call these *infinite chains*). It follows that every chain in your IE structure for any proposition you claim to know will have one of these shapes. The sceptical argument that I am presenting is based on the contention that having adequate evidence for p requires having an IE structure for p none of whose chains is of one of these forms. Since such IE structures are impossible, it follows from this contention that it is impossible to have adequate evidence for any proposition, and using the evidential constraint we can derive from this the conclusion that knowledge is impossible. This line of reasoning is known as the *epistemic regress argument*.[7]

---

[6] A non-obtaining state of affairs can also provide evidential support for p, and the account of evidence that I am going to defend in Chapter 4 will register this feature of the concept. Here I am assuming that the evidence provided by a non-obtaining state of affairs won't be adequate for the purpose of satisfying the evidential constraint on knowledge. See (Warfield 2005) for cases that might contravene this assumption.

[7] This presentation of the regress argument is derived from (Zalabardo 2008). The epistemic regress argument is often formulated in terms of reasons or justification, instead of evidence. If they are to yield the

As we have presented it, the epistemic regress argument has two (non-logical) premises:

1. The evidential constraint.
2. Having adequate evidence for p requires having an IE structure for p with no terminating, circular or infinite chains.

2, together with the logical fact that every evidential chain has to be of one of these forms, entails that you can't have adequate evidence for p. And this, together with the evidential constraint, entails that you can't know p. 1 and 2 validly entail that knowledge is impossible.

Attempts to refute this argument have traditionally targeted Premise 2, arguing that adequate evidence can result from IE structures with evidence chains of one or another of the types that the premise rules out.

The most intuitive and historically prominent line here is to vindicate IE structures with terminating evidence chains.[8] Given our account of inferential evidence, an evidence chain will have to end with a proposition that the subject knows, and in the presence of the evidential constraint this requires that the subject has adequate evidence for it. It follows that the vindication of terminating evidence chains will have to take the form of arguing that inferential evidence is not the only kind of evidence there is—that one can have, in addition, evidence that doesn't consist in facts that you know to obtain. If non-inferential evidence were possible, IE structures with terminating chains would not pose a problem, so long as their end points are propositions for which you have this kind of evidence.[9]

The other two types of evidence chain have also had their advocates. Circular chains have been defended by proponents of the coherence theory of knowledge. On the coherentist position, your evidence for a proposition is not invalidated by the fact that the chains of its IE structure eventually form loops. For the coherentist, an IE structure with this shape might still succeed in providing adequate evidence for a proposition.[10] Even infinite chains have some followers. The claim here is that an IE structure with indefinitely extensible chains can provide adequate evidence for a proposition.[11]

I am not going to try to assess here the prospects of any of these approaches to resisting Premise 2. My main concern is to highlight that resisting Premise 2 is not the only possible strategy for refuting the epistemic regress argument. Even if Premise 2 were correct, the argument against the possibility of knowledge would not hit the mark without the help of the evidential constraint. If the evidential constraint is not

result that knowledge is impossible, these versions of the argument will need to invoke a principle analogous to the evidential constraint, connecting reasons or justification with knowledge.

[8] An early instance of this position appears in (Aristotle 1994: chapter 3).

[9] Laurence BonJour has recently advocated this approach. See (BonJour 1999). For a classical version of the view, see (Price 1932).

[10] For a defence of this reaction to the regress argument, see (BonJour 1985).

[11] A view along these lines has been advocated by Peter Klein (Klein 1998, 1999).

assumed, we won't be able to derive the conclusion that you don't know a proposition from the premise that you don't have adequate evidence for it. If the evidential constraint is false, it is possible to have knowledge in the absence of adequate evidence.[12]

Notice also that the sceptic cannot react to this by settling for the contention that, although we might be able to know things, we won't be able to have adequate evidence for them. The argument for the impossibility of adequate evidence based on Premise 2 is also disturbed by the rejection of the evidential constraint. If knowledge does not require adequate evidence, then terminating chains do not pose a problem—IE structures with terminating chains will be able to generate adequate evidence, so long as their end points are propositions that the subject knows in the absence of evidence.

In sum, if the evidential constraint is false, the epistemic regress argument can't be used to show that knowledge is impossible or that we don't have adequate evidence for our beliefs.

## 1.3 Sceptical possibilities

I want to consider next sceptical arguments based on the observation that there are possible situations in which most of our beliefs would be undetectably false. Situations of this type are described by *sceptical hypotheses*. The most famous sceptical hypothesis is Descartes' evil demon hypothesis, according to which

[...] some malicious demon of the utmost power and cunning has employed all his energies in order to deceive me. [...] the sky, the air, the earth, colours, shapes, sounds and all external things are merely delusions of dreams that he has devised to ensnare my judgement. (Descartes 1984: 15)

More recently, Hilary Putnam has provided another illustration of the same idea:

[...] imagine that a human being (you can imagine this to be yourself) has been subjected to an operation by an evil scientist. The person's brain (your brain) has been removed from the body and placed in a vat of nutrients which keeps the brain alive. The nerve endings have been connected to a super-scientific computer which causes the person whose brain it is to have the illusion that everything is perfectly normal. There seem to be people, objects, the sky, etc; but really all the person (you) is experiencing is the result of electronic impulses travelling from the computer to the nerve endings. (Putnam 1981: 5–6)

As Anthony Brueckner points out, there are two different ways in which one might try to exploit the intuition that sceptical hypotheses describe real possibilities in an argument against your knowledge claims (Brueckner 1994). The first is based on the

---

[12] This strategy for using a reliabilist account of knowledge against the regress argument was first presented by David Armstrong (Armstrong 1973).

contention that sceptical possibilities undermine your claim to have adequate evidence for many propositions that you take yourself to know. The second seeks to derive the conclusion that you don't know these things from the premise that you don't know that sceptical hypotheses don't obtain. Let's consider each of these possibilities in turn.

The central premise of an argument that follows the first approach is the claim that any evidence that you might gather for many of your everyday beliefs is rendered inadequate by the existence of sceptical possibilities. A proper assessment of this claim will have to wait until we have an account of the conditions under which someone counts as having adequate evidence for a proposition. Here I only want to point out that the claim does not follow from the observation that your evidence is compatible with sceptical hypotheses and that these would make your beliefs false. As Brueckner observes (1994: 835), this entailment would hold only if adequate evidence for p had to be incompatible with any situation in which p is false, but this would be so only if evidence had to be deductive in order to count as adequate. All empirical evidence for a proposition is compatible with situations that would make the proposition false. If empirical evidence were incapable of bestowing on a belief the status of knowledge, many of our knowledge claims would be very vulnerable indeed. But this is not the line we are going to take here. We are going to assume that empirical evidence is capable of turning a true belief into knowledge, and hence that evidence can have this power even if it is compatible with situations that would make your belief false. A cogent refutation of our knowledge claims would have to respect this point.

It follows that sceptical hypotheses don't render your evidence for your beliefs inadequate simply by virtue of the fact that they are compatible with the evidence but would make your beliefs false. Showing that sceptical hypotheses have this effect would require a more involved argument. Several lines of reasoning are available at this point, but we will delay our discussion of them until we have a workable account of when someone counts as having adequate evidence for a proposition.

In any case, the outcome of this discussion doesn't have a direct bearing on our concerns. Even if sceptical hypotheses could be used to show that we can't have adequate evidence for many of the propositions we believe, deriving from this a refutation of our knowledge claims concerning these propositions clearly requires appealing to the evidential constraint. In its absence, the sceptic wouldn't be able to advance from the claim that you don't have adequate evidence for a proposition to the conclusion that you don't know it. Hence, since reliabilism invalidates the evidential constraint, it renders this kind of challenge to our knowledge claims thoroughly unpromising, whether or not sceptical hypotheses are taken to undermine the adequacy of our evidence for propositions that we think we know.

The second approach to using sceptical hypotheses to undermine knowledge claims seeks to obtain this result with the contention that we don't know that sceptical hypotheses don't obtain. The template for this line of reasoning is exemplified by the following argument, where BIV is the proposition that you are a brain in a Putnamian vat and HANDS is the proposition that you have hands:

1.  You don't know ~BIV.
2.  If you don't know ~BIV you don't know HANDS.

Therefore:

3.  You don't know HANDS.

Thus formulated, the argument is clearly valid. Hence it would only fail to establish its conclusion if its premises weren't all true.

Premise 2 is typically supported by reference to the principle of the closure of knowledge under known entailment (Closure, for short). Closure, in its simplest form, dictates that whenever you know that a proposition p entails a proposition q, if you know p you also know q:

Closure: If you know p and you know that p entails q, then you know q.

Contraposing on Closure yields Premise 2 immediately. Given that you know that HANDS entails ~BIV, since you know that envatted brains don't have hands, Closure dictates that if you didn't know ~BIV you wouldn't know HANDS either, as Premise 2 claims.

We are going to discuss Closure in some detail later on. Support for the principle is by no means unanimous, and some advocates of a principle along these lines would favour different formulations.[13] All that matters for our immediate purposes is that the plausibility of Premise 2 is directly dependent on the plausibility of principles along the lines of Closure. On the one hand, any principle recognizable as a version of Closure will underwrite Premise 2. On the other hand, the rejection of Closure principles will leave Premise 2 without obvious support, leading to the collapse of this line of sceptical reasoning.

Several authors have expressed the suspicion that Closure cannot be the right explanation of the plausibility of claims along the lines of Premise 2 (DeRose 1995: 32; Pryor 2000: 522). The problem is that Closure supports a claim of the form *if you don't know ~BIV you don't know p* only if you know that p is incompatible with BIV, and this requires, in turn, that p is as a matter of fact incompatible with BIV. However, it might seem that if knowing that you are not a brain in a vat is required for knowing that you have hands, it will also be required for knowing other propositions that are not incompatible with BIV. Take, for example, the proposition that there is a chair in the room. This proposition is not incompatible with BIV, as a vat containing a brain can be placed in a room that also contains a chair. Hence Closure cannot be invoked in support of the claim that if you don't know ~BIV you don't know that there's a chair in the room. However, this claim seems as plausible as Premise 2 of our sample

---

[13] Opponents of Closure include Fred Dretske and Robert Nozick (Dretske 1970; Nozick 1981). For alternative formulations of the principle see (Hawthorne 2005; Kvanvig 2006).

argument and one would expect both claims to be grounded in similar features of the situation.

One could try to provide a uniform treatment of these cases by appeal to principles that are stronger than Closure, but as Jonathan Vogel argues (2004: 435–6), this strategy faces serious difficulties.[14] An alternative approach would be to reflect that while Closure cannot be used to support the claim that if you don't know ~BIV you don't know that there is a chair in the room, one can easily formulate other sceptical hypotheses that are incompatible with the presence of a chair in the room. Take, for example, the proposition that you are a brain in a vat in a chairless room. Closure clearly supports the proposition that if you don't know that this hypothesis doesn't obtain you don't know that there's a chair in the room. But knowing that this hypothesis doesn't obtain seems to be just as problematic as knowing ~BIV. So long as we are flexible with which sceptical hypothesis we use in each case, Closure sustains a uniform treatment of all instances of this line of sceptical reasoning.

I have argued that, in the presence of Closure, Premise 2 of the sceptical argument is irresistible. How about Premise 1? How could one support the claim that you don't know you are not a brain in a vat? One obvious approach is to argue that you don't have adequate evidence for ~BIV. Once again, a proper assessment of this claim will have to wait until we have developed our account of evidence. Nevertheless, we can see that the claim that you don't have adequate evidence for ~BIV has more intuitive appeal than the corresponding claim for HANDS. One way to bring out this intuitive contrast is to reflect that prior to engaging in sceptical reasoning you are convinced that things would not look the way they look if HANDS were false, whereas anyone who understands the brain-in-a-vat hypothesis realizes that things would look just as they do if ~BIV were true. This suggests that it would be possible to be convinced that how things look doesn't provide you with evidence for ~BIV without accepting that you don't have adequate evidence for HANDS.

However, it is clear that a defence of Premise 1 along these lines is immediately vulnerable to the rejection of the evidential constraint. The result that you don't have adequate evidence for ~BIV would have no tendency to support the claim that you don't know this proposition unless adequate evidence were required for knowledge, as the evidential constraint dictates. Rejecting the evidential constraint opens the possibility of maintaining that you know ~BIV even though you don't have adequate evidence in support of this proposition. Hence, once more, reliabilism blocks this sceptical challenge to our knowledge claims.

This is not to say, however, that every version of reliabilism will allow us to say that you know ~BIV in the absence of evidence. Some versions of reliabilism might restrict the range of propositions that can be known in the absence of evidence in ways that exclude ~BIV from this treatment. These restrictions, if correct, would sustain a weaker

---

[14]  A strategy along these lines is discussed by Barry Stroud (1984: 25–30).

surrogate of the evidential constraint that would provide adequate support for Premise 1. We won't be able to assess the relevance of this point until we consider which version of reliabilism is correct. Our conclusion at this stage is simply that an argument that seeks to support Premise 1 with the evidential constraint, without restricting its scope, will not survive the adoption of reliabilism. It remains to be seen whether the version of reliabilism that I will recommend will sustain a modified version of this argument for Premise 1.

Premise 1 has also been defended with a different line of reasoning that doesn't rest on the assumption that knowledge requires adequate evidence. It appeals instead to the kind of fact that reliabilists invoke in their account of knowledge—the correlation between beliefs and the states of affairs that make them true. Let's say that your true belief that p is *sensitive* just in case the following subjunctive conditional holds: if p were false you wouldn't believe p. According to standard tracking accounts of knowledge, sensitivity is a necessary condition for knowledge: if it is the case that if p were false you would still believe it, then your belief that p can't be knowledge.[15]

The claim that sensitivity is necessary for knowledge sustains a straightforward argument against the claim that you know ~BIV. Notice that the following is an essential feature of the brain-in-a-vat hypothesis: if you were a brain in a vat, you would believe that you are not one. This means that your belief in ~BIV is not sensitive. If ~BIV were false you would still believe it. Hence, if sensitivity is necessary for knowledge, it follows that you don't know ~BIV, and this result has now been obtained without invoking the evidential constraint.

It follows from this that some versions of reliabilism sustain a line of reasoning in support of Premise 1 of the sceptical argument. However, it might be that embracing this line is ultimately detrimental to the sceptic's overall argumentative strategy (Brueckner 1994: 828). The reason is that the intuitions that support these versions of reliabilism can also be used to undermine the principle of Closure. If this is right, then the positions that sustain this argument in favour of Premise 1 would also deprive Premise 2 of support. We shall discuss this issue in some detail later on, but the basic point can be appreciated by considering a simplistic version of reliabilism that takes sensitivity as both necessary and sufficient for knowledge. In order for this account to accommodate Closure, sensitive belief would have to be closed under known entailment. That is, the following principle would have to hold universally:

If S's belief that p is sensitive and S knows that p entails q, then S's belief that q is sensitive.

On the simplistic reliabilist account that we are considering, any counterexample to this principle would be a counterexample to Closure. And this principle has

---

[15]   The idea, which we shall examine in great detail later on, is due to Robert Nozick (Nozick 1981). He refers to what we are calling *sensitivity* as *variation*, using the term *sensitivity* as synonymous with truth tracking. The label *sensitivity* is used as I am proposing by, e.g., Keith DeRose (1995: 27) and Tim Williamson (2000: 148).

counterexamples. Let p be the proposition that I'm typing on my computer, and let q be the proposition that my computer wasn't replaced with an identical replica (by invisible aliens, say) while I went to get a coffee. My belief in p is sensitive, since if it were false, if I wasn't typing on my computer, I wouldn't believe that I am. But my belief in q is insensitive: if invisible aliens had performed the swap in my absence I would still believe that I am typing on my computer.

The crucial point here is to realize that the sensitivity of my belief in p is not undermined by the fact that if aliens had done their trick I would believe p. The sensitivity of my belief in p depends on whether I would believe p if p were false, and everything else were, as far as possible, as it is in actuality. This is the application to sensitivity of a general point about the semantics of subjunctive conditionals.[16] The proposition that if I had had a puncture I would have been late for work is not made false by the fact that if I had had a puncture and the provost had sent a helicopter to take me to work I wouldn't have been late. In the same way, the proposition that if I wasn't typing on my computer I wouldn't believe that I am is not made false by the fact that if I wasn't typing on my computer and aliens had intervened I would believe that I am typing on my computer.

It follows that, on the simplistic version of reliabilism, Closure fails, and Premise 2 of the sceptical argument is deprived of its usual support. In fact, Premise 2 is not simply left unsupported. On this account of knowledge, Premise 2 is false, since your belief that you have hands is sensitive, but your belief that you are not a brain in a vat is not.

I have argued that the adoption of a version of reliabilism that takes sensitivity as its central notion would provide a line of support for Premise 1 that doesn't rely on the evidential constraint, but an account of knowledge along these lines might be detrimental to the sceptic's overall argumentative strategy, as it threatens to undermine Premise 2. This is exactly the situation for Robert Nozick's account of knowledge— the most prominent sensitivity-based version of reliabilism. Nozick uses his account of knowledge to defend the view that Premise 1 is true but Premise 2 is false. Nevertheless, other sensitivity-based accounts of knowledge have avoided this verdict, as they incorporate features that refute Premise 1 and/or save Premise 2. We shall consider some of the possibilities in great detail later on.

In sum, the overall situation concerning the form of sceptical reasoning under consideration is this: the rejection of the evidential constraint would deprive Premise 1 of one major source of support, although restricted versions of the principle might be invoked to plug the gap in the sceptical reasoning. Alternatively, the sceptic might try to find support for Premise 1 in a sensitivity constraint on knowledge. This line of reasoning would be accepted by some versions of reliabilism, but the features of the concept of knowledge that provide this support for Premise 1 might also be used to undermine Premise 2.

---

[16] I will discuss this point in more detail in Chapter 3.

## 1.4 The criterion

Let's consider next the line of reasoning against our knowledge claims that can be extracted from the observation that when we try to gather evidence for the reliability of our basic cognitive devices we seem forced to invoke evidence delivered by these very same devices. In order to assess this observation we would have to focus on specific cognitive devices. For the case of sense perception, the claim has been cogently defended by William Alston, and we shall assume here for the sake of the argument that the claim is correct (Alston 1993). I want to argue, however, that the crucial point is not that the evidence for the reliability of sense perception is obtained using sense perception, but that the sanction of sense perception is the only evidence that we can adduce in support of this evidence.[17] Let p be an essential component of your evidence for the proposition that sense perception is reliable, and suppose that the fact that it has been sanctioned by sense perception is your only evidence for p. Then the IE structure for the proposition that sense perception is reliable will contain a chain starting like this:

1. Sense perception is reliable
2. p
3. p is sanctioned by sense perception.

Let's assume that there is no problem concerning knowledge of the proposition that p has been sanctioned by sense perception. I want to consider, on this assumption, whether an IE structure containing this chain can provide adequate evidence for the reliability of sense perception.

I think it's clear that if there is a difficulty it concerns the involvement of 1 in the transition from 3 to 2. The issue here is that the sanction of sense perception provides evidence for a proposition only if sense perception is reliable. In fact, the claim that the sanction of sense perception provides evidence for a proposition can be taken to be *equivalent* to the proposition that sense perception is reliable. The question that we need to address is whether this circumstance invalidates this evidential chain.

Some epistemologists have argued that it doesn't—that there is a crucial difference between the kind of circularity that we obtain when we use as evidence a proposition that has already appeared in the chain (sometimes known as *premise circularity*) and the kind of circularity that obtains when the proposition that the evidence that you produce is adequate has already appeared in the chain (sometimes known as *rule circularity*). According to this position, while premise circularity invalidates an IE structure, rule circularity doesn't have this effect: IE structures with rule-circular chains might still provide adequate evidence.[18]

---

[17] On Stewart Cohen's influential presentation of the problem, the difficulty arises when knowledge of the reliability of, say, sense perception is based on knowledge that has been acquired with sense perception (Cohen 2002). I want to suggest that knowledge acquired with sense perception for which I had non-sensory evidence would be a perfectly legitimate basis for knowledge of the reliability of sense perception.

[18] Versions of this position have been defended by James Van Cleve and David Papineau (Van Cleve 1979, 1984; Papineau 1992).

From this point of view, the presence of the 1–2–3 sequence in the IE structure for 1 doesn't pose a problem. The involvement of 1 in the transition from 3 to 2 means that your evidence for 1 is rule circular, but if rule circularity is innocuous, this doesn't pose a threat to the adequacy of your evidence for 1.

I can't see that the distinction between premise circularity and rule circularity can be made to carry this weight. Notice that one consequence of this line is that the adequacy of your evidence for the reliability of sense perception would depend on a seemingly trivial point of formulation. If, on the one hand, we included the claim that sense perception is reliable as an additional premise in our argument for p, the resulting IE structure would be premise circular. If, on the other hand, the reliability of sense perception were treated as the inference principle that underwrites the transition from 3 to 2, the resulting IE structure would only be rule circular. I don't think one can plausibly claim that the second of these IE structures can produce adequate evidence but the first can't. A ban on circular IE structures should be extended to the inference principles that underwrite each inferential step, and if we take this step, it follows that we can't obtain adequate evidence for the reliability of sense perception.

The point that rule circularity is as detrimental as premise circularity can also be grounded in a claim about evidence that I shall endorse in subsequent chapters:

(*) q provides you with adequate evidence for p only if you know that q supports p.

If (*) is correct, assuming that evidence has to be inferential,[19] q will provide you with adequate evidence for p only if (a) you know q and (b) you know that q supports p. Now the only consequence of the contrast between premise circularity and rule circularity is which of these two necessary conditions for adequate evidence generates the problem. If your evidence for the reliability of sense perception is premise circular, it will violate condition (a). If it is rule circular, it will violate condition (b).

The result that we can't obtain adequate evidence for the reliability of sense perception can then be invoked to argue that we can't obtain adequate evidence for many of our beliefs. The problem here is that our IE structures for many propositions would reach sooner or later claims to the effect that a certain proposition has been sanctioned by sense perception. This can be argued to be an essential feature of evidence that we can classify as empirical. To see this as a problem we need to invoke principle (*). We are considering evidence chains with the following shape:

p
.
.
.
q
q has been sanctioned by sense perception.

---

[19] See Section 1.2, above.

If (⋆) is correct, this chain will produce adequate evidence only if you know that the sanction of sense perception supports q, that is, that sense perception is reliable. But in the presence of the evidential constraint this would require having adequate evidence for the reliability of sense perception and, as we have seen, such evidence is not to be had. It follows that empirical evidence is impossible and, by another application of the evidential constraint, that we can't know any proposition for which we can only provide empirical evidence.

As we have pointed out, there are some controversial steps in the line of reasoning that derives from the evidential constraint the impossibility of empirical knowledge. But be this as it may, if the evidential constraint were rejected the argument would collapse.[20] First of all, in the absence of the evidential constraint, the impossibility of empirical evidence would not threaten the possibility of empirical knowledge, since knowledge of empirical propositions would in principle be possible even if we didn't have adequate evidence for them.

Furthermore, empirical evidence might also be saved by the rejection of the evidential constraint. Rejecting the evidential constraint opens the possibility of knowing that sense perception is reliable in the absence of evidence for this proposition, and this would remove the difficulty that we have been discussing with empirical IE structures. On the resulting picture, we wouldn't be able to have adequate evidence for the proposition that sense perception is reliable, but we would still be able to know this proposition, and this would enable us to use the sanction of sense perception in adequate IE structures. Empirical knowledge and empirical evidence would both be saved.

Notice, however, that, as with the proposition that a sceptical hypothesis doesn't obtain, we might find that a restricted version of the evidential constraint restores the link between evidence and knowledge for the proposition that sense perception is reliable. An adequate assessment of the position that I am outlining will have to wait until this possibility has been considered.

My goal in the last three sections has been to provide an outline of the consequences of adopting a reliabilist account of knowledge for the assessment of the three main lines of sceptical reasoning. I have considered the bearing on these sceptical arguments of a prominent consequence of reliabilist accounts of knowledge—the rejection of the

---

[20] The involvement of the evidential constraint in the problem of the criterion is not so prominently displayed in Stewart Cohen's presentation. However, the constraint is also required for generating Cohen's version of the problem. According to Cohen, one of the sources of the problem is the following view:

(C) Our knowledge that sense perception is reliable has to be based on knowledge that we have acquired by sense perception (Cohen 2002: 309).

I think that we can safely assume that, by one piece of knowledge being based on another piece of knowledge, Cohen is referring here to an evidential link. Now, on the assumption that any otherwise plausible evidence for the reliability of sense perception will have been acquired by sense perception, the evidential constraint yields (C) immediately. However, it is hard to see how (C) could be supported in the absence of the evidential constraint, as we would have no obvious means of ruling out the possibility that knowledge that sense perception is reliable is not based on any other knowledge.

evidential constraint. I have argued that all three forms of sceptical reasoning rely heavily on the evidential constraint and hence that rejecting this principle would seriously undermine the prospects of the sceptical cause. We have seen that there are several ways in which the second and third lines might still be revived within the context of a reliabilist account of knowledge. The assessment of these strategies will have to wait until we have a much more detailed picture of the version of reliabilism that I am going to recommend. Once this picture is in place, we will see that none of these strategies can be used to reinstate these lines of sceptical reasoning. I will argue, however, that a form of sceptical argument different from the ones we have considered here does manage to pose a threat to our knowledge claims that doesn't collapse with the adoption of my favoured form of reliabilism. I shall concentrate on the assessment of this line of reasoning against the background of the version of reliabilism that I regard as correct.

# 2

# Reliabilism and the Evidential Constraint

We saw in Chapter 1 that reliabilist accounts of knowledge typically license the rejection of the evidential constraint—the principle that knowing p requires being in possession of adequate evidence for p. We also saw that the rejection of the evidential constraint seriously undermines the prospects of scepticism, as the evidential constraint plays an important role in the three main lines of reasoning against our knowledge claims.

The incompatibility of reliabilism and the evidential constraint is not generally questioned, but this connection can be invoked in both directions. The line I am going to take in this book is that, since a version of reliabilism provides the best analysis of knowledge, the evidential constraint should be abandoned. Others, however, have sought to invoke the same connection in the opposite direction. They have argued that, since the evidential constraint is independently plausible, the fact that reliabilism is incompatible with it should be treated as a reason for rejecting reliabilism.

The most prominent advocate of this line of reasoning against reliabilism has been Laurence BonJour. He has provided a sophisticated argument for the conclusion that reliabilism has to be rejected because it licenses the ascription of knowledge to subjects who have no evidence or reasons for their beliefs. The goal of the present chapter is to clarify and assess BonJour's line of reasoning.[1]

BonJour focuses his discussion on process reliabilism, and I shall follow him in this, although if his argument is successful other forms of reliabilism will also be undermined. As we saw in Chapter 1, the basic idea of process reliabilism is that whether a true belief has the status of knowledge depends on the reliability of the cognitive devices employed in forming (or sustaining) it. To have some plausibility, an account of knowledge along these lines would have to exhibit a considerable degree of complexity. However, for our immediate purposes, all that matters is that the account entails that if a true belief has been formed with a reliable procedure, then it is knowledge, at least in some circumstances in which the subject might not have adequate evidence for the

---

[1]  The argument of this chapter was first presented in (Zalabardo 2006).

belief. By (*process*) *reliabilism*, I shall refer to any account of knowledge which entails a principle along these lines.

The reliability of the procedure with which a belief has been formed wouldn't by itself furnish the subject with adequate evidence for the belief. Knowledge of the reliability of the procedure would have this effect, but a belief could have been reliably formed even if the subject doesn't know, or even believe, that this is so. Hence process reliabilism would license violations of the evidential constraint.

## 2.1 Intuitions

BonJour's attack on reliabilism is based on a series of well-known thought experiments involving subjects with the power of clairvoyance. The central case in BonJour's argument is that of Norman:

Norman, under certain conditions which usually obtain, is a completely reliable clairvoyant with respect to certain kinds of subject matter. He possesses no evidence or reasons of any kind for or against the general possibility of such a cognitive power or for or against the thesis that he possesses it. One day Norman comes to believe that the President is in New York City, although he has no evidence either for or against this belief. In fact the belief is true and results from his clairvoyant power under circumstances in which it is completely reliable. (BonJour 1985: 41)

BonJour clearly believes that our intuitions regarding this case undermine reliabilism. What is much less clear is the precise route by which he expects this conclusion to be reached.

A particularly straightforward strategy for adjudicating the contest between the evidential constraint and reliabilism is by appeal to our intuitions concerning the ascription of knowledge in specific circumstances. For this purpose, we would need to concentrate on cases in which a belief satisfies the sufficient condition for knowledge postulated by reliabilism, but not the necessary condition for knowledge laid down by the evidential constraint, that is, cases of reliably formed true belief for which the subject has no adequate evidence. If intuition regarding these cases dictated that the beliefs in question are knowledge, this could be taken as evidence against the evidential constraint and, less directly, for reliabilism. If, on the contrary, intuition dictated that these beliefs are not knowledge, we could take this result as undermining reliabilism and, less directly, as supporting the evidential constraint. I shall refer to this strategy as the *intuitive approach*. One way to construe BonJour's argument against reliabilism is as an application of the intuitive approach. My goal in this section is to articulate this construal and to assess the resulting antireliabilist argument.

One difficulty faced by the intuitive approach is that it is remarkably hard to find real cases which both parties agree to describe as satisfying the reliable-formation condition but not the evidential constraint. The reliable-formation condition would be satisfied by cases in which a belief was formed as a result of the operation of a basic cognitive device that is reliable, such as properly functioning perceptual devices, or introspection.

But the problem with these cases is that it is open to the proponent of the evidential constraint to argue that the subject has adequate evidence for these beliefs, typically taking the form of a belief identifying the procedure with which the target belief has been formed and a belief in the reliability of this procedure. Take, for example, Alicia's belief that a train is approaching the platform, formed by her highly reliable visual device for the detection of events of this kind. If the reliabilist tried to appeal to our intuition that Alicia knows that a train is approaching the platform as supporting her position, the advocate of the evidential constraint could reply that it would be illegitimate to interpret the intuition in this way. She would explain the intuition instead as resting on a background assumption to the effect that Alicia has adequate evidence for her belief. For in normal conditions we would expect Alicia to believe that her belief that a train is approaching the platform was formed with the relevant visual device, and that this device is reliable. Furthermore, we would expect these beliefs of hers to be knowledge. Clearly, if this assumption is playing a role in generating our intuition, it cannot be counted as lending support to reliabilism or undermining the evidential constraint.

We could of course stipulate that Alicia doesn't have adequate evidence for her belief, but it is questionable whether this stipulation would be effective in insulating our intuitions from the background assumption that the stipulation is meant to suspend. It is open to the proponent of the evidential constraint to argue that, if we still have the intuition that Alicia knows that a train is approaching the platform after stipulating that Alicia doesn't have adequate evidence for her belief, the reason is that the stipulation hasn't succeeded in neutralizing the effect on our intuitions of the background assumption that she does have adequate evidence. Let me refer to the possibility that our stipulations concerning a thought experiment might not have the intended effect on our intuitions as the problem of *intuition contamination*.

In sum, the attempt to use the intuitive approach to adjudicate the contest between reliabilism and the evidential constraint can be expected to generate the following dialectic. First, the reliabilist will claim that the method supports her position, on the grounds that we have stable intuitions to the effect that when a true belief has been formed by one of our basic cognitive devices, and the device is reliable, the belief has the status of knowledge. But even if she concedes that we have these intuitions, the evidentialist can object to the reliabilist's attempt to use them in her favour, arguing that they are to be explained instead by reference to a background assumption to the effect that in such cases the subject typically has adequate evidence for her belief. The reliabilist might then argue that these intuitions survive the stipulation that the subject doesn't have adequate evidence, but the evidentialist could question the significance of this fact, explaining it as a case of intuition contamination.

The only way forward for the intuitive approach appears to be to find cases of reliably formed belief where we have no overwhelming intuitive inclination to say that the subject has adequate evidence for her belief. If intuition favours the ascription of knowledge in these cases, the evidentialist won't be able to appeal to intuition contamination to rescue her position. If, on the contrary, intuition dictates that in these cases we shouldn't ascribe knowledge, the evidentialist could claim that her objections to the intuitions that appear to support reliabilism have been vindicated.

BonJour's introduction of his clairvoyance cases appears to be motivated by these reflections. His goal is to avoid the unfair advantage that intuition contamination would give to the reliabilist in more familiar cases. 'Cases involving sense-perception and introspection', he tells us 'are [...] not very suitable for an intuitive assessment of externalism, since one central issue between externalism and other [...] views is precisely whether in such cases a further basis for justification beyond the externalist one is typically present' (BonJour 1985: 37–8).[2] To avoid this difficulty, we need to concentrate on cases 'for which it will be easier to stipulate in a way which will be effective on an intuitive level that *only* the externalist sort of justification is present' (BonJour 1985: 38).

Norman's case appears to fit the bill perfectly. His true belief that the President is in New York City exhibits the features that are required for the application of the intuitive approach. On the one hand, the belief has been formed by a reliable procedure—Norman's powers—thereby satisfying the sufficient condition for knowledge postulated by the reliabilist.[3] On the other, the evidential constraint is not satisfied, as Norman doesn't have adequate evidence for his belief. BonJour considers two versions of the case (BonJour 1985: 41–2). In the first version, Norman takes himself to have evidence for his belief that the President is in New York City, since he believes it to have been formed with his clairvoyant faculty and he believes that this faculty is reliable. However this evidence is not adequate, as Norman's belief in the reliability of his clairvoyant faculty doesn't have the status of knowledge. In the second version, Norman doesn't even take himself to have evidence for his belief, since he doesn't believe that he has the power of clairvoyance.

Furthermore, applying the intuitive approach to this case won't raise the difficulties that we encounter when we consider more familiar cognitive devices such as sense perception. Reliabilists won't obtain an unfair advantage from intuition contamination in this case, since we have no irresistible inclination to assume that Norman has adequate evidence for his belief. Hence if intuition dictated that Norman doesn't know that the President is in New York City, the evidentialist could claim that, once it is properly applied, the intuitive approach adjudicates in favour of her position. I am not going to discuss whether intuition actually dictates that Norman's belief can't be knowledge. I am going to assume that it does,[4] and argue that it is open to the reliabilist to resist the thought that this outcome puts real pressure on her position.

---

[2] Cf. also (BonJour 1985: 50).

[3] Goldman has resisted this point. See below.

[4] At least in his initial reaction to BonJour's cases, Goldman seemed to concede the strength of this intuition. See below.

My proposal is that the reliabilist could contend that in moving from sense perception and introspection to clairvoyance, we may have removed one potential source of contamination—but only to replace it with another one which distorts our intuitions in the opposite direction. The problem is that many of us have a deep-seated conviction that clairvoyance doesn't exist, that its possibility is ruled out by some central elements of our world-view, and that evidence for this assessment is readily available. Of course, in the Norman case we stipulate that these assumptions are false, but it is open to the reliabilist to argue that these stipulations might not succeed in insulating our intuitions from the assumptions that they are meant to neutralize.

There are two particular aspects of the case where contamination might be suspected. The first is the claim that Norman has real clairvoyant powers. As some authors have suggested, many of us find it very hard to imagine a world in which clairvoyance is possible. If this is so, there is reason to suspect that our negative verdict on Norman's belief is informed by our inability to suspend disbelief in the existence of clairvoyance. According to this diagnosis, the reason why we don't think Norman knows is not that we don't take reliable formation to be sufficient for knowledge, but that we can't bring ourselves to assume that his belief has been formed with a reliable mechanism.[5]

The second feature of the case that might raise the suspicion of contamination is the claim that Norman doesn't have adequate evidence for the proposition that he doesn't have clairvoyant powers. Notice that if he had such evidence, then reliabilism could easily accommodate the intuition that Norman doesn't know that the President is in New York City. On Goldman's version of the position, the definition of knowledge incorporates a *non-undermining provision*, according to which a reliably formed belief wouldn't be knowledge if the subject had evidence against the reliability of the procedure with which it has been formed (Goldman 1986: 62–3).[6] Hence, if Norman had evidence against the proposition that he has clairvoyant powers, the intuition that his belief isn't knowledge would be in line with Goldman's account. BonJour accepts this, and the stipulation that Norman doesn't have any evidence or reasons against the existence of clairvoyance or against the hypothesis that he possesses it is explicitly designed to block this reliabilist rejoinder. Goldman's original response to the case was to maintain that Norman does have evidence against the hypothesis that he has clairvoyant powers, and hence that his non-undermining provision can deal with the case (Goldman 1986: 112), although he has later seemed less confident in this reply (Goldman 1991). However, even if we concede to the evidentialist the right to stipulate that Norman has no evidence against clairvoyance, we can still question the power of this stipulation to protect our intuitions from contamination, given that we

---

[5]   Robert Fogelin has endorsed this diagnosis (Fogelin 1994: 45). Cf. also (Vogel 2000: 608).

[6]   Notice that the non-undermining provision doesn't force the reliabilist to embrace the evidential constraint, since the resulting view still makes room for the possibility of knowing p when the subject lacks adequate evidence for p.

are inclined to assume that a standard belief system provides adequate evidence for the proposition that clairvoyance doesn't exist.[7]

In sum, the reliabilist can resist the anti-reliabilist application of the intuitive approach based on Norman's case with the same tools that the evidentialist deployed to resist the pro-reliabilist application. The anti-reliabilist significance of our intuitions in Norman's case, like the pro-reliabilist significance of our intuitions in the case of sense perception, is tainted by the suspicion of contamination.

## 2.2 Perfect pitch

One might feel at this point that the attempt to use the intuitive approach to adjudicate the contest between reliabilism and the evidential constraint should be abandoned, for lack of cases that neither party is likely to impugn as marred by contamination. However, I want to suggest that cases that don't raise this difficulty are not hard to find. In order to overcome the problems that we have encountered so far, we would need to focus on beliefs formed with a cognitive device exhibiting the following two features. On the one hand, its reliability should not be ruled out by fundamental aspects of our world-view. On the other hand, we should have no strong inclination to assume that the typical subject will have adequate evidence for or against its reliability.

One case that satisfies these desiderata is perfect pitch—the ability to recognize the pitch of a sound without having recently heard another sound whose pitch is known.[8] Perfect pitch satisfies the first constraint. It is perfectly compatible with our world-view, since we recognize it as a real phenomenon. However, a normal subject who hasn't studied the phenomenon may well have no evidence for or against its existence in general. One could argue that subjects with perfect pitch have introspective evidence for their possession of the faculty, since sounds will strike them as having a certain pitch. Notice, however, that what these subjects will be introspectively aware of in the first instance is a propensity to ascribe pitches to sounds, not the reliability of this procedure of belief formation. Someone with this propensity might in principle form systematically wrong pitch beliefs. If this situation were extremely unlikely, one could argue that awareness of the propensity would provide the subject with evidence of its reliability, but I am going to stipulate that this is not the situation—that many of the subjects who feel capable of detecting perfect pitch are highly unreliable.[9] Given this, a subject with the propensity would not have evidence for its reliability unless she had gathered independent information. Hence, in order to describe a case that satisfies

---

[7] See (Goldman 1991) for an alternative reliabilist diagnosis of clairvoyance intuitions.

[8] Jonathan Vogel has used this example in a similar context. Cf. (Vogel 2000: 608).

[9] Perfect pitch is actually quite rare in the population at large, and even among musically trained subjects (Dowling 1999). I am not aware of any studies on the correlation between seeming to oneself to have perfect pitch and actually having it. For all I know, my assumption might be in line with the facts. Nevertheless, the main point for our purposes is that we don't have a strong inclination to suppose that my assumption is false. For general information on perfect pitch see (Ward 1999).

the second desideratum, we would just need to introduce the further stipulation that she hasn't performed this task.[10]

We can now use perfect pitch to describe a case for the application of the intuitive approach that will be free of contamination in either direction. Consider Clara, a music student who is firmly convinced that she has perfect pitch. Whenever she hears a musical note, she identifies its pitch with a very high degree of subjective certainty and a very vivid phenomenology—the sound of, say, C#4, strikes her as simply unmistakable. She has never checked whether the beliefs that she has formed in this way are correct. She also has no evidence for or against the existence of perfect pitch in humans in general or in her own case. However, this lack of evidence doesn't diminish her certainty that she can identify the pitch of a note when she hears it.

Now suppose that Clara actually has perfect pitch: in normal circumstances she hardly ever misidentifies a note. One day she hears a bicycle bell and she forms the belief that the note is a C#4, having no reason for thinking that this is so other than the fact that it sounds to her like a clear C#4. Suppose that she is right.

So here we have a reliably formed true belief for which the subject lacks adequate evidence. If we have a stable intuition to the effect that Clara knows that the pitch of the bicycle bell is C#4, the reliabilist will be able to argue that the intuitive approach favours her position over the evidential constraint. And now the complaint that this intuition is the result of contamination will be much less plausible than in the straightforward perceptual case. We have no irresistible inclination to assume that Clara will have had access to adequate evidence for the presence in her of the relevant faculty.

It seems to me that intuition clearly supports the ascription of knowledge to Clara. Knowing the pitch of the notes you hear is the most natural characterization of what perfect pitch enables you to do, and that's precisely what we are inclined to say Clara has achieved by applying her faculty to the bicycle bell. In any case, my main goal in describing this case was not to support reliabilism, but to show that the intuitive approach can overcome the difficulties posed by intuition contamination.

## 2.3 BonJour and the intuitive approach

In Section 2.1 I developed a construal of BonJour's anti-reliabilist case as an application of the intuitive approach. I argued there that using Norman's clairvoyance thought experiments in this way wouldn't result in a very powerful anti-reliabilist argument. In this section I am going to question the attribution of this argument to BonJour.

---

[10] This stipulation won't be invalidated by intuition contamination, since we don't have a strong inclination to assume that everyone who has perfect pitch has performed independent checks of the reliability of their propensity to identify pitches.

BonJour manifests his attitude to an anti-reliabilist application of the intuitive approach when he is evaluating the attempt to deploy this strategy in defence of reliabilism. He characterizes the starting point of this argument in the following terms:

The basic factual premise of the argument is that in many cases which are commonsensically instances of justified belief and of knowledge, there seem to be no justifying factors present beyond those appealed to by the externalist. (BonJour 1985: 52)

A proponent of an anti-reliabilist application of the intuitive approach can be expected to reject this premise—to contend that in cases (like Norman's) in which no justifying factors are present beyond those appealed to by the reliabilist, intuition dictates that the beliefs in question don't have the status of knowledge. However, BonJour's assessment of this premise is completely different:

Though the precise extent to which it holds could be disputed, in the main the initial factual premise of this argument must simply be conceded. Any nonexternalist account of empirical knowledge that has any plausibility will impose standards for justification that many common-sensical cases of knowledge will fail to meet in any full and explicit way. (BonJour 1985: 52–3)

BonJour then goes on to question the strength of the support that reliabilism would receive from this premise, arguing that an account of knowledge might in principle be correct even if it forces us to revise some of our intuitive ascriptions of knowledge. A defence of reliabilism that takes these intuitions as the final arbiter for the correctness of an account of knowledge would rely on the following additional premise:

[ . . . ] that the judgments of common sense as to which of our beliefs qualify as knowledge are sacrosanct, that any serious departure from them is enough to demonstrate that a theory of knowledge is inadequate. (BonJour 1985: 53)

But this premise, BonJour tells us,

[ . . . ] seems entirely too strong. There seems in fact to be no basis for more than a quite defeasible *presumption* (if indeed even that) in favor of the correctness of common sense. (BonJour 1985: 53)

Although BonJour's intention is to undermine a defence of reliabilism along the lines of the intuitive approach, it is clear that his position would undermine to the same extent an attempt to use this strategy to attack reliabilism.

In light of these considerations, we have to conclude that BonJour takes a very dim view of the attempt to defend the evidential constraint by applying the intuitive approach to his clairvoyance cases. He thinks that conflict with our intuitive knowl-edge ascriptions wouldn't seriously undermine an account of knowledge and, even if it did, the proponent of the evidential constraint wouldn't be able to use this circum-stance to her advantage, as reliabilism provides a better match for our intuitive knowledge ascriptions than the evidential constraint. The argument that uses the intuitive approach to undermine reliabilism can't be BonJour's.

## 2.4 Epistemic rationality and responsibility

This raises the question of how we should construe the reasoning in which BonJour appeals to the clairvoyance cases to undermine reliabilism. He tells us that his goal in presenting these cases is to support and develop the following intuitive difficulty with reliabilism:

according to the externalist view, a person may be highly irrational and irresponsible in accepting a belief, when judged in light of his own subjective conception of the situation, and may still turn out to be epistemically justified [...] (BonJour 1985: 38)

This aspect of the argument is emphasized in a later passage, where he describes his anti-reliabilist argument as putting forward the following conception of epistemic rationality: 'of such rationality as essentially dependent on the believer's own subjective conception of his epistemic situation' (BonJour 1985: 49–50).

These passages suggest an anti-reliabilist argument based on the contention that reliabilism ascribes the status of knowledge to a belief in cases in which the subject is epistemically irrational and irresponsible in holding it (relative to his own subjective conception of the situation). According to this line of thought, reliabilism would have to be rejected on the grounds that this consequence is unacceptable. An argument against reliabilism along these lines would invoke the following two premises:

1. Reliabilism entails that a belief can be knowledge even if the subject is epistemically irrational and irresponsible in holding it (relative to his own subjective conception of the situation).
2. A belief can't be knowledge if the subject is epistemically irrational and irresponsible in holding it (relative to his own subjective conception of the situation).

I want to suggest that this is the main argument that BonJour is advancing against reliabilism, and that the role of the clairvoyance thought experiments in his discussion is to provide support for these premises. I shall consider each premise in turn.

Before we proceed, let me mention briefly a prominent line of reasoning that I shall not be considering here. One could object to this argument on the grounds that the notions of responsibility and rationality can't be applied to belief, because these notions can only be applied to items that are under the voluntary control of the subject, and belief doesn't satisfy this condition: we cannot decide what to believe. I shall not try to assess this line of reasoning here. I only want to point out that its success is open to question, and hence that the existence of other weaknesses in BonJour's reasoning would not be of merely academic interest.[11] In what follows I am going to waive this

---

[11] BonJour considers this objection in (BonJour 1985: 46). For an early defence of this line of thought see (Alston 1983). The argument has been attacked by Richard Feldman (Feldman 1988) and more recently by Matthias Steup (Steup 1996).

difficulty and assume for the sake of the argument that it makes perfect sense to ascribe to belief rationality and responsibility, as well as their opposites.

## 2.5 Premise 1

The core of BonJour's case for Premise 1 is the thought that the principle is instantiated by Norman's case. On the one hand, the reliabilist is committed to ascribing the status of knowledge to Norman's belief that the President is in New York City. On the other hand, Norman is epistemically irrational and irresponsible in holding this belief (relative to his own subjective conception). As we saw in Section 2.1, the first of these claims has not gone unchallenged. Nevertheless it is the second claim that I want to consider here. My goal is to assess the claim that, in holding his belief about the President's whereabouts, Norman is epistemically irrational and irresponsible (relative to his own subjective conception).

For this purpose we need to clarify the notion of rationality and responsibility that figures in the claim. The first point we need to note is that, according to BonJour, what distinguishes epistemic rationality or responsibility from other forms of rationality or responsibility is 'its essential or internal relation to the cognitive goal of truth' (BonJour 1985: 8). 'Our cognitive endeavors', he adds, 'are epistemically justified only if and to the extent that they are aimed at this goal' (BonJour 1985: 8). A precise construal of this goal raises familiar problems, but for our purposes we just need to assume that it is a goal that would be promoted, for any given proposition, by believing it if it is true, and not believing it if it is false.

This suggests that, for BonJour, epistemic rationality and responsibility are species of instrumental, or means–ends, rationality. The epistemic rationality of holding a belief depends, on this approach, on the extent to which doing so promotes the goal of truth. In this section I am going to consider whether there is a construal of the notion of epistemic rationality along these lines that can be invoked to show that Norman's belief is epistemically irrational and irresponsible. I am going to argue for a negative answer to this question. I will consider first a crude articulation of the conception of epistemic rationality as instrumental, in order to highlight the basic difficulty that I want to raise. Then I will argue that a more refined construal of the notion would raise the same difficulty.

The instrumental rationality of an action can be assessed from several points of view. One possibility is to assess it from an objective perspective, in terms of the objective likelihood of the action promoting the relevant outcome. Alternatively, we can assess it from the point of view of a certain conception of the relevant situation, independently of whether this conception is correct. The assessments of instrumental value that we would obtain from different conceptions of the situation can be expected to differ from each other, and the assessments that would result from an incorrect conception can be expected to differ from those that we would obtain from the objective point of view.

Thus, on this construal of instrumental rationality and responsibility, BonJour's claim about Norman is that from the point of view of his own conception of his situation, holding his belief that the President is in New York City is of little instrumental value, relative to the cognitive goal of truth. But the instrumental value of holding a belief relative to the cognitive goal of truth will depend on how likely it is that the belief is true. Hence, on my construal, BonJour's claim is that from the point of view of Norman's own conception of his situation, his belief that the President is in New York City is unlikely to be true.

In order to assess this claim, we need to reach a more precise understanding of the notion of 'Norman's conception of his own epistemic situation'. I want to start with a crude proposal as to how to understand this notion. According to this proposal, how likely it is, from the point of view of a subject's conception of her situation, that an action will promote a goal, is determined by how likely she believes it to be that the action will promote the goal. This thought yields the following account of subjective rationality and responsibility:

R1   From the point of view of a subject's conception of her situation, it is rational and responsible for her to perform action A in pursuit of goal G just in case she believes that A is likely to promote G.[12]

In the particular case of epistemic rationality and responsibility, the account would go as follows:

ER1   From the point of view of a subject's conception of her epistemic situation, it is epistemically rational and responsible to believe that p just in case she believes that p is likely to be true.

Notice that it follows from this account that for a subject who believes that p, holding this belief would be epistemically irrational and irresponsible from the point of view of her conception of her situation only if she didn't believe that p is likely to be true. One is entitled to wonder whether this is a coherent possibility—whether there is a possible cognitive state that we would want to describe by saying that the subject believes that p but doesn't believe that p is likely to be true. But even if we accept this as a genuine possibility, it is hard to see how it could be exploited to defend the epistemic irrationality and irresponsibility of Norman's belief, since nothing in BonJour's description of the case indicates that Norman fails to believe that it is likely that the President is in New York City. The point is particularly clear in the first of the two versions of the case that BonJour considers, on which I shall focus my discussion in the first instance. In this version, 'Norman *believes* himself to have clairvoyant power even

---

[12] I am simplifying matters by thinking of the rationality and responsibility of an action or belief as a yes-or-no question. It would probably be more adequate to construe them as a matter of degree, but it should be clear how to adapt my formulations to achieve this. Notice also that the simplification introduces an implicit reliance on a notional threshold for the likelihood that A will promote G.

though he has no justification for such a belief', and this belief 'contributes to his acceptance of the belief about the President's whereabouts' (BonJour 1985: 41–2). Clearly, if Norman believes that he has clairvoyant powers, he will believe that the propositions that are sanctioned by this faculty, including the proposition that the President is in New York City, are very likely to be true. I think we can conclude that on this crude construal of the notion of the subject's conception of her situation, there are no grounds for accusing Norman of irrationality and irresponsibility.

Since BonJour cannot exploit to his advantage the possibility of believing that p while failing to believe that p is likely to be true, we can simplify matters by ignoring it. Thus in what follows I shall assume, for the sake of simplicity, that a subject believes that p if and only if she believes that p is likely to be true.

This would be the end of the story if the account of subjective rationality and responsibility expressed by R1 and ER1 were correct. But the account needs to be refined. The problem is that, as it stands, it allows a subject to achieve rationality and responsibility by simply refusing to face the facts. Suppose that Alex drinks one bottle of whisky a day in order to improve his health, and he actually believes that drinking one bottle of whisky a day is likely to have this effect, but only because he has deliberately avoided exposure to medical opinion about the likely effects of this level of alcohol consumption. It seems to me that in these circumstances we might not want to say that from the point of view of Alex's conception of the situation, drinking one bottle of whisky a day is rational and responsible, relative to the goal of preserving his health, even though he believes that this policy is likely to promote the relevant goal. The same point can be made in the case of epistemic rationality. Suppose that Tracey believes that her husband liked the present she bought for him, but only because she hasn't asked him, although she believes that he would tell her the truth if she asked, but would otherwise act as if he had liked the present, whether he did or not. One could argue that from the point of view of Tracey's conception of the situation it is not rational for her to hold this belief, relative to the cognitive goal of truth.

These examples indicate that there are circumstances in which one can plausibly claim that the subject's beliefs do not determine what's rational and responsible for her to do in pursuit of a goal, from the point of view of her conception of her situation. I want to suggest that these are all cases in which the subject hasn't done her best, by her lights, to determine the likelihood that the course of action in question will bring about the relevant outcome. Alex may believe that one bottle of whisky a day will keep the doctor away, but he also believes that his doctor knows more about these things than he does, and he hasn't consulted her. Tracey may believe that her husband liked the present, but she also believes that she could easily check by asking him, and she has failed to do so. There are cognitive procedures that they haven't implemented, although they could have done so, which they think might have affected their assessment of the likelihood that the course of action in question will bring about the relevant goal.

We can accommodate this point by restricting the connection between the subject's conception of the situation and the beliefs she holds about it to cases in which she has done her best by her lights to determine the likelihood of the action in question promoting the relevant goal. This move would leave us with the following weaker principle:

> R2   If a subject has done her best by her lights to determine whether action A is likely to promote goal G, then from the point of view of her conception of her situation, it is rational and responsible for her to perform action A in pursuit of goal G just in case she believes that A is likely to promote G.

If we apply this general principle to the epistemic case we obtain the following:

> ER2   If a subject has done her best by her lights to determine the truth value of a proposition p, then from the point of view of her conception of her epistemic situation, it is epistemically rational and responsible to believe that p just in case she believes that p is likely to be true.

And by virtue of our simplifying assumption, this is equivalent to the following principle:

> ER2★   If a subject has done her best by her lights to determine the truth value of a proposition p, then from the point of view of her conception of her epistemic situation, it is epistemically rational and responsible to believe that p just in case she believes that p.

I want to suggest that this revised principle provides a very accurate constraint on the notion of the epistemic rationality and responsibility of a belief from the subject's point of view. According to it, if a subject believes that p, then this belief could only be epistemically irrational and irresponsible from the point of view of the subject's conception of her situation if she has failed to do her best by her lights to determine the truth value of p, that is, if she has failed to do something about it that she believes she could do and she believes might make a difference to her ultimate verdict.[13]

This gives us a very precise picture of how BonJour would have to proceed to substantiate his claim that from the point of view of Norman's conception of his epistemic situation his belief that the President is in New York City is epistemically irrational and irresponsible. He would have to argue that Norman hasn't done his best by his lights to determine whether the President is in New York City. In other words, he would have to argue that there is a corroboration procedure that Norman has failed to apply to the proposition that the President is in New York City of which Norman

---

[13] This conception of epistemic rationality and responsibility is closely connected to Richard Foley's notion of egocentric rationality (Foley 1993). The only important respect in which the two notions differ from each other concerns the role that Foley accords to reflection. Thus, according to ER2★ the beliefs of a subject who has done the best by her lights will be epistemically rational and responsible. The beliefs of such a subject will also be egocentrically rational provided that she trusts reflection—that she thinks that doing her best requires engaging in reflection. However, if the subject mistrusts reflection, her beliefs might be epistemically rational and responsible according to ER2★ but not egocentrically rational. On this point, cf. (Foley 1993: 97) and (Plantinga 1993: 133).

believes (a) that he could apply it to this proposition and (b) that doing so might make a difference to his verdict on its truth value.[14]

I can't see that there is any legitimate reason to conclude that this is the situation in which Norman finds himself. Nothing in BonJour's description of the case rules out the possibility that, concerning every corroboration procedure that Norman is aware of but has failed to apply to the proposition in question, he believes either that he can't apply it (e.g. tapping the President's phone might make him change his mind, but he can't really do it) or that it wouldn't make a difference to his verdict (e.g. he could ask his son, but what does he know . . . ). And if this is the situation, it follows from ER2★ that Norman's belief is epistemically rational and responsible from the point of view of his conception of his situation.

One line of reasoning that might be used in support of BonJour's claim goes as follows: there is a strong body of widely available scientific evidence against the existence of clairvoyance. Since Norman doesn't have evidence against the possibility of clairvoyance, he has failed to consider the verdict of science. But this means that Norman hasn't done his best to determine the truth value of his belief, and hence ER2★ doesn't entail that his belief is epistemically rational and responsible.

I suspect that this line of reasoning is responsible for much of the intuitive appeal of BonJour's verdict. However, it should be clear that it rests on an illegitimate assumption. By failing to consider the scientific evidence, Norman would only have failed to do his best by his lights if he believed about this procedure that he could apply it in this case and that the result of so doing might make a difference to his ultimate verdict. But it is not part of the case that Norman has either of these beliefs. The details of the case could be filled in in such a way that Norman believes that he has no access to the relevant scientific evidence. And even if he believes that he could consider the scientific evidence if he wanted, he might think that his belief that he has clairvoyant powers is so strong (or that his belief in science is so weak) that whatever the scientists might say would not make a difference to his conviction. And if his belief is not the result of dishonesty or negligence, in failing to take scientific evidence into account he wouldn't be failing to do his best *by his lights*.

To be sure, someone who holds science in such low esteem might be open to criticism, and we might even want to accuse them of irrationality or irresponsibility. But if their disdain of science results from the honest and conscientious pursuit of the cognitive goal of truth, the irrationality or irresponsibility they might be accused of is not irrationality or irresponsibility from the point of view of their conception of the situation. They might be irrational and irresponsible from our point of view, or even

---

[14] On an adequate construal of the notion of doing one's best by one's lights to determine the truth value of p, one could fail to do so not only by failing to apply a corroboration procedure that is related in this way to the proposition that p, but also by failing to apply a corroboration procedure that is related in this way to the proposition that there is a corroboration procedure that is related in this way to p . . . A simple induction would take care of all levels of iteration.

from the objective point of view. But from their own subjective perspective they are not doing anything wrong. From their own point of view their rationality and responsibility would not be open to question.

In his discussion of the first version of Norman's case, BonJour suggests a line of reasoning which it is tempting to regard as the real source of his conviction that Norman's belief is epistemically irrational and irresponsible. The starting point of this train of thought is what BonJour sees as the obvious irrationality of Norman's belief that he has clairvoyant powers:

> But is it not obviously irrational, from an epistemic standpoint, for Norman to hold such a belief when he has no reasons at all for thinking that it is true or even for thinking that such a power is possible? (BonJour 1985: 42)

Thus BonJour declares Norman's belief in his clairvoyance irrational on the grounds that he has no evidence or reasons to support it. Notice that the irrationality of Norman's belief that the President is in New York City cannot be established in quite the same way. In this version of the case Norman has evidence for his belief, since he takes it to be sanctioned by a highly reliable procedure. The problem in this case is that the evidence is not adequate. Norman has beliefs of which he believes that their truth would make it likely that the President is in New York City, but these beliefs are not knowledge. As BonJour tells us, 'this belief about his clairvoyance fails after all to have even an externalist justification' (BonJour 1985: 42). Thus this line of thought would derive the irrationality of Norman's belief that the President is in New York City from his lack of adequate evidence for it.[15]

I want to argue that this line of reasoning is unlikely to provide a significant contribution to BonJour's argumentative strategy. The problem is that it rests on the assumption that epistemic rationality requires adequate evidence. We can formulate the principle that is being invoked in the following terms:

> *Evidential constraint on epistemic rationality and responsibility*: If a subject doesn't have adequate evidence for a proposition p that she believes, then from the point of view of her conception of her situation she is epistemically irrational and irresponsible in believing that p.[16]

I don't want to discuss the intrinsic merits of this principle. I only want to remind the reader that BonJour's goal is to defend the evidential constraint on knowledge against

---

[15] The text actually suggests a different line of reasoning, according to which what follows from Norman's lack of adequate evidence for his belief is not that it is subjectively irrational, but that it is not knowledge. However, in the context of trying to support the evidential constraint on knowledge, this move would be utterly question begging.

[16] This principle could be seen as articulating a deontological alternative to the instrumental account of epistemic rationality that I have developed. According to this alternative, we would have a categorical duty to believe only propositions for which we have adequate evidence. Given BonJour's emphasis on the essential role played by the cognitive goal of truth in the notion of epistemic rationality, I don't think this account can be plausibly attributed to him.

reliabilist accounts of the notion, which seek to solve the epistemic regress problem by rejecting the constraint. And it is hard to see what argumentative strength would accrue to an argument for the evidential constraint on knowledge that uses as a premise the evidential constraint on epistemic rationality and responsibility. This line of reasoning would be effective just in case those who are inclined to reject the evidential constraint on knowledge could be expected to be more reluctant to reject the evidential constraint on epistemic rationality and responsibility. But I see no reason to expect this. In fact, the rejection of the evidential constraint on epistemic rationality and responsibility can be supported in independence of the fate of the evidential constraint on knowledge—by the adoption of an account of epistemic rationality and responsibility along the lines of ER2.[17]

I have focused so far on the first version of Norman's case. However, my conclusions apply equally to the second version, in which Norman finds himself strongly inclined to believe that the President is in New York City, but has nothing to say in support of his belief, since, unlike in the first version, Norman doesn't believe that he has the power of clairvoyance. However, as we have seen, according to ER2*, a belief can in principle be rational and responsible from the point of view of the subject's conception of her situation even if she has no evidence for it. This will be so if the subject has done her best by her lights to determine the truth value of the proposition in question. And we cannot rule out the possibility that Norman, in the second version of the case, as well as in the first, has applied to the proposition that the President is in New York City every corroboration procedure of which he believes that he could apply it and that doing so might make a difference.

It seems to me that BonJour's case at this point trades on an equivocation when he suggests that 'from [Norman's] standpoint, there is apparently no way in which he *could* know the President's whereabouts', that 'there is no way, as far as he knows, for him to have obtained this information' and that Norman's belief amounts to 'believing things to which one has, to one's knowledge, no reliable means of epistemic access' (BonJour 1985: 42). On one reading of these passages, they portray Norman as believing that he has no way of acquiring information about the President's whereabouts. If this is what Norman believes, then it is hard to see how he could fail to believe also that the chances of his belief being true are no better than random, and, according to ER2, this would make his belief subjectively irrational. But nothing in BonJour's description of the situation indicates that Norman believes that he has no way of obtaining information about the President's whereabouts. All that follows from the description of the case is that Norman can't identify a source of information about this matter, and it is perfectly

---

[17] For the possibility of subscribing to the evidential constraint on knowledge but not to the parallel constraint on epistemic rationality and responsibility, cf. Susan Haack's position on epistemological justification and moral justification: 'I do not think it is always morally wrong to believe on inadequate evidence. [ . . . ] however, I think it is always epistemically wrong to believe on inadequate evidence—in the sense that believing on inadequate evidence is always epistemologically unjustified belief' (Haack 1997: 138). Bruce Russell also makes room for this possibility. He writes: 'questions of epistemic blamelessness are separate from questions of the goodness of evidence' (Russell 2001: 38).

conceivable that Norman believes that he has a source of information about these matters even though he can't identify it. And in these circumstances Norman's belief that the President is in New York City might not be subjectively irrational.

So far in my discussion of epistemic rationality and responsibility I have argued that BonJour is not entitled to claim that from the point of view of Norman's own conception of his situation he is epistemically irrational and irresponsible in believing that the President is in New York City. But notice that it is open to BonJour to concede this point while still maintaining that Norman's case supports Premise 1. All that is required to establish Premise 1 is to show that it is possible that reliabilism ascribes the status of knowledge to a subjectively irrational belief, and although BonJour's description of the Norman case is compatible with a situation in which Norman would not be subjectively irrational, it is also compatible with a situation in which he is subjectively irrational. Suppose, for example, that he has failed to ask his wife, who works in the White House travel office and has always been willing to give Norman accurate details of the President's travel arrangements. Then the rationality of his belief would no longer be guaranteed by ER2*. But since reliabilism would bestow the status of knowledge on Norman's belief independently of how these details are filled in, Norman's case still supports Premise 1.

This is a perfectly legitimate move, and it will be effective so long as the reliabilist wants to maintain that the subjective irrationality of Norman's belief would leave its status as knowledge intact. However, the move would be ineffectual against a reliabilist who is prepared to give up this thought, arguing that the circumstances that would undermine the subjective rationality and responsibility of Norman's belief would also undermine its status as knowledge. This line could be pursued from within Goldman's version of reliabilism, since one could argue that the circumstances that would render Norman's belief subjectively irrational would also bring it under the non-undermining provision. Alternatively, the reliabilist could adopt a bolder strategy. She could simply modify her account of knowledge by treating epistemic rationality and responsibility, construed along the lines of ER2, as an additional necessary condition for knowledge. The resulting view would still be recognizably reliabilist, and, more importantly for our purposes, it would still license violations of the evidential constraint on knowledge. And, needless to say, this version of reliabilism would make Premise 1 immediately false, provided that, as I am suggesting, ER2 is correct.

## 2.6 Premise 2

Let's now turn briefly to Premise 2 of BonJour's argument against reliabilism. The first point to notice is that the claim stands in need of support. It is far from obvious that one cannot acquire knowledge 'against one's better judgment'. Thus, for example, Alvin Plantinga has argued that fulfilment of one's epistemic duties is not necessary for knowledge (Plantinga 1993: 45). Plantinga illustrates his point by asking us to suppose that he is convinced that forming the belief that he is seeing something red will deprive him of any chance of epistemic excellence. He argues that this conviction leads him to acquire an epistemic duty not to believe that he is seeing something red. However, he has the standard doxastic inclinations and it is only by heroic effort that he manages to refrain himself from forming this belief in the presence of fire engines, and so on. Then he describes the following situation:

On a given morning I go for a walk in London; I am appeared to redly several times (postboxes, traffic signals, redcoats practising for a reenactment of the American Revolution); each time I successfully resist the belief that I see something red, but only at the cost of prodigious effort. I become exhausted, and resentful. Finally I am appeared to redly in a particularly insistent and out-and-out fashion by a large red London bus. "Epistemic duty be hanged", I mutter, and relax blissfully into the belief that I am now perceiving something red. [ . . . ] in accepting [this belief] I would be going contrary to epistemic duty; yet could it not constitute knowledge nonetheless? (Plantinga 1993: 45)

The case can easily be adapted to support the rejection of Premise 2. In any case, I am not going to engage here in a general discussion of Premise 2. I am going to concentrate instead on the argument that BonJour adduces in its support. He presents the argument in his discussion of a possible reliabilist rejoinder. Before presenting Norman's case (case 4) BonJour presents three other cases of reliable clairvoyants. What distinguishes these cases from Norman's is that these subjects have reasons for thinking either that the President is not in New York City (case 1), or that they don't have clairvoyant powers (case 2), or that clairvoyance is impossible (case 3). The reliabilist strategy that BonJour is discussing consists in accepting that the subjects in the first three cases don't know that the President is in New York City, while refusing to extend this verdict to Norman. Here is BonJour's objection to this position:

But how can case 4 be successfully prised apart from the earlier ones? What the externalist needs at this point is a different account of *why* the beliefs in cases 1–3 are not justified, an account which does not invoke the notion of subjective irrationality, and hence does not extend readily to case 4. (BonJour 1985: 46)

In this passage, BonJour is taking for granted the subjective irrationality of Norman's belief, and arguing against the view that it might nevertheless be knowledge. In other words, he is arguing for the claim expressed in Premise 2 that subjective irrationality is incompatible with knowledge. BonJour argues for this conclusion on the grounds that subjective irrationality is the best explanation of why the subjects in cases 1–3 lack knowledge, and this explanation would not be available if subjective irrationality were compatible with knowledge. BonJour devotes most of his efforts to arguing against Goldman's alternative explanation of the absence of knowledge in cases 1–3, apparently thinking that the optimality of his preferred explanation could only be undermined by the existence of a better candidate. Here I want to pose a more basic objection to BonJour's claim. The hypothesis that the subjects in cases 1–3 are subjectively irrational wouldn't even be in the running for the post of the best explanation of their lack of knowledge unless it actually explained this phenomenon. And it wouldn't explain this phenomenon unless it was true. Hence BonJour's argument for Premise 2 would collapse if we could reject the claim that the subjects in cases 1–3 are subjectively irrational. This is precisely what I propose to do. I am going to argue that nothing in BonJour's description of his first three cases indicates that their subjects are subjectively irrational.

My reasons for making this claim are strictly parallel to the reasons I adduced for the Norman case. Let's concentrate on case 1. What makes Samantha's belief subjectively irrational, on BonJour's account, is the fact that she maintains it

appealing to her alleged clairvoyant power, even though she is aware of apparently cogent evidence, consisting of news reports, press releases, allegedly live television pictures, and so on, indicating that the president is at that time in Washington, D.C. (BonJour 1985: 38)

Let's consider what can be said about the epistemic rationality and responsibility of Samantha's belief from the point of view of ER2*. The most direct route to the conclusion that according to ER2* Samantha is epistemically irrational and irresponsible would involve arguing that she hasn't done her best by her lights to determine whether the President is in New York City. Then the epistemic rationality and responsibility of her belief would no longer be protected by ER2*. But on the basis of what we know about Samantha, this would require arguing that she has failed to consider the bearing of the 'media' evidence on her belief that the President is in New York City, and that she believes that implementing this procedure might make a difference to her final verdict on the truth value of this proposition. It is not clear whether this second point is part of BonJour's description of the case—that would depend on whether the evidence appears cogent *to Samantha*. If, having done her best by her lights to determine the reliability of media evidence, she believes that it is not to be trusted, then by failing to take it into account she wouldn't be failing to do her best by her lights to determine whether the President is in New York City—even if the media evidence appears cogent to us, or if it appears cogent in some objective sense.

Furthermore, we are not entitled to assume that Samantha hasn't considered the bearing of the media evidence on her belief that the President is in New York City. The only reason to assume this would be the thought that since the evidence appears cogent to her, if she had considered it she would have concluded that the President is unlikely to be in New York City, and hence, by our simplifying assumption, she wouldn't have the belief which by hypothesis she does have. But this reasoning rests on a mistake. From the assumption that the media evidence appears cogent to Samantha it doesn't follow that considering it will ineluctably lead her to believe that it is unlikely that the President is in New York City. Cogency is a relative matter. After considering the media evidence and realizing that it indicates that the President is unlikely to be in New York City, Samantha would have to weigh it against what she sees as her clairvoyance evidence for the opposite conclusion. We can't rule out the possibility that Samantha's belief that the President is in New York City emerges victorious from this contest, even if she conducts it honestly and conscientiously and with no goal other than truth. This possibility is not ruled out by BonJour's description of Samantha's case, and if this is the situation in which she finds herself, then according to ER2* her belief that the President is in New York City will be epistemically rational and responsible, from the point of view of her conception of the situation.

We have to conclude that BonJour's description of case 1 is compatible with situations in which Samantha's belief is epistemically rational and responsible, as well as with situations in which it isn't. However, there is no reason to doubt that BonJour would want to say in both situations that Samantha's belief is not knowledge. Hence, assuming that we require an explanation of the phenomenon that works in both situations, subjective irrationality is not the explanans we are looking for. Subjective irrationality can't explain why Samantha's belief is not knowledge because she might not be subjectively irrational in holding her belief.

We can make the same point with respect to cases 2 and 3. The outcome is that the absence of knowledge in cases 1–3 couldn't be explained in terms of subjective irrationality, even if knowledge were incompatible with subjective irrationality (i.e. even if Premise 2 were true). This result undermines completely BonJour's defence of Premise 2. He argues that it is entailed by what he takes to be the best explanation of the absence of knowledge in cases 1–3. But what he takes to be the best explanation of this phenomenon is no explanation at all, since its explanans is not even true in all instances of the phenomenon. Hence BonJour's argument for Premise 2 boils down to the claim that it is entailed by an explanation which doesn't work.

## 2.7  Two further arguments

I'd like to round up my discussion of BonJour's attack on reliabilism by considering two more aspects of his reasoning. The first concerns BonJour's attempt to bolster his anti-reliabilist case with an analogy with ethics. In ethics we find the same contrast between objective and subjective perspectives for the assessment of action that BonJour exploits in the assessment of belief. BonJour starts by considering an externalist account of moral assessment, according to which the moral justification of an action is determined by its actual consequences, independently of the subject's beliefs. As BonJour points out, saying that an agent's action is morally justified in this external sense 'is not at all inconsistent with saying that his action was morally unjustified and reprehensible in light of his subjective conception of the likely consequences' (BonJour 1985: 44).

Then BonJour suggests that the moral externalist might try to accommodate this subjective sense of justification by adding to her account of when an action is morally justified 'the further condition that the agent not believe or intend that it will lead to undesirable consequences' (BonJour 1985: 44). But BonJour finds this proposal unsatisfactory:

Since it is also, of course, not required by moral externalism that he believe that the action will lead to the best consequences, the case we are now considering is one in which the agent acts in a way that will in fact produce the best overall consequences, but has himself *no belief at all* about the likely consequences of his action. But while such an agent is no doubt preferable to one who acts in the belief that his action will lead to undesirable consequences, surely he is not morally justified in what he does. (BonJour 1985: 44–5)

For BonJour, the analogy with the epistemological case is perfectly clear:

And similarly, the fact that a given sort of belief is objectively reliable, and hence that accepting it is in fact conducive to arriving at the truth, need not prevent our judging that the epistemic agent who accepts it without any inkling that this is the case violates his epistemic duty and is epistemically irresponsible and unjustified in doing so. (BonJour 1985: 45)

I want to make two points about this. First of all, notice that the problem in the moral case arises only on the assumption that on an externalist account of moral justification it cannot be required that the agent 'believe that the action will lead to the best consequences'. BonJour doesn't see the need to support this assumption, but presumably he thinks that an account of moral justification that accepted this requirement would no longer qualify as externalist. There is little point in quibbling about what makes an account qualify as externalist. However, the analogue of this position in epistemology is explicitly classified by BonJour as externalist. It is Dretske's position, which requires, BonJour tells us, 'that the would-be knower also believe that the externalist condition is satisfied' (BonJour 1985: 233). Notice that, since it is not required that this belief has the status of knowledge, this position would still license counterexamples to the evidential constraint. I think there is little doubt that this position has nothing to fear from BonJour's ethical analogy.

The second point I want to make questions more generally the plausibility of the analogy. The problem that it raises for reliabilism in epistemology is that the reliabilist is committed to ascribing the status of knowledge to beliefs which the subject accepts 'without an inkling' that they are 'conducive to arriving at the truth'. Presumably this notion is to be construed in analogy with the situation in ethics of an agent who 'has himself *no belief at all* about the likely consequences of his action'. In other words, the reliabilist is committed to ascribing knowledge in cases in which the subject has no inclination to regard her belief as true. I want to suggest that the type of situation that this objection postulates simply doesn't arise. Believing a proposition is inextricably linked with the inclination to regard it as true. The externalist is not in danger of ascribing the status of knowledge to beliefs which aren't accompanied by this kind of inclination simply because there are no such beliefs.

Let me now turn to what is probably the key thought underlying BonJour's advocacy of the evidential constraint and his consequent rejection of reliabilism. Its starting point is a principle connecting epistemic justification and truth:

The distinguishing characteristic of epistemic justification is [ . . . ] its essential or internal relation to the cognitive goal of truth. It follows that one's cognitive endeavors are epistemically justified only if and to the extent that they are aimed at this goal. (BonJour 1985: 8)

Notice that this principle by itself doesn't lend any support to the evidential constraint. In fact, it wouldn't be surprising if a reliabilist invoked it in support of her account of justification, claiming that aiming at the cognitive goal of truth requires using cognitive processes that are sufficiently likely to bring it about.

Of course one could object to this objectivist reading of 'aiming at truth', on the grounds that it leaves the subject's conception out of the picture, and hence is not suitable for assessing the rationality and responsibility of her cognitive endeavours. A natural way of trying to bring that perspective into the picture would be to switch to a construal of aiming at truth in terms of the subject's beliefs and more basic inclinations concerning the extent to which her beliefs and cognitive processes bring her close to this goal. On this subjectivist construal, a subject would be aiming at truth so long as she didn't hold beliefs 'against her better judgment', that is, so long as she had done her best by her lights to determine the truth value of the propositions she believes. However, on this reading of 'aiming at truth' BonJour's principle would still not lend support to the evidential constraint. A reliabilist could accommodate the principle, on the subjective reading of aiming at truth, by adopting the proposal I made earlier to treat epistemic rationality and responsibility, construed along the lines of ER2$\star$, as an additional necessary condition for knowledge.

Thus neither on the objective nor the subjective reading of 'aiming at truth' does BonJour's principle lend support to the evidential constraint. To use the principle in this way requires the specific reading of the notion that BonJour puts forward in the continuation of the passage quoted above, where he informs us that aiming at the cognitive goal of truth 'means very roughly that one accepts all and only those beliefs which one has good reason to think are true'. Needless to say, on this reading of 'aiming at truth', BonJour's principle would support the evidential constraint. The problem for BonJour is that this reading stands itself in need of support, and I suspect that it is at least as vulnerable as the evidential constraint itself. For it is hard to see how someone who is inclined to reject the evidential constraint on knowledge can be expected to be more open to be persuaded to accept an evidential constraint on aiming at truth. The evidential constraint on knowledge can receive no effective support from this reading of aiming at truth, or a fortiori from BonJour's principle.[18]

We saw in Chapter 1 that a prominent feature of reliabilism is its incompatibility with the evidential constraint: if knowledge is construed along reliabilist lines, there will be instances of knowledge that don't satisfy the necessary condition imposed by the evidential constraint. We also saw that the evidential constraint plays a central role

---

[18] The same point can be applied to the deontological account of epistemic rationality mentioned in footnote 16. An effective argument for the evidential constraint on knowledge could not use as a premise the claim that we have a categorical duty not to believe in the absence of evidence.

in the main lines of sceptical reasoning against our knowledge claims. Hence its incompatibility with the evidential constraint places reliabilism in a favourable position for dealing with sceptical challenges.

In the present chapter I have considered a line of reasoning to the effect that its incompatibility with the evidential constraint should be treated as a refutation of reliabilism. According to this line of reasoning, reliabilism has to be rejected because it ascribes knowledge in cases in which the constraint is not satisfied. I have argued that this line of reasoning doesn't succeed—that the claim that the evidential constraint should be treated in this way as an adequacy condition for an account of knowledge has not received compelling support. This doesn't amount to a full defence of reliabilism, let alone of a specific version of the view. It simply removes what many have seen as an insurmountable obstacle to the acceptance of reliabilist accounts of knowledge.

Over the next four chapters, I am going to articulate and defend an account of knowledge with unmistakeable reliabilist credentials. In defending this account, I will not be assuming that knowledge has some kind of hidden essence that philosophical analysis can reveal. I take the analysis of knowledge to aim at the formulation of enlightening systematizations of our intuitions regarding the concept. According to this approach, an account of knowledge will be correct if it provides the most charitable and illuminating systematization of our intuitions concerning the circumstances under which people know things. This is the sense in which I shall claim my version of reliabilism to provide the right account of knowledge. The resulting analysis of knowledge will license violations of the evidential constraint. My goal in the present chapter has been to show that this is not a reason for rejecting the analysis.

# 3

# Knowledge and Truth Tracking

Reliabilism, in the wide sense in which we used the term in the first chapter, is the view that whether a true belief has the status of knowledge depends on how the natural order connects the state of affairs the belief consists in with the state of affairs whose obtaining determines the truth value of the belief—that is, S's belief that p with p. We saw there that the leading versions of reliabilism are process reliabilism and tracking accounts.

In the preceding chapter, I followed Laurence BonJour in focusing on process reliabilism. However, the version of reliabilism that I am going to defend in this book belongs firmly in the truth-tracking tradition. According to tracking accounts, whether S's true belief that p has the status of knowledge is determined by how the circumstances in which S would believe p covary with the circumstances in which p would be true.

The difference between process reliabilism and tracking accounts is less pronounced than it might appear at first. One apparent difference is that belief-forming mechanisms play a role in process reliabilism with no correlate in tracking accounts. However, when we look in some detail at Robert Nozick's seminal tracking account, we shall see that he assigns a role to belief-forming mechanisms not unlike the role that they play in process reliabilism.

The second prominent difference is that counterfactuals play a role in tracking accounts with no correlate in process reliabilism. This difference is also less deep than it might seem. Alvin Goldman, the main advocate of process reliabilism, construes the notion of the reliability of a belief-forming mechanism in probabilistic terms, but a construal of this notion in terms of counterfactuals would be possible in principle. Conversely, there is no reason in principle why we should follow Nozick in construing in terms of counterfactuals the features of the belief-world correlation on which he bases his account of knowledge. As Sherrilyn Roush has shown in an important recent book, there are natural probabilistic construals of these features (Roush 2005).

I think that the best way to introduce the version of reliabilism that I want to defend will be to consider in some detail Robert Nozick's tracking account of knowledge. My goal in the present chapter is to introduce the aspects of Nozick's proposal that will form the core of the account of knowledge that I want to defend, as well as the aspects of Nozick's position that I find unsatisfactory.

## 3.1 Nozick's analysis of knowledge

In a long chapter of his book, *Philosophical Explanations* (Nozick 1981), Robert Nozick put forward an account of knowledge in terms of the covariation between a belief and the state of affairs that determines its truth value. He posed the question of what conditions a true belief would need to satisfy in order to count as knowledge. His answer was that a true belief is knowledge if it satisfies two conditions concerning what the subject would believe in certain counterfactual situations. He first provided a basic preliminary formulation of these conditions and then argued that this formulation had to be modified.

In their preliminary formulation, these are Nozick's individually necessary and jointly sufficient conditions for S's true belief that p to have the status of knowledge:

If p were false S wouldn't believe p.
If p were true S would believe p.[1]

The first of these conditions represents the property that we called *sensitivity* in Chapter 1. For the second we shall use the label *adherence*.

In order to understand the consequences of these clauses we need to have a clear picture of the semantics of subjunctives that Nozick is presupposing. As he explains, the conditional *if p were true q would be true* can be true even if p doesn't entail q—even if it is possible for p to be true while q is false. The truth value of the subjunctive depends on whether q would be true in situations in which p is true that are otherwise fairly similar to the actual situation. Take, for example, the conditional *if I had had a puncture I would have been late for work*. This conditional may be true even though the antecedent doesn't entail the consequent. There are possible situations in which the antecedent is true and the consequent is false. Suppose, for example, that upon hearing of my puncture the provost sends a helicopter to take me to my office. But the fact that I wouldn't be late for work if this happened doesn't undermine the truth of the conditional. A situation in which the provost comes to my rescue is much more different from the actual situation than one in which I am left to fend for myself. The subjunctive is made true by the fact that I would be late for work in situations of the latter type.

Nozick uses the possible-worlds account of subjunctives to illustrate these points, although he expressly withholds commitment to the view. We can think of possible worlds as possible states of the world—ways things might stand. Possible worlds sustain relations of similarity. Thus, for example, a world in which I am left to deal with my puncture is more similar to the actual world than one in which the provost sends a helicopter. The possible-worlds account of subjunctives idealizes from these similarity comparisons to arrange possible worlds in a space in which the distance between two possible worlds represents their degree of similarity: the closer two worlds are to one

---

[1] One refinement of Nozick's proposal that I am ignoring is that the consequent of the adherence subjunctive requires not only believing p, but also failing to believe not-p (Nozick 1981: 178).

another the more similar they will be. Using this framework, Nozick provides the following explanation of the truth conditions of subjunctives: 'the subjunctive is true when (roughly) in all those worlds in which p holds true that are closest to the actual world, q is also true' (Nozick 1981: 173).[2] We can formulate this account in the following terms:

'If p were true q would be true' is true if and only if q is true in all the p-worlds whose distance to the actual world is no greater than the distance to the nearest p-world plus d.

d here represents how far into the range of p-worlds q would have to remain true in order for the subjunctive to be true.

Using this account we can provide alternative formulations of sensitivity and adherence.[3] We assume that S believes p and p is true. Sensitivity takes the following form:

S's true belief that p is *sensitive* just in case S doesn't believe p in any not-p-world whose distance to the actual world is no greater than the distance to the nearest not-p-world plus d.

Since the nearest p-world is the actual world, this account of subjunctives yields a somewhat simpler notion of adherence:

S's true belief that p is *adherent* just in case S believes p in all the p-worlds whose distance to the actual world is no greater than d.[4]

After introducing these notions, Nozick argues that they will need to be modified, to take into account the method used for forming the belief. The status of S's belief that p as knowledge, Nozick argues, depends on whether S would believe p, not in the nearest not-p-worlds, but in the nearest not-p-worlds in which she forms her opinion as to whether p with the method that she employed in actuality for forming her belief that p. Likewise, the status of S's belief that p as knowledge depends on whether S would believe p, not in the nearest p-worlds, but in the nearest p-worlds in which she forms her opinion as to whether p with the method that she employed in actuality for forming her belief that p. If S formed her true belief that p with method M, the method-relative notions of sensitivity and adherence can be formulated as follows:

S's true belief that p is *method-sensitive* just in case S doesn't believe p in any not-p-world in which she arrives at a belief as to whether or not p with method M whose

---

[2] This general account to counterfactuals originates in (Stalnaker 1968) and (Lewis 1973).

[3] Clearly, if adherence is not to be redundant as a condition of knowledge, it has to be possible for a true belief to be inadherent. On David Lewis's account of counterfactuals this is not a possibility, as he treats counterfactuals with true antecedents and consequents as true (Lewis 1973: 26–31).

[4] Sometimes Nozick gives the impression of treating as sufficient for adherence that S doesn't believe not-p in the closest possible worlds. Thus, at one point he tells us that in order for someone's belief to be adherent, 'he must come to the belief in a way that not only does but would yield a true belief (*when it yields any belief at all*)' (Nozick 1981: 186, my italics).

distance to the actual world is no greater than d plus the distance to the nearest not-p-world in which she arrives at a belief as to whether or not p with method M.

S's true belief that p is *method-adherent* just in case S believes p in all p-worlds in which she arrives at a belief as to whether or not p with method M whose distance to the actual world is no greater than d.

For situations in which the formation of the belief involves multiple methods, Nozick offers an account of which method is relevant in each case for assessing the status of the belief as knowledge. But for cases in which this complication is not present, method-sensitivity and method-adherence are taken to be necessary and sufficient for conferring on a true belief the status of knowledge.

I think that Nozick's proposal contains extremely valuable insights into the nature of knowledge. However, other aspects of the view strike me as much less plausible. My goal in the remainder of this chapter will be to provide an assessment of the main aspects of the proposal.

In my view, Nozick's most important contribution to the analysis of knowledge was to highlight the connection between knowledge and sensitivity. In many cases, the right explanation of why a belief doesn't have the status of knowledge is that the belief is not sensitive. Likewise the right explanation of why a belief is knowledge often has as an essential ingredient the sensitivity of the belief. The conviction that many of our beliefs are sensitive plays a major role in our epistemic optimism. We think we are well placed to form true beliefs because our cognitive devices are so related to our environment that we would be able to detect the falsehood of the propositions that we believe: if they were false, we wouldn't believe them.

Any plausible account of knowledge will have to assign to sensitivity pride of place. We cannot be very precise yet about the specific way in which sensitivity will be involved in our account of knowledge, but I can announce four main respects in which the role of sensitivity in the account that I want to present will differ from the role it plays in Nozick's.

First of all, as we have seen, on Nozick's account sensitivity is not individually sufficient for a true belief to have the status of knowledge. It is a necessary ingredient of a sufficient condition that also includes adherence. For Nozick, adherence has the same importance as sensitivity for determining whether a true belief has the status of knowledge. On the account that I want to recommend this parity won't be preserved. In the account of truth tracking that I am going to develop, sensitivity will be the central notion, and adherence will only play a minor role.

Second, on Nozick's account, truth tracking is necessary for knowledge. On the account that I am going to develop, truth tracking won't play this role. It will be instead one of several individually sufficient and jointly (disjunctively) necessary conditions for knowledge—one of several ways in which a true belief can achieve this status.

Third, as we have seen, Nozick employs a method-relative notion of tracking in his account of knowledge. The account that I am going to develop will not adopt this relativization. Our notion of when a belief tracks the truth won't make explicit reference to the method with which the belief has been formed.

Finally, instead of construing tracking, as Nozick does, in terms of counterfactuals, I will follow Sherrilyn Roush (2005) in providing a construal in terms of conditional probabilities, although the probabilistic account of tracking that I will endorse differs in important ways from Roush's proposal.

In the remainder of this chapter I want to do three things. First, I want to explain why a plausible account of knowledge based on truth tracking should not accord to adherence the importance that it has in Nozick's account. Second, I want to argue that sensitivity should not be relativized to methods. And third, I will argue for the need to contemplate a sufficient condition for knowledge that might be satisfied by beliefs that don't track the truth.

## 3.2 Adherence

Nozick tells us that he finds 'a pleasing symmetry' in his account of knowledge: in order to know p, S would have to believe p if p were true and to not believe p if p were false (Nozick 1981: 177).[5] I believe that this symmetry is illusory. Our concept of knowledge is not symmetric in this way. On the contrary, there is a fundamental asymmetry in the concept precisely at this point—whether or not you know p often depends crucially on what you would believe if p were false; what you would believe if p were true has a much less important influence on whether you know p.

In order to highlight this asymmetry I want to consider a family of cases, in which subjects form beliefs about someone's country of origin on the basis of their accent. I want to assume that it is generally possible to acquire knowledge about someone's provenance in this way—that accents are sufficiently correlated with regions to enable someone who can identify an accent to acquire knowledge about where the speaker comes from.

I want to consider first a case in which a subject's belief uncontroversially tracks the truth. In this first case, Scarlett is an American who is generally not very good at discriminating different English-language accents, except that she can detect very accurately a Scottish accent when she hears it. In addition to this discriminating skill, Scarlett knows from a very reliable and trusted source that most people who speak like that come from Scotland. As a result, whenever she hears that accent, she forms the belief that the speaker is Scottish. Furthermore, she never forms the belief that someone is Scottish on the basis of hearing them speak with any other accent.

---

[5] He adds, however, that he is not inclined to make too much of this symmetry (Nozick 1981: 177).

Suppose now that Scarlett is watching a talent show on TV with contestants randomly picked from several English-speaking countries. Suppose that the contest is won by Alistair, a Scottish contestant (with a Scottish accent). When Scarlett hears Alistair talk, she forms the belief that the winner is Scottish. Clearly, Scarlett's belief is both sensitive and adherent. It is sensitive because if the winner weren't Scottish, Scarlett wouldn't form the belief that he is Scottish, since he wouldn't speak in a Scottish accent. And it is adherent because in the nearest worlds in which the winner is Scottish Scarlett forms the belief that he is Scottish, since, subject to our assumptions on the correlation between accents and geographical origin, in these worlds the winner speaks with a Scottish accent.

It is clear that on Nozick's account Scarlett's belief would count as knowledge, and it is hard to see how any plausible version of the tracking account could fail to yield this verdict. I think this verdict is correct. Scarlett knows that the winner is Scottish, and the reason why she does is that her belief tracks the truth. What I want to consider is the relative weight that sensitivity and adherence should be accorded in this verdict. I am going to argue that sensitivity is much more important than adherence.

For this purpose I want to introduce another case. Consider now Gladys. Like Scarlett, Gladys is generally not very good at discriminating accents, except that she can detect very accurately a Glaswegian accent when she hears it. Suppose that Gladys has only vague geographical notions. She doesn't have a conception of Glasgow as the place people with that accent come from. She does know, however, from a very reliable source, that everyone who speaks like that is Scottish. As a result, whenever she hears that accent, she forms the belief that the speaker is Scottish. Furthermore, given her acknowledged incompetence at discriminating other English accents, she never forms the belief that someone is Scottish on the basis of hearing them speak with any other accent, Scottish or otherwise.

Suppose now that Gladys is watching the same talent show. Suppose that Alistair is from Glasgow and speaks with a Glaswegian accent. When Gladys hears him talk, she forms the belief that the winner is Scottish. Gladys's belief, like Scarlett's, is sensitive: if the winner weren't Scottish she wouldn't have formed the belief that he is Scottish, since if he weren't Scottish he wouldn't speak with a Glaswegian accent. However, unlike Scarlett's, Gladys's belief is not adherent. The immediate neighbourhood of worlds in which her belief is true contains worlds in which she doesn't form the belief—all those worlds in which the contest is won instead by a contestant from somewhere in Scotland other than Glasgow.

On Nozick's account, this circumstance would in principle undermine the status of Gladys's belief as knowledge. It can't be knowledge because it doesn't track the truth, since adherence is a necessary condition for truth tracking. I want to suggest, however, that this is the wrong verdict on Gladys's belief. The natural thing to say is that Gladys knows that the winner is Scottish. The procedure that she uses for forming beliefs on these matters latches on to a feature of the situation that guarantees, subject to our assumptions, that her belief will be true. And that is what knowledge requires, according to the intuitions on which tracking accounts rely.[6]

Clearly, Gladys's epistemic situation is generally inferior to Scarlett's. If a contestant from Aberdeen won the show, Scarlett would form the belief that the winner is Scottish, and this belief would have as much of a claim to count as knowledge as her actual belief about the winner from Glasgow. Gladys, by contrast, would fail in this situation to form the true belief that the winner is Scottish.

I am claiming, however, that Scarlett's general epistemic superiority over Gladys is of no consequence when it comes to assessing the epistemic status of their actual belief that the winner is Scottish. Both beliefs enjoy the same level of protection against the risk of error, and for that reason they deserve the status of knowledge to precisely the same degree. The fact that Scarlett's belief is adherent and Gladys's isn't is of no consequence on this point.

In order to underline the asymmetry between sensitivity and adherence I want to consider another case. Brenda can identify a British accent very accurately, but believes that everyone who talks like that comes from Scotland. Brenda is watching the same talent show as the others, and when she hears Alistair speak she also forms the belief that the winner is Scottish. Now, Brenda's belief is adherent. In all the nearby worlds in which her belief is true, worlds in which the contest is won by other Scots, she forms the belief that the winner is Scottish. However, her belief is not sensitive. There are nearby worlds in which the belief is false but she still has it—worlds in which the contest is won by non-Scottish Brits. I want to argue that there is a fundamental difference between the status of Gladys's sensitive, inadherent belief, on the one hand, and that of Brenda's adherent, insensitive belief, on the other. Unlike the sensitivity of Gladys's belief, the adherence of Brenda's provides no protection against the risk of error, as it poses no obstacle to her falsely believing that the winner is Scottish. Sensitivity produces knowledge because it protects your belief from the risk of error. Adherence doesn't produce knowledge because it doesn't have this effect.

I am not denying that adherence provides a general epistemic advantage. We have seen how it does that with beliefs that are also sensitive, and it's easy to see that it has the same effect in the absence of sensitivity. For this purpose consider our final case.

---

[6] One might try to argue, on Nozick's behalf, that Gladys's belief is method adherent, but this proposal faces serious difficulties. Suppose first that arriving at a belief as to whether or not p with M includes suspending judgement with M. Then Gladys's belief won't be method adherent, as there are nearby worlds in which her belief is true and she forms her belief as to whether the winner is Scottish with her accent method, but she doesn't form the belief that the winner is Scottish, i.e. worlds in which the contest is won by a Scot from somewhere other than Glasgow. Suppose now that arriving at a belief as to whether or not p with M includes only forming with M the belief that p or the belief that not-p. Then Gladys's belief will be method adherent, but we only need to modify the case slightly to block this result. Suppose that Gladys is inclined to believe that someone is Scottish if they speak with a Glaswegian accent, and to believe that they are not Scottish if they speak with any other accent. Now we have once again that Gladys's belief is not method adherent, although it strikes me as fully deserving of the status of knowledge. In any case, as I shall argue in Section 3.4, relativizing sensitivity to methods brings in serious problems.

Wendy can detect very reliably a working-class British accent although she can't discriminate between regional varieties. She mistakenly believes that everyone who speaks with that accent comes from Scotland. She can't identify any other accents, so if someone doesn't speak in a British working-class accent she doesn't form the belief that the speaker comes from Scotland. Wendy is watching the same talent show. Like the others, she forms the belief that the winner is Scottish when she hears Alistair talk, since he speaks, as it happens, with a working-class Glasgow accent. Wendy's belief is neither sensitive nor adherent. There are nearby worlds in which her belief is false but she still has it—worlds in which the contest is won by working-class non-Scottish Brits. And there are nearby worlds in which her belief is true but she doesn't have it—worlds in which the contest is won by an upper-class Scot. I don't think anyone would have any inclination to treat Wendy's true belief as knowledge.

Wendy's general epistemic situation is inferior to Brenda's in the same way in which Gladys's is inferior to Scarlett's. Brenda would form true beliefs in situations (upper-class Scots) in which Wendy would fail to do so. I am suggesting, however, that this advantage doesn't have any consequences for the status as knowledge of their belief in the proposition that the winner of the contest is Scottish. The reason is that the epistemic advantage that Brenda enjoys over Wendy doesn't offer her belief any protection against the risk of error. Error is only possible in situations in which the proposition is false, and the adherence of Brenda's belief has no effect on what she believes in those situations.

The following table provides an overview of the four cases that I have presented:

|            | Sensitive | Insensitive |
|------------|-----------|-------------|
| Adherent   | Scarlett  | Brenda      |
| Inadherent | Gladys    | Wendy       |

I have argued that the sensitive beliefs should be classified as knowledge and the insensitive ones shouldn't, independently of whether they are adherent or not. The inadherence of a sensitive belief doesn't detract from its claim to the status of knowledge, and the adherence of an insensitive belief doesn't boost its claim to this status. In these cases, sensitivity makes all the difference; adherence makes no discernible difference. This is the fundamental asymmetry that Nozick's account fails to reflect.

I have suggested that the source of this asymmetry lies in the power that sensitivity has and adherence lacks to protect a belief from the risk of error. How well protected you are from this risk depends on what happens in counterfactual situations in which the belief is false, and these are the situations that determine the sensitivity of a belief. The level of risk protection enjoyed by your belief doesn't depend in any way on what happens in other situations in which your belief is true, but these are the situations that adherence describes. Insofar as truth tracking is a means of achieving knowledge, sensitivity is its main ingredient. When I present in Chapter 6 the account of truth tracking that I am going to defend, we shall see that something like adherence will play a limited role in how a belief in p can have the status of knowledge by tracking p. But this involvement of adherence in tracking won't restore the symmetry. Knowledge by truth tracking will remain, essentially, a matter of sensitivity.[7]

## 3.3  Nozick's defence of adherence

Nozick motivates the introduction of adherence in his account of knowledge with a couple of examples—cases of sensitive belief that intuitively we don't want to count as knowledge. In the first case he invokes, a person who is raised from birth floating in a tank, being brought to believe things by direct electrical and chemical stimulation of his brain, is brought in this way to believe 'that he is in the tank and is being brought to believe things in this way' (Nozick 1981: 175). This true belief, Nozick contends, should not be counted as knowledge. However, it is sensitive: if the person wasn't floating in a tank and brought to believe things in this way, he wouldn't believe that he is. Hence, Nozick argues, we need to introduce an additional necessary condition for knowledge, and he proposes adherence as the condition that will do the job. The reason that the person doesn't know is, on this approach, that his belief is not adherent. There are nearby possible worlds in which he is floating in a tank and brought to believe things in this way but he is not brought to believe in this way that this is the situation he finds himself in.

I want to assess the support that this case provides for the introduction of adherence as an additional necessary condition for knowledge. I want to start by accepting two central aspects of Nozick's description of the case. First, I agree with Nozick that this subject doesn't know. Second, I agree that his belief is sensitive. Hence, a sensitivity-based account of knowledge will yield the wrong verdict in this case. This is certainly a weakness of sensitivity-based accounts of knowledge. It means that they don't provide a perfect match for our intuitions concerning who knows what. However, an imperfect match may well be the best we can get. I want to argue that this limitation of sensitivity-based accounts doesn't justify their rejection, and that supplementing them with an adherence clause produces a generally inferior match for our epistemic intuitions.

First of all it is important to understand the source of the problem exemplified by Nozick's case. I want to start by asking why what you would believe in counterfactual situations should be considered relevant for the epistemic status of your actual beliefs. It seems to me that the reason why counterfactual beliefs are relevant for the epistemic status of actual beliefs is that your counterfactual beliefs reflect the belief-forming patterns and dispositions from which your actual beliefs arise. It follows from this

---

[7] See (Bird 2003) for another line of reasoning against adherence.

answer that the only counterfactual situations that are relevant to the epistemic status of your actual beliefs are those in which you have the same belief-forming patterns and inclinations that you have in actuality. What you would believe in counterfactual situations in which you have significantly different belief-forming inclinations won't reflect your actual inclinations, and should not be treated as relevant to the epistemic status of your actual beliefs.

These points apply, in particular, to the relevance of sensitivity for the status of a belief as knowledge. Sensitivity is relevant to knowledge insofar as whether you would believe p if p were false reflects your actual patterns of belief formation—insofar as you would still have the same belief-forming inclinations if p were false. Sensitivity cannot be used for determining whether you know in cases in which if your belief were false you would have significantly different belief-forming inclinations. What you would believe in these circumstances will not accurately reflect your actual belief-forming inclinations. Consequently it shouldn't be taken into account when assessing the epistemic status of your actual beliefs. In these cases, sensitivity does not determine whether you know or not.

Now, there are propositions whose content guarantees that what you would believe if they were false will be irrelevant to the epistemic status of your belief in these propositions. These are propositions that provide a sufficiently general true description of your actual belief-forming patterns.[8] Call these propositions *cognitively reflective (CR)*. If your belief in a CR proposition were false, you would have significantly different belief-forming inclinations. Hence what you would believe in that situation will not reflect your actual belief-forming inclinations, and should be regarded as irrelevant to the epistemic status of your belief in the CR proposition. The sensitivity of your belief in a CR proposition cannot be used to determine whether your belief has the status of knowledge.[9]

This is an intrinsic limitation of any sensitivity-based account of knowledge: these accounts won't provide an accurate match for our epistemic intuitions concerning beliefs in CR propositions. This is the limitation that Nozick's case exposes. The proposition that he is in a tank being brought to believe things by direct electrical and chemical stimulation is, for the person in the tank, a CR proposition. If it were false, his belief-forming inclinations would be radically different. Hence what beliefs he would form in that situation won't reflect his actual cognitive inclinations, and should not be expected to represent the epistemic status of his actual belief in the proposition. Even though his belief is sensitive, it should not be counted as knowledge.

Other things being equal, this limitation should count against sensitivity-based accounts of knowledge. However, the problem has a very specific source, and should not in principle undermine our confidence in the ability of these accounts to match our

---

[8] In this connection, see Nozick's discussion of believing that you are applying method M via the application of method M itself (Nozick 1981: 215).

[9] Doing so might be described as an instance of the conditional fallacy (Shope 1978).

epistemic intuitions in the vast majority of cases, where CR propositions are not involved. An account that overcame this limitation without creating more serious problems elsewhere would certainly be preferable to one that is afflicted by it. Introducing adherence as an additional necessary condition for knowledge does appear to solve the problem posed by CR propositions. However, this is achieved at a price. I am going to argue that the move would produce the wrong verdict in many other cases. And the new problems don't concern relatively recherché cases, like belief in CR propositions, but perfectly mundane beliefs.

In order to appreciate the consequences of invoking adherence to solve the problem posed by Nozick's case, I want to consider a slight modification of the scenario he presents. In the situation that Nozick contemplates, the psychologists that are in charge of your cognitive economy while in the tank bring you to believe things randomly—with no connection with the facts that these beliefs purport to represent. I think that this randomness is the main obstacle to ascribing to the beliefs formed in this way the status of knowledge. Normally this shortcoming is reflected in the insensitivity of the beliefs. But the connection between randomness and insensitivity breaks down for beliefs in CR propositions.

The point I want to make is that if instead of being randomly produced, the beliefs of the tank-dweller were suitably correlated with the states of affairs that make them true, a proponent of a tracking account of knowledge should have no problem according them this status. Here, I take it, Nozick and I are on the same side. My disagreement with Nozick concerns how 'suitably correlated' should be understood in this context, and, in particular, whether the notion should include an adherence condition.

Suppose then that in a situation that is in other respects as Nozick describes, the psychologists set things up so that at least some of the beliefs of the tank-dweller are systematically correlated with the states of affairs that would make them true. Suppose, for example, that they fit the computer that generates his beliefs with a sensor that reliably detects the presence of a male (other than the tank dweller) in the room where he lies in his tank, and brings him to believe that there is a male in the room precisely if there is a male in the room. It seems to me that it is possible to fill in the details of the case in such a way that his true belief that there is a male in the room counts as knowledge on Nozick's account, since it would be both sensitive and adherent. And I believe this is the right verdict. The male-sensor, if reliable, would enable him to acquire knowledge of whether there is a male in the room.

However, while Nozick's account would yield the right result in this case, the adherence requirement will prevent us from treating as knowledge cases that deserve this status. Suppose, for example that the psychologists decide to fit the belief-generating computer with another sensor that will determine when the person in the tank is brought to believe that there is a female in the room. Suppose that the positive reliability of the female-sensor is virtually perfect: it never produces the belief that there is a female in the room unless this is so. Suppose, however, that its negative reliability has an important shortcoming: it fails to be triggered by women with a cold.

In my view, the tank dweller's (true) belief that there is a female in the room, generated in this way, has as strong a claim to the status of knowledge as his true belief that there is a male in the room. The sensors generating both beliefs protect them from error in equal measure. The subject is as unlikely to believe falsely that there is a female in the room as that there is a male in the room. As in the TV-contest cases, the male-sensor is generally preferable to the female-sensor, since it will enable the subject to form the true belief that there is a male in the room whenever there is a male in the room, whereas the female-sensor won't enable him to form the belief that there is a female in the room on many occasions on which this is the case. But this difference should not be allowed to affect the epistemic status of the true beliefs that he actually forms as a result of the operation of each of the sensors. They both confer on the true beliefs they produce the status of knowledge because they both offer the same degree of protection from the risk of error.

In sum, introducing adherence as a necessary condition for knowledge may succeed in overcoming the difficulty faced by sensitivity-based accounts concerning CR propositions. However, the price of solving this problem is introducing a more serious difficulty. We can easily describe cases of sensitive, inadherent belief in everyday propositions that we would want to count as knowledge. By introducing adherence in our account of knowledge we may be able to match our epistemic intuitions concerning CR propositions, but we will be unable to match our intuitions concerning these other cases. It seems to me that the problem generated by adherence is much more pervasive and fundamental than the problem that it solves. I conclude that the introduction of adherence is insufficiently motivated by Nozick's example. The proponent of a sensitivity-based account of knowledge should bite the bullet and accept that the problem concerning CR propositions is an intrinsic limitation of her position.

The second line of reasoning that Nozick offers in support of adherence is based on a version of a case originally presented by Gilbert Harman:

The dictator of a country is killed; in their first edition, newspapers print the story, but later all the country's newspapers and other media deny the story, falsely. Everyone who encounters the denial believes it (or does not know what to believe and so suspends judgment). Only one person in the country fails to hear any denial and he continues to believe the truth. (Nozick 1981: 177)

Nozick tells us that we are reluctant to say that this person knows the truth, and he appears to assume that an adequate account of knowledge has to yield the result that he doesn't. A sensitivity-based account violates this constraint: if the dictator hadn't died, the newspapers wouldn't have printed the story of his death, and the subject wouldn't believe that he has died. Nozick concludes that an additional necessary condition for knowledge needs to be included in the account, and proposes adherence as the condition that will do the job. The subject's belief is not adherent, as there are nearby possibilities in which he doesn't believe that the dictator is dead—those in which he encounters reports that deny the story.

Clearly this line of reasoning for adherence is only as strong as the assumption that the subject in the example shouldn't count as knowing that the dictator is dead. If this assumption is rejected, we haven't been offered a cogent reason for treating adherence as a necessary condition for knowledge. I want to argue that the assumption should be rejected: in the situation described, the subject knows that the dictator is dead.

The question turns on the epistemic consequences of evidence one doesn't possess. Harman originally presented the case as one of several examples of the following situation: You have evidence for a true proposition p that you believe which would suffice, in the absence of other factors, for conferring on your belief the status of knowledge. However, there's cogent evidence against p, of which you are not aware, although it is easily accessible to you, such that if you were aware of it you would no longer know p (Harman 1973: 142–54). Let me refer to cases that satisfy this description as *Harman cases*.

The example that Nozick borrows from Harman is a Harman case. If it weren't for the deception, the evidence that the subject obtains by reading the newspaper would confer on his belief the status of knowledge. However, the deception produces evidence that is easily available to him, although he is not aware of it, against the dictator's death. If he were aware of this evidence and continued to believe that the dictator is dead, the body of evidence that would then be at his disposal would no longer confer on his belief the status of knowledge.

The question that we need to ask is whether we should say in Harman cases that the subject doesn't know. The first point we need to mention is that intuitions on this point are much less unanimous than in other central thought experiments in epistemology. Nozick and Harman's intuitions sanction the verdict that these subjects don't know. However, I find it much more natural to say in these cases that the subject knows, and I'm not alone in this. Bill Lycan, who reports similar intuitions, adds that sampled opinion is evenly split. He writes:

> I have informally tested a fair number of epistemologists, philosophers generally, students, and non-philosophers. Less than half of those questioned responded with a clear intuitive denial of knowledge, while at least half judged firmly that [Harman cases] are cases of knowledge. (Lycan 1977: 121)

Obviously it would be desirable if the issue didn't boil down to a clash of intuitions. One way in which we might be able to adjudicate the issue is in connection with the principle that Carnap called the *requirement of total evidence* (Carnap 1962: 211–13). It is undeniable that in order to determine whether your evidence confers on your true belief that p the status of knowledge we need to take into account all the evidence at your disposal that is relevant to p. Suppose that you have evidence for and against p, and that the favourable evidence, in the absence of evidence to the contrary, would confer on your belief the status of knowledge. It doesn't follow from this that you know p. The net support that p receives from all the relevant evidence at your disposal, both positive and negative, might be very weak or even negative.[10] If this is the situation, your evidence should not be treated as conferring on your true belief that p the status of knowledge.

One can plausibly claim that this point should be extended in some cases to evidence that you don't have. Suppose that you listen to the defence lawyers present their case and you obtain in this way excellent evidence for the true proposition that the defendant is innocent, but you leave the courtroom before the prosecution presents even stronger (although misleading) evidence against this proposition. One could argue that in this situation your claim to know that the defendant is innocent is undermined by the evidence presented by the prosecution, even though it isn't in your possession.

The crucial question for our purposes is whether we should treat in this way the misleading evidence that the subject in the dead-dictator case doesn't have. I want to suggest that this question should be answered in the negative. The reason why it is plausible to say that the evidence presented by the prosecution should affect the epistemic status of your belief is that you are aware that adding that evidence to the evidence already in your possession is likely to result in weaker overall support for your belief. This feature is missing from the dead-dictator case. When the subject reads in the newspaper that the dictator is dead, he has no reason for thinking that reading other newspapers or listening to the radio news bulletins is likely to produce a state of information from which his belief would receive weaker support. Media reports on these matters tend to agree with one another, and the subject has no reason to believe that this case will be an exception. Given that the subject has no reason to believe that the additional evidence would be likely to result in weaker support, taking it into account for assessing the epistemic status of his belief would seem totally arbitrary. The misleading evidence may be readily available, but there is no reason, as far as the subject knows, why he should take the trouble to access it.

As Lycan suggests, lack of clarity on this point might lend spurious support to the intuition that the subject in a Harman case doesn't know (Lycan 1977: 124–5). One can easily slip into assuming that the subject should realize that the additional sources of evidence are likely to make a difference. With this assumption in place, the claim that the misleading evidence is relevant to the status of the subject's belief starts to seem plausible. But, this assumption is entirely out of place, and once we see this clearly the epistemic relevance of the misleading evidence might lose much of its intuitive appeal.

In sum, I think that the example that Nozick borrows from Harman doesn't lend cogent support to the introduction of adherence in our account of knowledge. The move is defended with the contention that a sensitivity-based account is forced to ascribe knowledge to the subject in the example, while adherence would enable us to

---

[10] Your evidence for p might be weakened, not only by evidence against p, but also by evidence against your favourable evidence.

avoid this result. But this result doesn't have to be avoided. The subject knows that the dictator is dead. Sensitivity produces the right verdict on this case.

The third argument that Nozick deploys in support of adherence invokes its ability to accommodate knowledge of necessary truths. Knowledge of necessary truths poses a problem for sensitivity-based accounts of tracking. If p is a necessary truth, the antecedent of the sensitivity schema is necessarily false—there are *no* not-p-worlds. But on the standard accounts of the semantics of subjunctives, subjunctives with necessarily false antecedents are vacuously true. It follows that every belief in a necessary truth will vacuously satisfy the sensitivity condition. Clearly, not every belief in a necessary truth can be treated as knowledge. Therefore, sensitivity cannot be in general a sufficient condition for a true belief to have the status of knowledge.

If we want to save the role of sensitivity in our account of knowledge, we have in principle two options. The first would be to restrict the scope of the sensitivity-based account of knowledge to knowledge of contingent truths. The second would be to find an additional necessary condition for knowledge which, together with sensitivity, can be seen as jointly sufficient for knowledge. The second route is in principle more appealing, since it doesn't abandon the aspiration to provide a unified account of knowledge. This is the route that Nozick takes, and his proposal is that adding adherence to sensitivity will enable his account of knowledge to deal with necessary truths.

He argues for this point by considering the contrast between two methods by which one might come to believe a mathematical truth (Nozick 1981: 186). The first is mathematical proof. If S forms a belief in a mathematical truth p using this method, Nozick argues, her belief will be method adherent—in every nearby world in which S arrives at a belief as to whether p using this method, she forms the belief that p. Since this true belief is adherent as well as (vacuously) sensitive, Nozick's account treats it as a case of knowledge, as desired. The second method that Nozick considers is dogmatically believing what your parents tell you concerning p. If S forms her belief in p with this method, her belief won't be method-adherent. There are nearby worlds in which S forms her opinion on whether p with this method and comes to believe not-p instead of p, because in these worlds her parents tell her not-p. On the assumption that S's parents are unreliable informants on whether or not p, the inadherence of S's belief in p is unquestionable. It follows that on Nozick's account this belief won't have the status of knowledge, as desired.

We are about to raise some issues concerning the relativization of sensitivity and adherence to methods that could cause problems at this point. But leaving these concerns aside for now, we will have to concede that the introduction of adherence produces the right result in these two cases. Clearly Nozick needs and expects that this situation applies to all cases of belief in a necessary truth—that those that we should count as knowledge are method adherent and those that we shouldn't count as knowledge are not. I want to argue that this is not the situation. We can easily describe cases of method-adherent belief in a mathematical proposition that intuitively should not be counted as knowledge.

Luper-Foy describes a case of this kind. He considers a subject who believes $\sqrt{4} = 2$ using the method consisting in believing the proposition just in case John is not both fat and not fat (Luper-Foy 1984: 31). Clearly this belief is method adherent—in every world (at any distance) in which the subject forms her belief on whether or not $\sqrt{4} = 2$ using this method, she will believe $\sqrt{4} = 2$. However, intuitively, this (vacuously) method-sensitive, method-adherent true belief is not knowledge. The subject does not know in this way that $\sqrt{4} = 2$. Notice that it is not an essential component of this case that there are no worlds in which the method fails to produce true belief. It would be enough if true belief was produced in every nearby world. Suppose, for example, that our subject forms her belief on whether or not $\sqrt{4} = 2$ with the following method: believing $\sqrt{4} = 2$ if and only if her crystal ball remains in a solid state at room temperature. There are worlds in which this method fails to produce true belief, but they are presumably too remote to affect the method-adherence of the belief. This is another method-sensitive, method-adherent true belief that should not be counted as knowledge.

I conclude that adding adherence to sensitivity doesn't produce an adequate treatment of knowledge of necessary truths. The resulting account will classify as knowledge many beliefs in necessary truths that intuitively shouldn't have this status. Adherence doesn't enable us to extend the scope of our sensitivity-based account of knowledge to necessary truths. Hence the desirability of extending the account in this way provides no support for the introduction of adherence.

In this section I have considered the three lines of reasoning that Nozick offers in support of adherence. I have argued that they all fail. First, I have argued that even though adherence may produce the right results concerning knowledge of CR propositions, it produces a much more pervasive clash with our intuitions. Second, I have argued that adherence doesn't receive legitimate support from its power to classify Harman cases as cases in which the subject doesn't know, since, *pace* Nozick, Harman, and others, it seems to me that some Harman cases are genuine cases of knowledge. Finally, I have argued that adherence receives no support from the desirability of including knowledge of necessary truths in the scope of a sensitivity-based account of knowledge, since adherence doesn't produce a satisfactory treatment of these cases. I conclude that Nozick hasn't offered cogent support for the introduction of adherence. We shall see later on that a concept that might be recognized as a version of adherence will figure in our account of tracking, but it will only play a marginal role. Truth tracking is, first and foremost, sensitivity.

## 3.4 Methods

As we've seen, Nozick believes that an adequate account of truth tracking needs to relativize sensitivity and adherence to the method that was used in forming the belief.

He defends this move by considering two kinds of difficulty that afflict the unmodified position.

The first problem concerns adherence: there are cases that we want intuitively to count as knowledge in which adherence is not satisfied:

[...] the bank-robber's mask slips off as he is escaping and the bystander sees it is Jesse James, whose picture is on many wanted posters. [...] The bystander knows that Jesse James is robbing the bank. (Nozick 1981: 193)

As Nozick realizes, the bystander's belief is not adherent—there are nearby worlds in which he doesn't have the belief, because the robber's mask doesn't slip off. Nozick's proposal is to save adherence from this kind of counterexample by introducing the method-relative version of the notion. The bystander's belief, Nozick argues, is method-adherent. The method employed in forming the belief, he explains, is 'looking and concluding that it is Jesse James on the basis of seeing certain things' (Nozick 1981: 193). And in every nearby world in which he forms a belief on whether or not the robber is Jesse James using this method he forms the belief that he is Jesse James.[11]

The second problem concerns sensitivity: there are true beliefs that we intuitively want to count as knowledge in which sensitivity is not satisfied:

A grandmother sees her grandson is well when he comes to visit; but if he were sick or dead, others would tell her he was well to spare her upset. (Nozick 1981: 179)

In this case, once more, intuition dictates that the grandmother knows that her grandson is alive. Nevertheless, her belief is not sensitive, since in the nearest worlds in which he is not alive her relatives would make sure that she doesn't find out.

Once again, methods save the day. In the nearest worlds in which her grandson is dead *and* she forms her belief on whether or not he is alive with the method she actually employed for forming her belief on this question, the grandmother doesn't believe that he is dead. Her belief is method-sensitive.

The first of these arguments need not detain us. The difficulties with adherence that Nozick seeks to solve by appealing to methods are precisely the difficulties that I have invoked to argue against treating adherence as necessary for knowledge. If, as I am recommending, we refrain from treating adherence as necessary for knowledge, cases like Jesse James's don't pose a problem: the bystander knows that the robber is Jesse James because if the robber wasn't Jesse James he wouldn't believe that he is.

The second problem will require much more attention. Surely the grandmother's belief should count as knowledge, but it is obviously insensitive. Hence sensitivity can't be necessary for knowledge. If we want to preserve the involvement of sensitivity in our account of knowledge something has to be done. Nozick's proposal is to shift to the method-relative formulation of sensitivity. I am going to recommend a different

---

[11] The ability of method relativization to deal with these cases has been called into question. See, e.g., (Forbes 1983: 47–8).

approach, but before I present my preferred alternative I'd like to consider some of the difficulties raised by the introduction of methods.

Clearly, one problem with the appeal to methods is that it forces us to formulate principles of method individuation, since the method-sensitivity of a belief will often be affected by how we individuate the method with which the belief was formed. This is a version of the problem of generality raised against process reliabilism (Feldman 1985). I am not going to present this as a reason against appealing to methods. The problem of method individuation might be a specific manifestation of a general problem that any version of reliabilism will have to address.

The problem on which I want to concentrate arises from the fact that, as Nozick acknowledges, many belief-forming methods capable of producing knowledge are what Nozick calls *one-sided methods*. A one-sided method, Nozick tells us, 'is incapable of recommending belief in not-p; it either recommends belief in p or yields no recommendation' (Nozick 1981: 183). Consider, for example, a medical test for a condition with virtually no false positives but lots of false negatives. A positive result in the test virtually guarantees that the condition is present, but a negative result provides only very weak support for the hypothesis that the condition is absent, since lots of people with the condition test negative. This test can recommend belief in the proposition that the condition is present, but it can only recommend very weakly belief in the proposition that the condition is not present.

Luper-Foy has presented an objection to Nozick's account of knowledge based on the consequences of one-sidedness for the method-relative notion of sensitivity. Here is his presentation of the problem:

> The problem that arises when we apply (3) [method sensitivity] to a one-sided method M is that (3) can never be met. Its antecedent requires that M come to believe that p or that not-p via M. But in order to do so, when M is one-sided, S must come to believe that p via M. And then the consequent of (3) cannot be satisfied. (Luper-Foy 1984: 27)

Luper-Foy is using here a plausible construal of the notion of arriving at a belief as to whether or not p with method M as either forming the belief that p with M or forming the belief that not-p with M (Luper-Foy 1984: 28). It follows from this that a world in which the antecedent of the method-sensitivity subjunctive is true is a not-p-world in which either S forms the belief that p with M or she forms the belief that not-p with M. But since M is one-sided, Luper-Foy argues, S cannot form the belief that not-p with M. Hence a world in which the antecedent of the method-sensitivity subjunctive is true will have to be a not-p-world in which S forms the belief that p with M. But then the consequent of the subjunctive will be false in that world.[12] It follows that in all (nearby) worlds in which the antecedent is true the consequent is false. Therefore the method-sensitivity subjunctive is false. Whenever a belief is formed with a one-sided method, method sensitivity cannot be satisfied.

---

[12] Assuming that the subject doesn't have contradictory beliefs.

I find a couple of problems in Luper-Foy's reasoning. Let's concentrate first on necessarily one-sided methods, that is, cases in which there is no world in which S forms with M the belief that not-p (abbreviated $\text{Bel}_M$ not-p). There are two situations compatible with the necessary one-sidedness of M. The first is that there are worlds in which not-p & ($\text{Bel}_M$ p ∨ $\text{Bel}_M$ not-p). This is the situation that Luper-Foy is contemplating. Take the nearest world in which not-p & ($\text{Bel}_M$ p ∨ $\text{Bel}_M$ not-p). In this world, since M is necessarily one-sided, we have that not-p & $\text{Bel}_M$ p, from which it follows that S's belief that p is not method sensitive, as Luper-Foy concludes.

However, this is not the only scenario compatible with the one-sidedness of M. We might find instead that there are no worlds in which not-p & ($\text{Bel}_M$ p ∨ $\text{Bel}_M$ not-p), that is, in every not-p world, S fails to form a belief with M on whether or not p. In this case, the antecedent of the method-sensitivity subjunctive is necessarily false, and on the standard account subjunctives with necessarily false antecedents are true (Lewis 1973: 16). In this way, a belief formed with a necessarily one-sided method can be method sensitive, contrary to Luper-Foy's claim.

My second point concerns contingently one-sided methods. Presumably when we assert that S formed the belief that p with a one-sided method M we don't mean to rule out very remote worlds in which S forms the belief that not-p with M. All we are claiming is that there is a sphere H of possible worlds centred on the actual world, in which S doesn't form the belief that not-p with M. For contingently one-sided methods the situation is more complicated than Luper-Foy suggests. Assume that M is (contingently) one-sided. Now there are three cases to consider. First, if there are no worlds satisfying the antecedent of method sensitivity (i.e. not-p & ($\text{Bel}_M$ p ∨ $\text{Bel}_M$ not-p)), we have once more that S's belief that p will be method sensitive. Second, suppose that the nearest world satisfying the antecedent of method sensitivity is inside H. Then, since M is one-sided, this will be a world in which not-p & $\text{Bel}_M$ p, rendering S's belief that p method insensitive. But now we have a third possibility. Suppose that the nearest world w satisfying the antecedent of method sensitivity is outside H. Now the one-sidedness of M won't interfere with method sensitivity. Whether or not S's belief that p is method sensitive will depend on whether among the worlds that are no further away than the distance to w plus d there are worlds in which not-p & $\text{Bel}_M$ p. If there are such worlds the belief will be method insensitive. If, on the contrary, there are no such worlds, then the belief will be method sensitive.

In sum, there are two ways in which a belief formed with a contingently one-sided method might be method sensitive. The first is if there are no not-p-worlds in which S forms a belief as to whether or not p using M. The second is if the nearest not-p-world in which S forms a belief as to whether or not p is outside the sphere or worlds that determine the one-sidedness of M. Neither of these possibilities is contemplated by Luper-Foy.

Nevertheless, it seems to me that Luper-Foy's general concern is perfectly legiti-mate. What we've found is that with respect to beliefs formed with one-sided methods, relativizing sensitivity to methods has an important consequence: satisfaction of the method-relative condition can depend on what happens in worlds that are much more remote than those that determine satisfaction of the unrelativized condition.

Let's go back to our clinical test with virtually no false positives but lots of false negatives. Let's assume that false positives could only arise in situations that are significantly different from the actual situation. Suppose, for example, that some law of nature would have to be violated in order for someone who tests positive to be free from the condition. Clearly, if a doctor's belief that the condition is present is based solely on the positive result of this test, her belief will be sensitive—in the nearest worlds in which the condition is absent she won't believe that it is present. Once we relativize to methods, what happens in the nearest worlds in which the condition is absent no longer settles the issue. Now we need to look at the nearest worlds in which the condition is absent *and* the doctor forms a belief as to whether or not the condition is present using the test. Since the method is one-sided, it won't produce a negative result in any nearby worlds, and since false positives can only arise in radically different circumstances, it won't produce a positive result in any nearby worlds in which the condition is absent. It follows that relativizing to methods makes the sensitivity of the doctor's belief hostage to what happens in remote worlds, in which the method starts producing beliefs (positive or negative) on the presence of the condition when the condition is actually absent. If in the nearest world in which the condition is absent and the method produces a belief, it produces the belief that the condition is present, the doctor's actual belief won't have the status of knowledge, after all.

This strikes me as the wrong result. If she forms the belief with the method that we have described, the doctor's belief that the condition is present should count as knowledge by virtue of the fact that she won't form the belief that the condition is present in any nearby world in which the condition is absent, independently of what happens in the more remote worlds in which the condition is absent and the method produces a belief. Method relativization doesn't work for one-sided methods because it forces us to look at the wrong worlds for determining whether a true belief has the status of knowledge.

Luper-Foy proposes to avoid the problems posed by one-sided methods with a reformulation of method sensitivity. His idea is to remove mention of the method employed from the antecedent of the sensitivity subjunctive (Luper-Foy 1984: 28–9). His account of method sensitivity is equivalent to this:

> S's true belief that p is method sensitive just in case, if p were false, S would not form the belief that p with M (i.e. just in case S doesn't form the belief that p with M in any not-p-world whose distance to the actual world is no greater than d plus the distance to the nearest not-p-world).[13]

---

[13] See (Williamson 2000: 154), where a similar formulation of sensitivity is discussed as a necessary condition for knowledge.

Unfortunately, Luper-Foy's proposal doesn't work. There are cases in which a belief that shouldn't count as knowledge because it was formed with a method that would easily produce false beliefs would nevertheless count as method sensitive on Luper-Foy's account. Suppose, for example, that the grandmother of Nozick's case forms her belief that her grandson is well by consulting her crystal ball, and does so in a way that would produce the belief that he is well in every nearby world (imagine, for example, that the crystal ball tells her that he is well by failing to shatter when lightly stroked with a feather). Now suppose that, as in Nozick's case, if the grandson were unwell or dead, others would make sure that she doesn't find out. For this purpose they would remove and destroy her crystal ball, fearing that it might actually work and break the sad news to her.

It seems obvious to me that in this case we don't want to say that the grandmother knows that her grandson is well. One can't come to know these things by consulting a crystal ball. Nevertheless, the grandmother's belief satisfies Luper-Foy's sensitivity condition: in all nearby worlds in which her grandson is not well she doesn't form the belief that her grandson is well using the crystal-ball method. Luper-Foy's proposal has to be rejected.

Another way in which one might try to save method sensitivity from these difficulties is to use a different construal of the notion of forming a belief as to whether or not p with method M, including not only cases in which S forms the belief that p or the belief that not-p with M, but also cases in which S suspends judgement on whether or not p with M. But it is not clear how this proposal could be made to work. The decision to suspend judgement on a question is typically taken either when the subject believes that she has insufficient information at her disposal or when she believes that in the information at her disposal support for p is evenly balanced with support for not-p. The failure of a one-sided source of information to produce a positive verdict will contribute to the decision to suspend judgement only in a negative sense—by failing to provide support for (or against) p. But the decision will always have to take into account the deliverances of other sources of information, and it is hard to see how we are supposed to single out the worlds in which suspension of judgement should be attributed to an individual method.

The problem is perhaps particularly acute in cases in which S forms the belief that p on the basis of information that she obtained not by applying a method, in the non-technical sense of the notion, but as a result of serendipity. In the case of the clinical test that we considered earlier, if the test produced a negative result and the doctor decided to suspend judgement on the presence of the condition, the responsibility of this decision would be borne jointly by all the sources of information which, along with this test, failed to provide significant support for or against the presence of the condition. But in this case, at least the involvement of the method would be marked by the performance of the test. In other cases, however, it is hard to see how the method with which a belief was formed could be said to be involved in a counterfactual decision to suspend judgement on the question. Suppose that Mary's husband was kidnapped years ago, and nothing has been heard from him since then. One day, Mary finds on the street a page of today's newspaper with what she positively identifies as her husband's signature on it, and she forms as a result the belief that her husband is alive. Here, presumably, finding a page of the day's newspaper with her husband's signature is the method by which her belief was formed. Now consider a counterfactual situation in which she doesn't find a page of the day's newspaper with her husband's signature and she suspends judgement on whether or not her husband is alive. It seems to me that we can't make any clear sense of the method being involved in her suspension of judgement. Her failure to find a page of today's paper with her husband's signature is just one of indefinitely many potential sources of information on the question that would fail to produce a verdict. In cases like these, the notion of suspending judgement on p with one-sided method M is particularly problematic.

I have argued that relativizing sensitivity to the method employed in forming the belief produces unacceptable results in the case of one-sided methods. One way in which one might try to save Nozick's position from this point is to contend that, while the problem may be real, it is only a minor limitation of the proposal, as one-sidedness is a marginal phenomenon. However, this line is highly implausible. One-sidedness is a widespread phenomenon. If we insist on describing all cases of belief formation as involving methods, in many cases the only candidate for the job is a one-sided method.

Furthermore, it could be argued that two-sidedness, when it occurs, is merely coincidental, and contributes nothing to the epistemic status of the belief. Consider our doctor who has formed the belief that the condition is present in a patient as a result of the positive result obtained in the test with virtually no false positives but lots of false negatives. Suppose that the patient goes to another doctor for a second opinion. This doctor also forms the belief that the condition is present, but she bases her belief on a different clinical test—one with the same very low incidence of false positives but an equally low rate of false negatives. In this test, like in the previous one, a positive result virtually guarantees that the condition is present, and a negative result, unlike in the previous test, virtually guarantees that the condition is absent. It seems to me that the second doctor's belief that the condition is present doesn't have a stronger claim to count as knowledge than the first doctor's belief does. The difference between a one-sided and a two-sided method is irrelevant to the epistemic status of beliefs. We have here, in effect, another manifestation of the asymmetry that we identified when we discussed adherence. S's true belief that p achieves the status of knowledge thanks to the method with which it was formed when S wouldn't form the belief that p using that method if p were false. Whether or not S could also use the method to form the belief that not-p is irrelevant to the epistemic status of her belief that p. One-sidedness is not a marginal phenomenon. One-sided methods have all that's required in every case for the production of knowledge. The difficulties that method relativization encounters with one-sided methods are fundamental. The move should be rejected on these grounds.

## 3.5  Evidence

As we've seen, Nozick supports his proposal to relativize sensitivity and adherence to methods with two kinds of considerations: cases that we intuitively want to treat as knowledge that don't satisfy the adherence condition (e.g. the Jesse James case) and cases that we intuitively want to treat as knowledge that don't satisfy sensitivity (e.g. the grandmother case). As I explained in the previous section, the first kind of case doesn't pose a problem for the account that I am developing, since I don't think that adherence should be treated as a necessary condition for knowledge. However, the second kind of case does pose a problem that I need to deal with. I need to explain why the grandmother's belief counts as knowledge even though it is not sensitive.

Nozick's approach to this problem consists in revising the definition of sensitivity so that the grandmother's belief counts as sensitive, after all. I have rejected Nozick's proposed revision in terms of methods. There might be other more promising revisions of the notion that achieve the intended result, but this is not the approach that I am going to take. I am going to accept instead that the grandmother's belief is not sensitive, and hence that some insensitive beliefs count as knowledge: sensitivity is not a necessary condition for knowledge.

I am going to argue that sensitivity, in the formulation that I will provide in Chapter 6, is a sufficient condition for knowledge. However, sensitivity is not the only sufficient condition for knowledge that my account will contemplate. There will be two other individually sufficient conditions for knowledge that can be satisfied by insensitive beliefs. The grandmother gets to know, in spite of the insensitivity of her belief, by satisfying one of these additional conditions.

I want to introduce the condition that will confer on the grandmother's insensitive belief the status of knowledge by reference to the traditional distinction between inferential and non-inferential knowledge. Inferential knowledge is knowledge that you have by virtue of knowing other things that provide you with evidence for your belief. Non-inferential knowledge, by contrast, does not rest on other items of knowledge in this way. My proposal is that sensitivity should be invoked in the explication of non-inferential knowledge, while inferential knowledge should receive a separate construal.

Nozick and other more recent advocates of tracking accounts of knowledge don't subscribe to this approach. Naturally they accept that knowledge is often inferential, but they don't think of the phenomenon as requiring separate treatment.[14] On this view, when you know inferentially that p, this is so because possessing adequate evidence for p makes your belief that p track the truth. On my proposal, by contrast,

---

[14] On Nozick's view, acquiring evidence for p will allow S to know p by ensuring that her belief in p tracks the truth (Nozick 1981: 249). Keith DeRose appears to accept the same picture of the relationship between evidence and truth tracking (DeRose 1995: 25). As we shall see in due course, Sherrilyn Roush (2005) rejects this approach in the case of deductive evidence, but accepts it for non-deductive evidence. I have discussed this issue in (Zalabardo 2009b: 76–7).

whether you have inferential knowledge will not depend on whether your belief tracks the truth. In many cases the conditions that produce inferential knowledge will also make your belief track the truth, but there will be exceptions to this correlation—cases of inferential knowledge in which your belief does not track the truth.

It is this feature of the account that will enable us to explain why the grandmother's insensitive belief has the status of knowledge. She knows that her grandson is well because during his visit she came to know other things that provide her with adequate evidence for her belief. And being in possession of this evidence enables her to know that her grandson is well even though her belief in this proposition doesn't track the truth.

The possibility of knowing inferentially without tracking the truth is not merely a technical trick for dealing with problem cases. It reflects what I regard as an important role that evidence can play in our cognitive economy: evidence enables us to overcome the cognitive handicap posed by insensitivity. Suppose that you are an experienced police interrogator and that after years on the job you have developed the skill to make remarkably accurate intuitive judgements on who is lying and who is telling the truth. Nevertheless, in spite of the general reliability of your judgements on this matter you have discovered a marked bias affecting a specific category of subjects. Whenever you interrogate someone from your village you find yourself convinced that he is lying. You realize that this doesn't correspond with reality—the proportion of liars in your village is similar to the proportion of liars in the population at large.

Suppose that you are interrogating someone from your village, and that you find yourself once more predictably convinced that he is lying. Suppose that he is, as a matter of fact, lying. Nevertheless intuition dictates that you don't know this, and the natural explanation of this verdict is that your belief is not sensitive: if he were telling the truth you would still believe that he is lying.

I want to suggest that the epistemic handicap posed by the insensitivity of your belief can be overcome, and that acquiring adequate evidence for the subject's mendacity is the obvious way to achieve this. If, for example, you could test your subject with a reliable lie-detector, and it dictated that your subject is lying, you would know as a result that he is lying. Your bias would no longer be an obstacle to knowledge.

Now, it seems to me that the possibility of acquiring knowledge in this way is not open to question, but it might seem that the case doesn't support the claim that evidence can confer on an insensitive belief the status of knowledge, since the process of evidence acquisition will have made your belief sensitive. If he weren't lying, the argument goes, the lie-detector test would have had a negative result, and then you wouldn't believe that he is lying. I'd like to discuss two important assumptions made by this argument.

The first assumption made by the argument is that if your intuition and the lie-detector test recommended different verdicts, you would go along with the lie-detector recommendation. This is not a factual assumption. Proponents of this line of thought will accept that your inclination to follow your intuition might be stronger than your inclination to accept the verdicts of the lie-detector. But they will argue that if this is the situation the evidence provided by the lie-detector test will not confer on your belief the status of knowledge.

This is the line that Nozick takes in his treatment of cases of overdetermination, where more than one method is involved in the production of a belief. Suppose that the production of your true belief that p involved two methods: M1, relative to which your belief tracks the truth, and M2, relative to which your belief doesn't track the truth. In this situation, on Nozick's account, your belief will have the status of knowledge just in case if M1 recommended believing not-p and M2 recommended believing p you would believe not-p (Nozick 1981: 182). Thus suppose that in the counterfactual situation in which the lie-detector says your subject is telling the truth but your instinct tells you he is lying you believe that he is lying. Then, according to Nozick, your actual belief that he is lying doesn't count as knowledge, in spite of the evidence provided by the lie-detector test.

I don't find this view very plausible. It seems to me that so long as you are in possession of strong evidence for the proposition you believe, as provided by the lie-detector test, your belief should count as knowledge even if your inclination to follow your instinct is stronger than your inclination to bring your belief in line with the evidence. In the actual situation, your evidence enables you to ascertain that the chances of your belief being in error are very small. I am claiming that this circumstance should confer on your belief (if true) the status of knowledge even if in any conflict between the lie-detector and your instinct you wouldn't be able to resist going along with your instinct. If this is the situation you find yourself in, your insensitive belief will have the status of knowledge.[15]

The second assumption made by the argument linking evidence with sensitivity concerns the character of the evidence at your disposal. The argument assumes that the fact that you have adequate evidence for p entails that if p were false you would have adequate evidence for not-p. Of course there are many cases that answer to this description, but there are many other cases that don't, and we can fill in the details in our example to reflect this point. Suppose that your lie-detector is only one-way reliable. If it says that someone is lying, it is virtually impossible that they are telling the truth, but if it doesn't say that they are lying, the probability that they are lying is only marginally lower than random. Suppose, as before, that the lie-detector test gives a positive result for your subject.

Filling in the details in this way means, in effect, that the lie-detector method is a one-sided method. As Nozick realizes, his general treatment of cases of overdetermination doesn't work in these cases (Nozick 1981: 183). Here we can't look at what you would believe if M1 recommended believing not-p and M2 recommended believing

---

[15] In taking this line, I am rejecting the view that, in order to confer on a belief the status of knowledge, evidence has to be somehow causally responsible for the belief. However, as we'll see in Chapter 4, it will be required that the subject believes (in fact, knows) that the evidence supports the belief.

p because if M1 is one-sided it will never recommend believing not-p. He proposes that in these cases knowledge will require instead that you believe p in the counterfactual situation in which M1 recommends believing p and M2 recommends believing not-p.

This requirement strikes me as no more plausible than the one in force for two-sided methods, and I reject it on the same grounds. If in the counterfactual situation in which the lie-detector tells you that the suspect is lying but your intuition tells you that he is telling the truth you believe that he is telling the truth, your actual belief that he is lying will still receive the status of knowledge from the evidence provided by the lie-detector.

However, the point that I want to make now applies even if the requirement is satisfied. I take it that if the lie-detector method outweighs the intuitive method, there is no reason for withholding from your belief the status of knowledge. Evidence provided by a one-sided lie-detector has the same power to confer on your true belief the status of knowledge as evidence provided by a two-sided model. If the lie-detector test has a positive result, you now know that your subject is lying, notwithstanding the unreliability of the negative verdicts of the device. However, this evidence would not render your belief sensitive. If the suspect were telling the truth, the test would have a negative result, but a negative result from the one-sided lie-detector doesn't provide a significant recommendation for believing that the subject is not lying. In the absence of a recommendation from the lie-detector, your bias would prevail, and you would believe that he is lying. The evidence provided by the one-sided lie-detector test enables you to know that your subject is lying, at least when the lie-detector method outweighs the intuitive method, but it does so without making your belief sensitive. This is a second way in which evidence can confer the status of knowledge on an insensitive belief.

## 3.6  Conclusion

At the beginning of this chapter I declared my support for Nozick's idea that sensitivity should play a crucial role in our theory of knowledge. However, the bulk of the chapter has been devoted to arguing against other aspects of Nozick's position. I have argued first that adherence should not be accorded the same importance as sensitivity. Then I have argued against Nozick's proposal to relativize sensitivity to methods. Finally I have argued that inferential knowledge should be possible in cases of insensitive belief. We can see how the outline of a positive picture starts to emerge from these negative points. On this picture, inferential and non-inferential knowledge will receive separate accounts. Sensitivity will be the central notion of our account of non-inferential knowledge, while inferential knowledge will not require sensitive belief.

The next few chapters will fill in the details within this outline. Chapters 4 and 5 will present a theory of inferential knowledge. In Chapter 4 I will put forward a theory of when your evidence provides adequate support for one of your beliefs. In Chapter 5

I will consider how you need to be related to evidence that supports a true proposition you believe in order for this evidence to confer on your belief the status of knowledge.

Then in Chapter 6 I will present a theory of non-inferential knowledge. I start by providing a construal of truth tracking in which sensitivity plays the leading role, and adherence receives much less importance. I shall put forward truth tracking, on this construal, as a sufficient condition for non-inferential knowledge (for true beliefs). Then I shall argue that we need to contemplate a second form of non-inferential knowledge—a sufficient condition for non-inferential knowledge that can be satisfied by beliefs that don't track the truth.

With this theory of knowledge at our disposal, we'll be able to return to the sceptical problem and assess the prospects of different forms of sceptical argument against our knowledge claims. This will be our main task in the rest of the book.

# 4

# Evidence

At the end of the preceding chapter I argued that inferential and non-inferential knowledge should receive separate accounts. My goal in this chapter and the next is to provide an account of inferential knowledge.

One way to know that a liquid is an acid is to see that the litmus paper that we have dipped in it turns red. This is a paradigm case of inferential knowledge. You know that the liquid is an acid by virtue of the evidence provided by the fact that the litmus paper has turned red. Let ACID be the proposition that the liquid is an acid, and let RED be the proposition that the litmus paper that you have dipped in the liquid has turned red. In order for you to know ACID on the strength of the evidence provided by RED, two types of condition need to be satisfied. The first type concerns the connection between RED and ACID. The second concerns your relationship to RED and to the connection between RED and ACID. We can characterize conditions of the first type as objective, and conditions of the second type as subjective. Objective conditions for inferential knowledge will be the subject matter of the present chapter. Subjective conditions will be discussed in the next.

Why does (the state of affairs represented by) RED provide adequate evidence for (the state of affairs represented by) ACID? I am going to answer this question in probabilistic terms. ACID is very likely to be true if RED is true, and very likely to be false if RED is false, and RED is very likely to be true if ACID is true, and very likely to be false if ACID is false. I am going to explicate the fact that RED provides adequate evidence for ACID in terms of these probabilistic facts.

## 4.1 Probability

Both in everyday life and in science we appear to be committed to the existence of probabilistic facts. We say, for example, that snow is more probable in January than in April, that red-haired parents are more likely to have red-haired children than other parents, or that people who exercise regularly are less likely to have heart attacks than those who don't. In many cases we feel that probabilities can be given precise values. We say that the probability that a coin lands heads in a fair toss is 1 in 2, and that a child of a 30-year-old mother has a 1 in 910 chance of being born with Down's syndrome.

The status and nature of these facts are controversial issues that fall beyond the scope of this book. Here I only want to make a few remarks to indicate the conception of probability facts that I am going to invoke in my account of evidence. The probabilities that figure in my explanandum are neither logical, a priori discoverable facts about events, nor subjective degrees of belief by actual or ideally rational subjects. They are instead objective, contingent facts about states of affairs, knowable only by empirical investigation. They arise from the nomological order: the probability of states of affairs is determined by the laws of nature (Lewis 1986, 1994).

Some authors, following Lewis, have argued that this approach makes the existence of non-trivial probabilities (higher than 0 but lower than 1) contingent on whether the universe is ultimately deterministic (Lewis 1986, 1994; Schaffer 2007). On this position, in a deterministic world, every possible event would have probability 1 or 0. But others have argued that this outcome can be avoided without abandoning Lewis's basic approach (Hoefer 2007; Glynn 2010). One appealing strategy for achieving this goal is to argue that probabilities should be generated not only by fundamental laws, but also by the laws of high-level or special sciences, such as statistical mechanics, genetics, economics, or meteorology. These sciences ascribe non-trivial probabilities that are not contingent on the universe being ultimately probabilistic.

The crucial question for this approach is whether these non-trivial probabilities can be regarded as genuine objective chances or should be dismissed instead as merely epistemic. To establish the objectivity of these probabilities within the Lewisian paradigm would require showing that the laws of the special sciences should be treated as part of the best system of laws of nature. According to Lewis, objective chances are what the probabilistic laws of the best system say they are (Lewis 1994: 480). Hence, if the best system contained the laws of the special sciences alongside fundamental laws, it would produce non-trivial objective chances even if the fundamental laws of the system were deterministic.

Luke Glynn has argued persuasively that the laws of the special sciences should be included in the best system, even by Lewis's criteria of what the best system should contain. According to Lewis, the best system is the system that gets the best balance of simplicity, strength, and fit (Lewis 1994: 480). But as Glynn argues, the inclusion in the system of at least some special laws can be expected to enhance the satisfaction of these criteria. He writes:

[ . . . ] it seems that a system that yields the special scientific laws as theorems will be much stronger or more informative than one that yields merely the fundamental microphysical laws. This is because the microphysical laws tend to fall silent about the higher-level properties that the special scientific laws relate. (Glynn 2010: 59)

And he adds:

Nor need the addition, to a system, of axioms required to entail the special scientific laws cost much in terms of simplicity. (Glynn 2010: 60)

And the point doesn't depend on the acceptance of Lewis's Humean account of laws. Glynn argues that the special scientific laws 'ought [ ... ] to be accommodated as genuine laws by any adequate account of lawhood' (Glynn 2010: 65).[1]

Another feature of Lewis's proposal is that probabilities are time-indexed, since the probability of p at t is determined, not only by the best system of laws, but also by the complete history of the universe up to t. One consequence of this is that even if the best system contains probabilistic laws, the probability of a proposition about past events will always be trivial—1 if the proposition is true and 0 if it is false.

This outcome renders probabilities unsuitable for the explication of evidential support. Propositions about the past can sustain relations of evidential support independently of their truth value. The proposition that it rained last night receives more support now from the proposition that the streets were wet in the morning than from the proposition that the sky was red the previous morning, independently of the truth value of the propositions involved.

I propose to avoid this outcome by rejecting Lewis's idea that the history of the universe should play a role in the determination of probabilities. Probabilities will be determined by the laws alone, and will, as a result, not change with time.[2]

Parallel to the philosophical controversies about its nature, the concept of probability has received a sophisticated formal treatment. Here the question can be posed in the following terms. If probabilities are represented numerically, what formal principles would need to be satisfied by the function that pairs each proposition with the number that represents its probability? The answer to this question would take the form of a set of axioms that a function from propositions to numbers would need to satisfy in order to count as a probability assignment.

There are many axiomatizations of probability, but one, due to A. N. Kolmogorov, is generally treated as the standard system (Kolmogorov 1933). Kolmogorov's axioms concern a function taking as arguments not propositions, but the elements of a field. A field F on a non-empty set $\Omega$ is a set of subsets of $\Omega$ that includes $\Omega$ itself and is closed under complementation (with respect to $\Omega$) and union, i.e. if A and B are in F, $A \cup B$ is in F, and if A is in F, $\Omega - A$ is in F.

Kolmogorov's axioms provide a contextual definition of the concept of a *probability function*, as any function p from a field F on $\Omega$ to the real numbers satisfying the following conditions:

1. For every A in F, $p(A) \geq 0$.
2. $p(\Omega) = 1$.
3. If $A \cap B = \emptyset$, $p(A \cup B) = p(A) + p(B)$.[3]

---

[1] An alternative to Glynn's approach, advocated by Carl Hoefer (2007), is to maintain that not all objective chances follow from laws of nature, fundamental or higher-level.

[2] Carl Hoefer has also rejected the view that probabilities are time indexed while retaining some features of Lewis's basic approach (Hoefer 2007).

[3] Kolmogorov added to these, with some reservations, an axiom that is equivalent to a correlate of Axiom 3 for the union of a countable collection of pairwise disjoint sets.

Kolmogorov's approach can be easily applied to functions taking, not elements of a field, but propositions as arguments. I'll take propositions to be individuated semantically, by their truth conditions. Thus, for example, '~(A & B)' and '~A ∨ ~B' will denote the same proposition. Similar results could be achieved if the elements of the domain were individuated syntactically. Let Π be a set of propositions closed under truth-functional composition. Then we can adapt Kolmogorov's axioms by saying that a function p from Π to the real numbers is a probability function just in case it satisfies the following axioms:

*Axiom 1*: p pairs each element of Π with *a non-negative* real number.
*Axiom 2*: p pairs the logically true proposition with 1.
*Axiom 3*: p pairs the disjunction of two logically incompatible propositions with the sum of their respective images under p.

In what follows I am going to assume that probabilities can be represented by a function from propositions to real numbers that satisfies these axioms.[4]

Satisfaction of these axioms by p has some immediate consequences that we will invoke later on. Notice, first, that the probability of a proposition and the probability of its negation will always add up to one (Theorem 1, see Appendix). Second, the logically false proposition has probability 0 (Theorem 2). Third, the probability of a proposition is no greater than the probability of any of its logical consequences (Theorem 3). Fourth, the probability of every proposition is no less than 0 and no more than 1 (Theorem 4). Finally, the probability of a disjunction is the sum of the probabilities of the disjuncts less the probability of their conjunction—that is, the probability that the first disjuncts is true, plus the probability that the second is true, less the probability that both disjuncts are simultaneously true (Theorem 5).

Nevertheless, the axioms are compatible with a huge range of probability assignments. In particular, the axioms do not dictate that logically indeterminate propositions have to have probabilities greater than 0 and less than 1. A function that pairs each logically indeterminate proposition with 0 or with 1 can still satisfy the axioms.

## 4.2 Conditional probability

The formal theory that we have sketched concerns the assignment of probabilities to individual propositions. However, the notion that we want to exploit in our theory of evidence is the notion of conditional probability—the probability of a proposition given another proposition, for example the probability that the liquid is an acid given that the litmus paper has turned red.

---

[4] If we took as the domain of the function a set of sentences of a formal language, in order to achieve the same result we would need to add another axiom:

If A and B are logically equivalent, p(A) = p(B).

The standard approach here is to define conditional probability in terms of categorical probability. Thus, *the conditional probability of a proposition A on a proposition B*, written p(A | B), where A and B have probabilities and the probability of B is greater than 0, is defined by the following equation:

(CP)   p(A | B) = p(A & B)/p(B)

Thus, for example, according to CP, the probability of the liquid being an acid conditional on the litmus paper turning red equals the probability that the liquid is an acid and the litmus paper turns red divided by the probability that the litmus paper turns red.

If conditional probability is defined in these terms, from the assumption that categorical probability satisfies the Kolmogorov axioms it follows that conditional probability displays a very similar behaviour, assuming, for each instance of p(X | Y), that p(Y) ≠ 0. Notice first that conditional probability satisfies straightforward correlates of the axioms: the probability of A on B is non-negative (Theorem 6), the conditional probability of the logically true proposition on any proposition is 1 (Theorem 7), and if C entails that two propositions are logically incompatible, the probability of their disjunction equals the sum of their respective probabilities conditional on C (Theorem 8).

Conditional probability also satisfies straightforward correlates of the theorems that we presented in the previous section. First, the probability of A on B and the probability of ~A on B always add up to one (Theorem 9). Second, the probability of the logically false proposition on any proposition is zero (Theorem 10). Third, if C entails a material conditional, then the probability of its antecedent conditional on C is no greater than the probability of its consequent conditional on C (Theorem 11). Fourth, conditional probabilities are at least 0 and at most 1 (Theorem 12). And finally we have a conditional correlate of Theorem 5: the probability of a disjunction conditional on a proposition C is the sum of the probabilities of its disjuncts conditional on C less the probability of their conjunction conditional on C (Theorem 13).

Two further consequences of (CP) and the Kolmogorov axioms are worth mentioning, since they will play an important role in our subsequent discussion. They concern the relationship between conditional and categorical probabilities. The first is known as the *mixing principle*. It says that if $A_1, \ldots, A_n$ and B are propositions such that B entails that $A_1, \ldots, A_n$ are pairwise contradictory and that at least one of them is true, the (categorical) probability of B equals the sum of the conditional probability of B on each of the $A_i$ times the probability of $A_i$ (Theorem 14). The second, known as *Bayes's Theorem*, connects the conditional probability of A on B with the conditional probability of B on A. It says that the conditional probability of A on B divided by the categorical probability of A equals the conditional probability of B on A divided by the categorical probability of B (Theorem 15).

Thus, on the standard approach, conditional probability is defined in terms of categorical probability by means of (CP). This way of proceeding has serious shortcomings.

One obvious source of difficulties is the impossibility of defining p(A | B) when p(B) = 0. If only logical falsehoods had probability 0 the problem would not be particularly serious. However there are good reasons for thinking that some logically indeterminate propositions also have to be assigned probability 0. Take, for example, the probability that a continuous random variable X takes a particular value x. The probability of X = x has to be zero, but, as Alan Hájek has argued, there would seem to be many well-defined probabilities conditional on this outcome, for example the probability that X = x given that X = x or the probability that this coin will land heads given that X = x (Hájek 2003: 286).

A more general difficulty with introducing conditional probability in this way is that there are many cases where the conditional probability of A on B seems well defined and precise but the probability of B is either vague or indeterminate. Consider, for example, the probability that the coin lands heads if I toss it fairly. This value would seem to be perfectly determinate, thanks to the macroscopic laws governing the behaviour of coins in these circumstances. But what is the probability that I toss the coin fairly? There doesn't seem to be any incoherence in maintaining that this probability doesn't have a determinate value even though the probability that the coin will land heads if I toss it fairly is 0.5. In fact this kind of situation wouldn't be at all unusual on the construal of probability that I am recommending. If the history of the universe doesn't play a role in the assignment of probabilities, it is hard to see how propositions describing individual events could be assigned probabilities. However, this difficulty doesn't arise for the probability of an event given some other event. Assigning conditional probabilities is something that probabilistic laws seem capable of doing directly, without the intervention of categorical probabilities.

These considerations recommend rejecting the idea that conditional probability should be defined by (CP), and, more generally, that conditional probability should be defined in terms of categorical probability. Conditional probability should be treated instead as the fundamental notion, with categorical probability then trivially defined as conditional probability on logical truth.[5] On this approach, (CP) should not be treated as the definition of conditional probability, but as a constraint that conditional probability will have to satisfy whenever p(A & B) and p(B) are well defined and the latter is non-zero. Taking this route would involve providing a set of axioms for p(A | B), and there are several extant proposals.[6] I am not going to discuss these options. I am simply going to assume that all the theorems of the Kolmogorov system plus (CP) are theorems of the theory of conditional probability, leaving to one side the question of how the theory should be axiomatized.

---

[5] A more comprehensive argument in favour of this approach has been provided by Alan Hájek (Hájek 2003).

[6] An influential axiomatization of conditional probability as a primitive notion was presented by Karl Popper (Popper 2002: appendix *iv). See also (van Fraasen 1995), with an appendix on the previous literature.

I have argued that treating conditional probability as the fundamental notion will enable us to assign a definite value to p(A | B) even in cases in which p(A) and p(B) are undefined. Nevertheless, we cannot expect that the account of probability I have endorsed will yield a value for p(A | B) for any arbitrary pair of propositions A and B. Whether it does or not will depend on the presence in the best system of probabilistic laws connecting the states of affairs represented by A and B. For cases in which there are no determinate conditional probabilities involving A and B, my account won't be able to postulate relations of evidential support between A and B. The importance of this limitation will depend on the details of which special laws are treated as generating objective probabilities. This is not a question we can address here, and I am going to assume that the requisite probabilities exist whenever a relation of support is intuitively present.[7] Notice in this connection that probabilities don't need to receive particularly precise values in order to sustain relations of evidential support.

## 4.3 Evidence and probability

My proposal, then, is that whether evidence E provides adequate support for hypothesis H depends on the values of the conditional probabilities linking E and H. The next question that we need to address is the precise form of this dependence. Clearly the strength of E's support for H will be a matter of degree, but when it reaches a certain threshold it will sustain inferential knowledge of H. This is the notion that we are ultimately interested in—a degree of evidential support that can be exploited to obtain inferential knowledge.

One factor on which E's support for H will unquestionably depend is the value of p(H | E). Other things being equal, E's support for H will increase with the value of p(H | E), and the connection between E and H won't be able to produce inferential knowledge of H unless this value is sufficiently high. It wouldn't make much sense to try to set a precise threshold for this, but notice that if p(H | E) is less than 0.5, p(~H | E) will be higher than p(H | E)—H will be more likely to be false than true if E is true (see Theorem 9). In this situation the connection between E and H wouldn't sustain inferential knowledge of H. Hence the threshold for p(H | E) to sustain inferential knowledge would have to be higher than 0.5.[8]

On the other hand, the threshold should be lower than 1. Inferential knowledge can arise from non-deductive support. Hence it will have to be possible to know H on the basis of the connection between E and H when the value of p(H | E) is less than 1. It follows that the threshold for p(H | E) should be greater than 0.5 but less than 1.

My claim is that a value for p(H | E) above this threshold is a necessary condition for the connection between E and H to sustain inferential knowledge of H. However, it

---

[7] Thanks to Carl Hoefer for pressing me on this point.

[8] My claim is not that the threshold for p(H | E) should be 0.5, but that the threshold itself, not just the value of p(H | E), should be higher than 0.5.

can't be a sufficient condition. To see this, notice that two propositions A, B are said to be probabilistically independent of one another if $p(A \mid B) = p(A)$. When this condition is met, the probability of A is unaffected by the truth value of B. Clearly, if E and H are probabilistically independent of one another, we don't want the connection between them to give rise to inferential knowledge of H. However, treating a lower bound for $p(H \mid E)$ as a sufficient condition for adequate support would have this effect for every hypothesis H whose probability is above the threshold. H would receive adequate support from any proposition that is probabilistically independent from H. It follows that we need to look for other necessary conditions for E providing adequate support for H which, together with a lower bound on $p(H \mid E)$, can be plausibly seen as jointly sufficient conditions.

One possibility that we might consider at this point is to set an upper bound on $p(H \mid {\sim}E)$ as an additional necessary condition for adequate support. However, I want to argue that this would be a mistake. E can provide excellent support for H in cases in which $p(H \mid {\sim}E)$ is not particularly low. Consider the kind of example that we discussed in Chapter 3 in connection with methods—a clinical test for a condition with virtually no false-positives but lots of false-negatives. I think it is undeniable that the evidence provided by a positive result in such a test can sustain inferential knowledge of the presence of the condition. In this situation the probability that the condition is present if the test result is positive will be very high. However the probability that the condition is present if the test result is negative need not be particularly low. The probability that the condition is present in a patient that has tested negative could be nearly as high as the probability that the condition is present in a random individual.

Another place we can look for probabilistic necessary conditions of adequate support is the inverse probabilities, of the evidence on the hypothesis, often known as *likelihoods*.

We can ask first whether it is a necessary condition for E to provide adequate support for H that the conditional probability of E on H is above a certain threshold. I want to argue that this question has to be answered in the negative. There are cases in which intuitively we would want to say that E provides adequate support for H but the probability of E on H is not particularly high. Consider again our clinical test with virtually no false-positives but lots of false-negatives. A positive result in this test will provide adequate support for the presence of the condition, but the probability of a positive test result if the condition is present won't be particularly high.

Notice, though, that for each evidence–hypothesis pair there will be a threshold for $p(E \mid H)$ such that below this threshold E cannot provide adequate support for H. The lower bound for $p(E \mid H)$ will be dictated by our lower bound on $p(H \mid E)$ by virtue of Bayes's Theorem. If b is our lower bound for $p(H \mid E)$, it follows that E won't provide adequate support for H unless $p(E \mid H)$ is greater than $b \cdot p(E)/p(H)$. This means that if $p(E)$ is greater than $p(H)$, $p(E \mid H)$ will have to be above our threshold for $p(H \mid E)$ if E is to provide adequate support for H. However, when $p(E)$ is much smaller than p(H), E will be able to provide adequate support for H with very small values for p(E | H). This is the situation in our clinical test. A positive test result can provide adequate support for the presence of the condition with a very low value for p(E | H) because a positive test result is much less likely than the presence of the condition.

We ask next whether it is a necessary condition for E to provide adequate support for H that the conditional probability of E on ~H is low. I think that a low p(E | ~H) (i.e. high p(~E | ~H), see Theorem 9) should be treated as a necessary condition for adequate support. If a clinical test gave a positive result in many cases in which the condition is not present, a positive result would not provide adequate evidence for the presence of the condition. E providing adequate evidence for H requires that if H were false, E would be unlikely to obtain.

Notice that the points I have made about the relationship between p(H | E) and p(E | H) apply also to the relationship between p(~E | ~H) and p(H | ~E). For every E–H pair, our lower bound for p(~E | ~H) will enjoin an upper bound for p(H | ~E).[9] If p(E) is greater than p(H), E won't provide adequate support for H unless p(~H | ~E) is above the threshold for p(~E | ~H) (and hence p(H | ~E) below one less the threshold). But if p(E) is much smaller than p(H), the upper bound on p(H | ~E) will be correspondingly insubstantial. This is the situation with our clinical test. Since a positive test result is much less probable than the presence of the condition, the former can provide adequate support for the latter even though the value of p(H | ~E) is high.

So my proposal so far is to treat high values for p(H | E) and p(~E | ~H) are necessary conditions for E to provide adequate support for H, and to impose no restrictions on the values of p(E | H) or p(H | ~E). Notice that our two necessary conditions are independent of one another. Contraposition does not apply to conditional probabilities. We could have, on the one hand, that p(H | E) is high and p(~E | ~H) is low. This would happen, for example, if H and E were both very likely, but independent of one another. On the other hand, we could have a high p(~E | ~H) and a low p(H | E). We would have this situation, for example, if E and H were both very unlikely, but independent of one another.

However, these independently necessary conditions for adequate support cannot be treated as jointly sufficient. E could fail to provide adequate support for H even if both p(H | E) and p(~E | ~H) were arbitrarily high. To see this, suppose that E and H are probabilistically independent of one another, but p(H) and p(~E) are above our thresholds for p(H | E) and p(~E | ~H), respectively. If E and H are probabilistically independent of one another, clearly E won't provide adequate support for H, but both p(H | E) and p(~E | ~H) will be above the thresholds for adequate support. Here our necessary conditions will be satisfied in cases that we don't want to treat as instances of adequate support. More conditions will need to be added to obtain a set of individually necessary and jointly sufficient conditions for adequate support.

---

[9] If c is our lower bound for p(~E | ~H), the upper bound for p(H | ~E) will be $1 - (c \cdot p(\sim H)/p(\sim E))$.

# 4.4 Incremental confirmation

The natural place to look for additional probabilistic conditions for adequate support is the notion of incremental confirmation. Incremental confirmation corresponds to the intuitive idea that adequate evidence should increase the probability of the hypothesis—that the probability of the hypothesis given the evidence should be greater than the unconditional probability of the hypothesis. Thus, if $p(H \mid E) > p(H)$, we say that E incrementally confirms H, if $p(H \mid E) < p(H)$, E incrementally disconfirms H, and if $p(H \mid E) = p(H)$, E neither confirms nor disconfirms H, since E and H are probabilistically independent.

There are a couple of equivalent formulations of the condition $p(H \mid E) > p(H)$. Notice first that it follows from Bayes's Theorem that $p(H \mid E) > p(H)$ if and only if $p(E \mid H) > p(E)$. It can also be easily shown that $p(H \mid E) > p(H)$ if and only if $p(E \mid H) > p(E \mid {\sim}H)$ (Theorem 16).

It is hardly controversial that incremental confirmation should be treated as a necessary condition for adequate support—E won't provide adequate support for H unless E incrementally confirms H.[10] In fact, it seems natural to introduce a stronger condition. Notice that E will incrementally confirm H so long as $p(H \mid E) > p(H)$ (i.e. $p(E \mid H) > p(E \mid {\sim}H)$), no matter how small the gap between the two values might be. It would seem reasonable to demand that E won't provide adequate support for H unless $p(H \mid E)$ is substantially greater than $p(H)$, or $p(E \mid H)$ is substantially greater than $p(E \mid {\sim}H)$. Notice that there are in principle two ways of measuring how much greater the first value is than the second—in terms of the *difference* between the two and in terms of the *ratio*. It follows that we have to consider four different proposals as to how to express how much E incrementally confirms H, depending on which magnitudes we use ($p(H \mid E)$ and $p(H)$ or $p(E \mid H)$ and $p(E \mid {\sim}H)$) and on whether we look at their difference or their ratio. The four possibilities are represented in the following table:

|  | Differences | Ratios |
|---|---|---|
| *Probabilities* | $PD(H, E) = p(H \mid E) - p(H)$[11] | $PR(H, E) = p(H \mid E) / p(H)$[12] |
| *Likelihoods* | $LD(H, E) = p(E \mid H) - p(E \mid {\sim}H)$[13] | $LR(H, E) = p(E \mid H) / p(E \mid {\sim}H)$[14] |

---

[10]  The condition is not redundant. E might fail to incrementally confirm H even if E satisfies with respect to H the conditions for adequate support that we introduced in the previous section, since, as we saw, these conditions can be satisfied when E and H are probabilistically independent.

[11]  See (Earman 1992; Gillies 1986; Jeffrey 1992).

[12]  See (Milne 1996). Milne argues for log(PR) as the true measure of confirmation. Log(PR) is ordinally equivalent to PR. See below.

[13]  LD hasn't received much support among confirmation theorists but it is the account of weak evidential support put forward by Robert Nozick (Nozick 1981).

[14]  See (Fitelson 2001a; Roush 2005). Fitelson argues for log(LR), which is ordinally equivalent to LR.

Treating a substantial level of incremental confirmation as a sufficient condition for adequate support would involve setting a lower bound on one of these measures. Which one should we choose? The first point we need to make is that our choice would make a difference, as the four options disagree with each other on the degree to which evidence confirms hypotheses. We can express this point precisely with the help of the following notion. Two measures M1 and M2 of incremental confirmation are *ordinally equivalent* just in case for all evidential propositions E, E⋆ and all hypotheses H, H⋆, M1(H, E) < M1(H⋆, E⋆) if and only if M2(H, E) < M2(H⋆, E⋆). Hence, when two measures of incremental confirmation are ordinally inequivalent, they produce different orderings of evidence–hypothesis pairs according to degree of confirmation.

Our four measures of incremental confirmation are ordinally inequivalent. Any two of them will order some evidence–hypothesis pairs differently according to the degree to which the evidence confirms the hypothesis. In fact, disagreements can be found even when we restrict ourselves to considering the degree to which two hypotheses are confirmed by a single evidential proposition (Theorem 18, Theorem 19, Theorem 20).

In order to choose between our candidate measures, we need to look in some detail at how they behave in specific contexts. We can appreciate the difference between the two probability measures if we consider how their verdicts are affected by the probability of the hypothesis. Consider two hypotheses H, H⋆ such that H is much more probable than H⋆, for example p(H) = 0.7, p(H⋆) = 0.000000001. Notice that here similar values for PD(H, E) and PD(H⋆, E⋆) will result in much larger values for PR(H⋆, E⋆) than for PR(H, E). Thus, for example, if evidential propositions E, E⋆ are such that p(H | E) = 0.7095, p(H⋆ | E⋆) = 0.01, we have that PD(H, E) = 0.0095, PD (H⋆, E⋆) = 0.009999999, whereas PR(H, E) ≈ 0.99, PR(H⋆, E⋆) = 10,000,000.

I want to suggest that in these cases intuition strongly favours PR over PD. A piece of evidence that increases the probability of a hypothesis from 0.000000001 to 0.01 provides much more support than one that increases the probability of a hypothesis from 0.7 to 0.7095. And the issue does not concern only how much more confirmation E⋆ provides for H⋆ than E provides for H. This difference between the behaviours of PD and PR is the source of their ordinal inequivalence: it will produce disagreements on the ordering of evidence–hypothesis pairs by degree of confirmation.

We can show this with an example provided by George Schlesinger (Schlesinger 1995). Schlesinger asks us to compare two scenarios. In the first, we consider a type of aircraft which is regarded as extremely safe, with a $1/10^9$ probability of crashing in a single flight. However, further inspection of the structure of the aircraft reveals a flaw as a result of which the probability of one of these planes crashing is actually 1/100. The second scenario concerns troops landing gliders behind enemy lines. We start from the assumption that someone taking part in one of these operations has a 26 per cent chance of perishing, but one day the commander announces that due to peculiar weather conditions the risk has increased from 26 per cent to 27 per cent.

As Schlesinger argues, the degree to which the inspection of the aircraft confirms the hypothesis of a plane crash is intuitively much higher than the degree to which the unusual weather conditions confirm the hypothesis of a glider mission resulting in death. This intuition is preserved by the probability-ratio account. If H is the hypothesis of a plane crash and E is the inspection of the aircraft, PR(H, E) is $1/100$ divided by $1/10^9$, that is $10^7$. On the other hand, if H$\star$ is the hypothesis of a glider mission ending in tragedy, and E$\star$ is the unusual weather, PR(H$\star$, E$\star$) is $27/100$ divided by $26/100$, that is 1.038. PR(H, E) is much higher than PR(H$\star$, E$\star$). The probability-difference measure, by contrast, does not preserve the intuition. PD(H, E) is $1/100 - 1/10^9$, that is 0.00999... and PD(H$\star$, E$\star$) is $27/100 - 26/100$, that is 0.01. PD(H, E) is slightly smaller than PD(H$\star$, E$\star$).

In sum, PD and PR provide conflicting verdicts on the degrees to which two hypotheses are supported by evidence when one of the hypotheses is significantly more probable than the other. And in these cases, intuition is firmly in favour of PR and against PD. If confirmation is to be measured in terms of how much the evidence increases the probability of the hypothesis, this increase has to be considered as a ratio, not as a difference. PR is the only probability measure that holds any promise.

We turn now to comparing the likelihood measures. Here an important difference arises when we consider the degree to which two evidential propositions confirm a single hypothesis. When we focus on this special case, LR and the two probability measures agree with each other—they always produce the same verdicts on whether E provides more or less confirmation for H than E$\star$ does. Their verdicts in these cases can be characterized in the following terms: they all dictate that E confirms H more strongly than E$\star$ does whenever the probability of H on E is greater than the probability of H on E$\star$ (Theorem 21). This feature of LR, PD, and PR can be plausibly treated as an adequacy condition for a measure of confirmation—if H is made more probable by E than by E$\star$, then H should be counted as receiving more confirmation from E than from E$\star$. However, LD doesn't satisfy this constraint. There are cases in which the probability of H on E is greater than the probability of H on E$\star$ but LD dictates that E$\star$ confirms H more strongly than E does (Theorem 22). This is a highly counterintuitive outcome and I propose to rule out LD as a measure of confirmation on these grounds.[15] This leaves us with LR as the only likelihood measure of confirmation in contention.

With the difference measures out of the running, we are faced with a choice between the ratio measures. In order to make this choice we need to look at the circumstances in which the two measures produce conflicting verdicts. For this purpose, notice that PR(H, E) can also be expressed as $p(E \mid H)/p(E)$. This enables us to see PR and LR as fractions with the same numerator and different denominators. Notice that if we concentrate on the degree to which a single evidential proposition E confirms two hypotheses H and H$\star$, according to PR this will depend exclusively on the probability of the evidential proposition on each of the hypotheses, that is PR(H, E) $>$ PR(H$\star$, E) if and only if $p(E \mid H) > p(E \mid H\star)$. Let's assume that $p(E \mid H) > p(E \mid H\star)$, and hence

---

[15] Fitelson (2001b) has shown that the same shortcoming is present in another popular account of confirmation: $p(H \mid E) - p(H \mid {\sim}E)$. This account has been defended by (Joyce 1999; Christiensen 1999).

that PR(H, E) > PR(H★, E), and consider under what circumstances we would have LR (H, E) < LR(H★, E). Notice that this will happen when the denominators of LR(H, E) and LR(H★, E) compensate for the gap between their numerators, that is when $p(E \mid \sim H)/p(E \mid \sim H^\star) > p(E \mid H)/p(E \mid H^\star)$ (Theorem 23).

A similar situation obtains when we remove the restriction to cases in which only one evidential proposition is involved. With respect to LR the situation is unchanged: LR(H, E) will be greater than LR(H★, E★) whenever the ratio of $p(E \mid H)$ to $p(E^\star \mid H^\star)$ is greater than the ratio of $p(E \mid \sim H)$ to $p(E^\star \mid \sim H^\star)$. With respect to PR, we have that PR(H, E) will be greater than PR(H★, E★) just in case the ratio of $p(E \mid H)$ to $p(E^\star \mid H^\star)$ is greater than the ratio of $p(E)$ to $p(E^\star)$.

It follows from this that LR gives to $p(E \mid \sim H)$ an importance that it lacks in PR. Let's simplify matters by assuming that E and E★ are equiprobable evidential propositions. If $p(E \mid H)$ is greater than $p(E^\star \mid H^\star)$, PR will dictate that E provides more confirmation for H than E★ provides for H★, irrespective of the values of $p(E \mid \sim H)$ and $p(E^\star \mid \sim H^\star)$. For LR, by contrast, no matter how much greater than $p(E^\star \mid H^\star)$ $p(E \mid H)$ might be, it will be possible for E★ to provide more confirmation for H★ than E provides for H, if the value of $p(E^\star \mid \sim H^\star)$ is sufficiently smaller than the value of $p(E \mid \sim H)$. If $p(E \mid H) = n \cdot p(E^\star \mid H^\star)$, LR(H★, E★) will be greater than LR(H, E) if $p(E \mid \sim H)$ is greater than $n \cdot p(E^\star \mid \sim H^\star)$.

We can appreciate the intuitive relevance of this point by thinking of E and E★ as positive results in clinical tests for the presence of conditions H and H★. Then $p(E \mid H)$ will correspond to the ratio of true-positives of the test—how many cases of the condition it detects—and $p(E \mid \sim H)$ to the ratio of false-positives—how often it produces a positive result when the condition is not present. Now we can see the disagreement between PR and LR as concerning the relevance of the ratio of false-positives to the degree to which a positive test result confirms the presence of the condition. According to PR, the false-positive ratio has no direct effect on the degree of confirmation. If the true-positive ratio of E with respect to H is higher than the true-positive ratio E★ with respect to H★, then E provides more confirmation for H than E★ provides for H★, irrespective of what the corresponding false-positive ratios might be. For LR, by contrast, the false-positive ratio plays a decisive role in confirmation. No matter how much higher the true-positive ratio of E with respect to H might be than the true-positive ratio of E★ with respect to H★, E★ might still provide more confirmation for H★ than E provides for H, if the gap between the false-positive ratios outweighs the gap between the true-positive ratios.

I take this difference to support a preference for LR. The degree to which a positive test result confirms the presence of a condition has to be directly affected by the likelihood of a positive result if the condition is not present. A plausible measure of confirmation has to satisfy this constraint, but PR violates it. I want to extract from this general constraint two adequacy conditions for a measure of confirmation.[16]

---

[16] The argument that follows was first presented in (Zalabardo 2009a).

The first condition concerns the degree to which two evidential propositions confirm a single hypothesis. Consider the degree to which a diagnosis of asthma is supported by two standard symptoms: wheezing and a dry cough. Both symptoms have a very high ratio of true-positives: most people with asthma wheeze and most people with asthma have a dry cough.[17] Let's assume that the true-positive ratio is identical in each case. However, with respect to false-positives, the two symptoms rate very differently. Very few people who don't have asthma wheeze, whereas quite a few people who don't have asthma have a dry cough. Hence wheezing and a dry cough have the same ratio of true-positives, while wheezing has a significantly lower ratio of false-positives than a dry cough does.

I want to suggest that a plausible measure of confirmation should yield the result that the features of the example that we have described suffice for concluding that wheezing confirms a diagnosis of asthma to a higher degree than a dry cough does. In general, a plausible measure of confirmation should take same true-positive ratio with a lower false-positive ratio as a sufficient condition for a higher degree of confirmation. This yields my first adequacy condition for a measure of confirmation:

(1) If $p(E \mid H) = p(E^\star \mid H)$ and $p(E \mid \sim H) < p(E^\star \mid \sim H)$, then E confirms H to a higher degree than $E^\star$ does.

Clearly, treating LR as our measure of confirmation would satisfy (1), since if $p(E \mid H) = p(E^\star \mid H)$ and $p(E \mid \sim H) < p(E^\star \mid \sim H)$, LR(H, E) and LR(H, E$^\star$) have the same numerator, but LR(H, E) has a smaller denominator than LR(H, E$^\star$) does. However, this gives no advantage to LR over PR. As we saw above, LR and PR always agree in their verdicts when a single hypothesis is involved. Hence taking PR as our measure of confirmation would also satisfy (1).

I want to argue next that intuition sanctions the same verdict when we are comparing the degree to which two evidential propositions confirm different hypotheses. Compare now the degree to which wheezing confirms a diagnosis of asthma with the degree to which weight loss confirms a diagnosis of lung cancer. Most lung cancer patients lose weight. Hence, as evidence for lung cancer, weight loss has a very high true-positive ratio, which we can assume to be identical to the true-positive ratio of wheezing or a dry cough as evidence for asthma. However, lots of people who don't have lung cancer also lose weight. Hence, as evidence for lung cancer, weight loss has quite a high ratio of false-positives, which we can assume to be identical to the false-positive ratio of a dry cough as evidence for asthma.

I want to suggest that intuition dictates that when we compare the degree to which wheezing supports a diagnosis of asthma with the degree to which weight loss supports a diagnosis of lung cancer, we should draw the same conclusion as when we compared wheezing and a dry cough as evidence for asthma. Wheezing has the same ratio of true-

[17] I'm grateful to Jonathan Grigg and Sabine Kleinert for the medical examples.

positives with respect to asthma as weight loss does with respect to lung cancer, but the former has a lower false-positive ratio than the latter does. Hence a plausible account of confirmation should treat wheezing as confirming the asthma hypothesis to a higher degree than weight loss confirms the lung cancer hypothesis. In general, a plausible theory of confirmation should take same true-positive ratio with a lower false-positive ratio as a sufficient condition for a higher degree of confirmation, even when we are dealing with different hypotheses. This yields my second adequacy condition for a theory of confirmation:

(2)   If $p(E \mid H) = p(E^\star \mid H^\star)$ and $p(E \mid {\sim}H) < p(E^\star \mid {\sim}H^\star)$, then E confirms H to a higher degree than $E^\star$ confirms $H^\star$.

Clearly, the same reasoning that we gave for (1) establishes that treating LR as our measure of confirmation would satisfy (2). Notice, however, that LR might not be the only measure of confirmation that satisfies (2). (2) says nothing about the orderings that the confirmation function should yield when the true-positive ratios are different. The question that we need to ask is whether treating PR as our measure of confirmation would also satisfy (2). I am going to argue that this question should be answered in the negative.

Notice that, since PR(H, E) can be expressed as $p(E \mid H)/p(E)$, to show that PR doesn't satisfy (2) it would suffice to establish that $p(E) > p(E^\star)$ is compatible with $p(E \mid H) = p(E^\star \mid H^\star)$ and $p(E \mid {\sim}H) < p(E^\star \mid {\sim}H^\star)$. In these cases, (2) would dictate that E confirms H to a higher degree than $E^\star$ confirms $H^\star$, but treating PR as our measure of confirmation would yield the opposite result. I am going to argue that this is the situation.

Suppose that E, as evidence for H, and $E^\star$, as evidence for $H^\star$, have the same high ratio of true-positives, say 95 per cent, but that E has a lower ratio of false-positives (2.5 per cent) than $E^\star$ does (20 per cent). Hence we have:

$p(E \mid H) = p(E^\star \mid H^\star) = 19/20$
$p(E \mid {\sim}H) = 1/40$
$p(E^\star \mid {\sim}H^\star) = 1/5$

Is this compatible with $p(E) > p(E^\star)$? Clearly, if we assumed that $p(H) = p(H^\star)$, the situation would be the same as in the one-hypothesis scenario. The mixing principle would entail that $p(E) < p(E^\star)$.

However once we remove the assumption that $p(H) = p(H^\star)$, the result no longer follows. Suppose, for example, that $p(H) = 1/3$ and $p(H^\star) = 1/20$. Then the mixing principle tells us that $p(E) = 1/3$, while $p(E^\star) = 0.2375$. Using our reformulation of PR, we have that PR(H, E) = 2.85 and PR($H^\star$, $E^\star$) = 4. Hence in this case, although $p(E \mid H) = p(E^\star \mid H^\star)$ and $p(E \mid {\sim}H) < p(E^\star \mid {\sim}H^\star)$, taking PR as our measure of confirmation would yield the result that E confirms H to a lesser degree than $E^\star$ confirms $H^\star$, in violation of our adequacy condition.

We can extract from these considerations a reply to Peter Milne's argument in support of PR (Milne 1996). Milne has defended PR on the grounds that it is the only measure of confirmation satisfying five desiderata. The premise of Milne's argument is correct: PR is the only measure of confirmation satisfying his five conditions. Hence to resist his conclusion we would need to reject his contention that an adequate measure of confirmation would need to satisfy these conditions. This is the line I am going to take. In fact, that Milne's conditions should be rejected is a consequence of what we have already said, since they are incompatible with my condition (2).

The source of the incompatibility is Milne's condition 5:

M5  If $p(E \mid H) = p(E \mid H^\star)$, then E confirms H and $H^\star$ to the same degree.

Notice that the following is a special case of (2), above:

(2$^\star$)  If $p(E \mid H) = p(E \mid H^\star)$ and $p(E \mid \sim H) < p(E \mid \sim H^\star)$, then E confirms H to a higher degree than $H^\star$.

Clearly M5 and (2$^\star$) are incompatible. They produce conflicting results whenever $p(E \mid H) = p(E \mid H^\star)$ and $p(E \mid \sim H) \neq p(E \mid \sim H^\star)$.[18] Hence, if, as I have argued, (2) is correct, it follows that M5 should be rejected, and PR receives no support from the fact that it uniquely satisfies Milne's desiderata.[19]

My proposal, then, is to treat a high value for LR as a necessary condition for adequate support.[20] Using LR has some distinct advantages over some of the main alternatives. One valuable feature is the fact that, unlike probability measures, LR uses only conditional probabilities. If, as I suggested above, there are many cases in which conditional probabilities are well defined but the corresponding unconditional probabilities are not, LR will yield a measure of confirmation in many cases that the probability measures cannot cover.

LR is also free from a difficulty afflicting the probability measures. The problem concerns very probable hypotheses. If we use probability measures of confirmation, no evidence will confirm these hypotheses to any substantial degree. Consider first the probability difference measure. Notice that the highest possible value of PD(H, E) is $1 - p(H)$. Hence if $p(H)$ is very close to 1, the highest possible value of PD(H, E), for any E, will be very low. It follows that if we set PD(H, E) $> n$ as a necessary condition for adequate support, if $p(H) > 1 - n$, no evidential proposition will be able to provide adequate support for H. A similar problem arises for PR. If $p(H)$ is very close to 1, PR (H, E) will also be very close to 1, that is, negligible, for any E. The highest possible value of PR(H, E) is $1/p(H)$. Hence, if we set PR(H, E) $> m$ as a necessary condition for adequate support, if $p(H) > 1/m$, no evidential proposition will be able to provide

---

[18] If E confirms H, this will happen whenever $p(E \mid H) = p(E \mid H^\star)$ and $p(H) \neq p(H^\star)$ (Theorem 24).

[19] Franz Huber has presented a similar reply to Milne's argument (Huber 2008).

[20] Notice that this proposal can in principle be accepted by those for whom LR is not the right measure of confirmation.

adequate support for H. LR, by contrast, doesn't face this difficulty. For any lower bound that we set on LR(H, E) and any value for p(H) lower than 1,[21] it would be possible for an evidential proposition to satisfy the condition with respect to H (Theorem 25).

PR faces a similar difficulty with respect to very probable evidential propositions (Roush 2005: 75–6). Here the problem is that if p(E) is very high, E won't be able to provide much support for any proposition. As we've seen, PR(H, E) can also be written as p(E | H)/p(E). Hence, if p(E) is very close to 1, PR(H, E) won't be much higher than 1 for any H. The highest possible value of PR(H, E) is 1/p(E). Hence, if we set PR(H, E) > m as a necessary condition for adequate support, if p(E) > 1/m, then E won't satisfy our necessary condition for support with respect to any H. The problem doesn't arise for LR. No matter how close to 1 p(E) might be, p(H | E) can be arbitrarily high (Theorem 26).

Another virtue of LR is its ability to treat deductive support as a limiting case of non-deductive support (Roush 2005: 163). Notice that, for any given positive value for p(E | H), as p(E | ~H) approaches 0, LR(H, E) will approach infinity. Now, if E entails H, we have that p(E | ~H) = 0. In this case LR(H, E) is not defined, but it is natural to think of it as taking the value that LR(H, E) approaches as p(E | ~H) approaches 0, that is, infinity. We shall register this intuition with an amendment of our measure of support, stipulating that if p(E | H) ≠ 0, p(E | ~H) = 0, E supports H to an infinite degree.[22] The probability measures, by contrast, cannot replicate this treatment of deduction.[23] If E entails H, we have that p(H | E) = 1. Hence PD(H, E) will be 1 − p(H), and PR(H, E) will be 1/p(H). It follows that E won't provide much support at all for its highly probable logical consequences.[24]

## 4.5 What adequate evidence is

When we started our discussion of incremental confirmation, we identified two necessary conditions for adequate support—a high value for p(H | E) and a low value for p(E | ~H). To these we now add a third—a high value for LR(H, E). We saw that the first two conditions do not render the third redundant, as (H | E) can be arbitrarily high and p (E | ~H) arbitrarily low in cases in which E doesn't confirm H. We need to consider now whether either of the previous conditions is rendered redundant by the new one. With respect to a high value for p(H | E) the answer is no. An arbitrarily high

---

[21] For p(H) = 1, see below.

[22] Notice that if p(E | ~H) = 0, we have that p(E | H) > 0 if and only if p(E) > 0.

[23] According to Roush (2005: 163), Fitelson has shown that LR is the only plausible measure of confirmation with this feature.

[24] If H is necessarily true, CP does not give a value to the denominator of LR(H, E), for any E. However, since H will be entailed by E, it is natural to adopt the same treatment as in other cases of logical entailment, saying that necessary truths are supported to an infinite degree by any proposition that's not necessarily false.

value for LR(H, E) is compatible with an arbitrarily low value for p(H | E).[25] With respect to a low value for p(E | ~H) the situation is different. A lower bound on p(E | H)/p(E | ~H) does impose an upper bound on p(E | ~H). If p(E | H)/p(E | ~H) > n, then it will have to be the case that p(E | ~H) < 1/n. So, unless we have a reason for imposing an upper bound on p(E | ~H) lower than 1/n, this condition will be rendered redundant by our lower bound on LR(H, E). Hence I propose to drop a low value for p(E | ~H) as a condition for adequate support.

This leaves us with two conditions—high values for p(H | E) and LR(H, E), treating the latter as taking an infinite value when E entails H. I propose to treat these as individually necessary and jointly sufficient conditions for adequate evidential support. This proposal is very close to the account of evidence provided by Sherrilyn Roush, who offers additional support for the approach (Roush 2005: chapter 5). The only difference between Roush's position and mine on this point is that she replaces a lower bound on p(H | E) as a necessary condition for adequate evidence with a lower bound on p(E) (Roush 2005: 165–78). She shows that sufficiently high values of p(E) and LR (H, E) will enjoin a high value for p(H | E). This is an interesting result, and it entails that replacing a lower bound on p(H | E) with a lower bound on p(E) won't force us to treat as cases of adequate support cases that we wouldn't treat in this way if we stuck to p(H | E). Notice, however, that, as Roush acknowledges, the converse doesn't hold: there are cases in which p(H | E) and LR(H, E) are high but p(E) is low (Roush 2005: 175). Hence, Roush's move will not let us treat as instances of adequate support some cases that would be treated in this way by my account. And cases of adequate support in which p(E) is low are not in any way marginal or farfetched. In fact a kind of case that has already figured in our discussion would seem to fit this description. Suppose that testing positive in a certain clinical test (E) is a highly improbable occurrence, but that subjects with a certain condition (H) are vastly more likely to test positive than those without the condition.[26]

It is in fact not easy to see what Roush is claiming concerning the role of p(E) in the concept of evidence, since she accepts that cases in which p(H | E) and LR(H, E) are high but p(E) is low are cases of good evidence. In any case, I am not convinced by her argument for using p(E) instead of p(H | E). Her thought appears to be that p(E) fares better than p(H | E) with respect to what she calls the *leverage* intuition:

Evidence would be useless to us if in order to judge its relation to the hypothesis it supports we had to know whether the hypothesis was true. (Roush 2005: 158)

Roush is surely right to suggest that an account of evidence needs to respect this intuition, and that the intuition would not be respected if in order to determine the

---

[25] My discussion in Chapter 6 of the relationship between the tracking ratio of a belief and its safety level can be easily adapted to provide a more accurate picture of the relationship between LR(H, E) and p(H | E).

[26] See (Fennell and Cartwright 2010) for an interesting discussion Roush's views on the desirability of a high value for p(E).

degree to which an evidential proposition supports a hypothesis we needed to determine the probability of the hypothesis. What is not so clear is that leverage should be in conflict, not only with p(H), but also with p(H | E).

The issue here might turn on whether we think of conditional probability as defined in terms of unconditional probability or, as I am proposing, as a fundamental notion. If we take the former view, then determining p(H | E) would seem to require determining p(H & E), which would violate leverage.[27] If, on the other hand, we think of the conditional probability of H on E as resulting from probabilistic laws that might not even assign a probability to H, it becomes clear that determining that the probability of H on E is high doesn't require determining the probability of H, and hence that the involvement of the former in the notion of evidence doesn't violate the leverage thought. Furthermore, on the view that I am recommending of the relation between conditional and unconditional probabilities, replacing a conditional probability, p(H | E), with an unconditional probability, would be a step in the wrong direction.

---

[27] Notice, though, that if this is the source of the conflict with leverage, it is hard to see why the same reasoning wouldn't apply to LR.

# 5

# Inferential Knowledge

In the preceding chapter I put forward a construal of the notion of adequate evidence. I have argued that an evidential proposition E provides adequate support for hypothesis H when p(H | E) and LR(H, E) have sufficiently high values. Inferential knowledge exploits these evidential links. If E provides adequate support for H, we can know H inferentially by being suitably related to E and to the connection between E and H. The nature of this relation is the subject matter of the present chapter. How does a subject have to be related to adequate evidence for H in order to know H inferentially?

Assume that H and E are both true and that E provides adequate support for H. These conditions will have to be satisfied in order for inferential knowledge of H based on E to be possible. The truth of H is required for knowledge of H, and inferential knowledge would have to be based on evidence that actually exists and provides genuine support for H.[1] What we need to ask is how S would have to be related to these facts in order to obtain inferential knowledge of H. Clearly S will have to believe H, as required for knowledge. I want to argue that S will need to believe, in addition, both E and that E supports H. Notice that on the conception of belief that I sketched in Chapter 1, this doesn't require that S has entertained either proposition in consciousness. Hence an actual process of conscious inference from E to H won't be required for inferential knowledge. Notice also that believing that E supports H won't require being aware of the analysis of the evidential link that I am recommending, just as believing that the person that sat next to me on the tube this morning on the way to work is the same person that sat next to me on the way back doesn't require being aware of the correct analysis of personal identity.

I want to suggest next that truly believing E, H, and that E supports H won't suffice for inferential knowledge of H. If S's true beliefs in E and in E's support for H were epistemically deficient, her true belief in H would not acquire the status of knowledge as a result. In order to produce this outcome, S's true belief in E, and in E's support for

---

[1] Ted Warfield (Warfield 2005) has argued that inferential knowledge can sometimes be based on false premises.

H, would have to have some positive epistemic status. I am going to assume that knowledge is the status that plays this role.[2,3]

So the proposal so far is that S's true belief in H will be an instance of inferential knowledge when there is a proposition E such that S knows E and S knows that E supports H.[4] This corresponds to a fairly traditional and natural account of inferential knowledge. I believe this account is along the right lines. It faces important challenges, but these can be met with relatively minor modifications, or so I will argue in this chapter.

## 5.1  Foundationalism

On the standard foundationalist picture, your body of knowledge has an inductive structure. The base is constituted by the propositions you know non-inferentially, and the inductive clause is provided by inferential knowledge. The inductive clause can be applied repeatedly in the usual way—the propositions that you know inferentially on the basis of the evidence provided by non-inferentially known propositions can then be used as evidence to ground inferential knowledge of other propositions, and so on. In this way your body of knowledge would grow by successive stages of inferential knowledge based on evidence provided by inferentially known propositions.

There is a central aspect of this picture that I want to endorse: inferential-knowledge claims will always have to start with non-inferentially known evidence. Notice that this restriction ensures that knowledge won't result from a circular chain. It won't be possible to have inferential knowledge of H based on evidence that includes H, on evidence that is known inferentially on the basis of evidence that includes H, and so on. Inferential knowledge will ultimately have to rest on non-inferentially known propositions.

However, there is another standard feature of foundationalism that I cannot endorse. On the foundationalist picture that I have sketched, an inferential-knowledge chain involving true propositions H, $E_1, \ldots, E_n$, will always produce knowledge of H, so long as $E_n$ is non-inferentially known and you know of each subsequent link that it receives adequate support from the preceding link. The plausibility of this aspect of the picture crucially depends on whether the support relation can be assumed to be transitive, that is, on whether A provides adequate support for C whenever A provides adequate support for B and B provides adequate support for C. On the assumption of

---

[2]  See (Luzzi 2010) for a defence of the idea that inferential knowledge can sometimes result from evidence that is not known.

[3]  Paul Boghossian has argued that, at least in the case of deductive inference, requiring knowledge of the support that E provides for H leads to an infinite regress or a vicious circle (Boghossian 2000, 2001, 2003). I have argued elsewhere that Boghossian has failed to show that the requirement has these consequences (Zalabardo 2011).

[4]  Inferential knowledge will also have to be subject to a constraint along the lines of Carnap's requirement of total evidence (Carnap 1962: 211–13). I shall not mention this constraint explicitly in what follows.

transitivity, the situation generated by an inferential-knowledge chain of any length is not substantially different from cases of inferential knowledge directly based on non-inferentially known evidence. Transitivity entails that in any inferential-knowledge chain involving H, $E_1, \ldots, E_n$, H will receive adequate support from $E_n$.[5]

The transitivity assumption is obviously legitimate on versions of foundationalism that incorporate concepts of inferential knowledge for which only deductive support counts as adequate. However, when non-deductive support is also treated as a suitable basis for inferential knowledge, transitivity will no longer hold in general. This is the situation that obtains for the account of adequate support that I have defended. It is easy to see that there will be cases in which $p(H \mid E_1)$ and $LR(H, E_1), \ldots, p(E_{n-1} \mid E_n)$ and $LR(E_{n-1}, E_n)$ are all sufficiently high, but $p(H \mid E_n)$ and $LR(H, E_n)$ are not sufficiently high.[6] I want to suggest that if this is the situation, you shouldn't count as knowing H on the basis of this chain of evidence even if you know $E_n$ non-inferentially, and you know that $E_1$ supports $H, \ldots, E_n$ supports $E_{n-1}$.

In order to get this result we need to curtail the iterative aspect of the foundationalist picture. This is achieved with the constraint that an inferential-knowledge chain ending with (true) H will produce knowledge of H only if it starts with non-inferentially known E that provides adequate support for H.[7] I am proposing to adopt this constraint.

## 5.2 Gettier

The next issue that I want to consider arises from Edmund Gettier's argument against the claim that every true justified belief is an instance of knowledge. In his famous paper (Gettier 1963), Gettier provided two counterexamples to this claim—cases of justified true belief that we intuitively would not want to count as instances of knowledge.

In the first of Gettier's cases, Smith believes with justification that Jones will get the job for which he is applying and that Jones has ten coins in his pocket. By inference from this, Smith forms the belief that the person who will get the job has ten coins in his pocket. As it turns out, the job doesn't go to Jones, but to another applicant who has ten coins in his pocket. Gettier argues, convincingly, that Smith's true belief that the man who will get the job has ten coins in his pocket is justified, since it was produced

---

[5] Notice that even if the relation of adequate support is transitive, known adequate support might not be—we might have that S knows that A supports B and that B supports C but fail to know that A supports C, even if as a matter of fact it does. See below.

[6] Roush (2005: 150–2) argues that, in a tracking chain, errors don't multiply or grow exponentially: they no more than sum.

[7] Notice that it doesn't follow from this constraint that the subject must know that E supports H, so long as one can fail to know this while knowing that each link in the chain supports the next link. If we wanted to require that the subject knows that E supports H, we would have to abandon altogether the iterative aspect of the foundationalist picture, demanding that inferential knowledge can be based only on non-inferentially known evidence. We shall not take this step here.

by valid inference from a justified premise. However, it seems intuitively wrong to say that Smith knows that the man who will get the job has ten coins in his pocket. Hence we have a case of justified true belief that we don't want to count as knowledge.

In the second case, Smith believes with justification that Jones owns a Ford. By inference from this, he forms the belief that either Jones owns a Ford or Brown is in Barcelona, in the absence of any information about Brown's whereabouts. In fact, Jones doesn't own a Ford, but Brown is in Barcelona. Once again, Smith's true belief that either Jones owns a Ford or Brown is in Barcelona is justified, but intuition dictates that it doesn't qualify as knowledge.

It will be useful to describe a variant of Gettier's second case. As before, Smith believes with justification that Jones owns a Ford. By inference from this, he now comes to believe that someone in the office owns a Ford. As in the previous case, Jones doesn't own a Ford, although someone else in the office does own one. Once again the natural verdict would seem to be that Smith has a justified true belief in the proposition that someone in the office owns a Ford, but that this belief doesn't have the status of knowledge.

I want to argue that the phenomenon exemplified by these cases poses a challenge to the account of inferential knowledge that we are considering. The problem is that the Gettier phenomenon will force us to treat as instances of knowledge beliefs that intuitively should not receive this treatment.

On the face of it, the cases that we have described don't really have this effect. The proposition that Jones is going to get the job and has ten coins in his pocket clearly provides adequate support for the proposition that the man who will get the job has ten coins in his pocket, since the former entails the latter, and we can assume that Smith knows that it does. But in order for our account to count this as an instance of inferential knowledge Smith would also have to know that Jones is going to get the job and has ten coins in his pocket, and although Smith believes this, his belief, being false, cannot have the status of knowledge. Our account does not treat this case as an instance of inferential knowledge. The same situation obtains for the other cases. Smith's belief in his evidence—that Jones owns a Ford—cannot have the status of knowledge, since it is false.

Nevertheless, a closer look at the cases reveals that our account is vulnerable to them. Let E be a proposition that describes Smith's adequate evidence for the proposition that Jones will get the job and has ten coins in his pocket. E will include, for example, as Gettier suggests, the assurances given by the president of the company that Jones will get the job and a count of the coins in Jones' pocket recently performed by Smith. Clearly, E provides adequate evidence for the proposition that the person who will get the job has ten coins in his pocket, and we can assume that Smith knows this. Furthermore, E itself is true, and there is no reason to suppose that Smith doesn't know it. Hence it follows from our account that Smith knows inferentially that the person who will get the job has ten coins in his pocket, with the role of evidence played by E.[8]

The same situation obtains in both versions of the second case. Let E now describe Smith's evidence for the proposition that Jones owns a Ford, including, for example, as Gettier suggests, information about Jones' long history of ownership of Fords, and his recent offer of a ride while driving a Ford. E provides adequate evidence for the proposition that either Jones owns a Ford or Brown is in Barcelona, as well as for the proposition that someone in the office owns a Ford, and we can assume that Smith knows this. Moreover, E is true, and there is no obvious reason why Smith shouldn't know it. If he does, we are committed to treating his beliefs that either Jones owns a Ford or Brown is in Barcelona and that someone in the office owns a Ford as instances of knowledge, in violation of Gettier's intuition.

It follows that our account of inferential knowledge cannot be right as it stands. However, I want to argue that a minor modification of the view will enable us to overcome the difficulty. I want to start with a proposal concerning the nature of the problem. Notice that a salient feature of Gettier's cases is that the contentious proposition can be made true by several recognizably distinct states of affairs. The proposition that either Jones owns a Ford or Brown is in Barcelona can be made true by Jones owning a Ford and by Brown being in Barcelona. Likewise, the proposition that someone in the office owns a Ford can be made true by each of the states of affairs consisting in A owning a Ford, for any person A in the office. And the proposition that the person who will get the job has ten coins in his pocket can be made true by each of the job candidates getting the job and having ten coins in his pocket.[9]

This feature of these propositions is reflected in their logical form, at least in Gettier's second case and in my modified version. Each of the ways in which the proposition that Jones owns a Ford or Brown is in Barcelona can be made true corresponds to one of its disjuncts, and each of the ways in which the proposition that someone in the office owns a Ford can be made true corresponds to one of its substitution instances. The point can also be applied to the first case, on a Russellian construal of definite descriptions. Now each of the ways in which the proposition that the person who will get the job has ten coins in his pocket can be made true corresponds to one of the substitution instances of the proposition that there is a unique person getting the job with ten coins in his pocket.

<hr />

[8] See, in this connection, Keith Lehrer's argument for the claim that reasoning that produces Gettier cases need not involve false lemmas (Lehrer 1965: 170).

[9] Sometimes, the term 'Gettier case' is applied to any case in which intuition dictates that a belief is true and justified but not knowledge. There is of course nothing wrong with this terminological convention, but cases that fall under this category arise from a range of quite different phenomena, and we shouldn't expect a uniform treatment covering all these cases. Here I am concerned only with cases of justified true belief that is not knowledge arising from the phenomenon I've just described. I deal with cases arising from the phenomenon exemplified by Goldman's fake-barn cases in Chapter 6.

Now, in each of the cases, Smith's evidence concerns one of the ways in which the proposition can be made true—Jones getting the job and having ten coins in his pocket, in the first case, and Jones owning a Ford, in the second. On the diagnosis that I want to recommend, the problem exemplified by Gettier's cases arises from a mismatch between the possible way of making the proposition true that actually makes it true and the possible way of making it true for which Smith has evidence. If this is right, Gettier's cases are not instances of knowledge because they violate a principle to the effect that if a proposition p can be made true in several different ways, evidence for one way of making p true will not produce knowledge of p unless it is the way in which it is actually made true. I believe that this principle is correct, and that it explains why Gettier's cases are not instances of knowledge.

What we need now is a way of modifying our account of inferential knowledge to make it comply with this principle. I am going to start with a proposal that exploits the syntactic dimension of the situation. I've pointed out that the contentious propositions in Gettier's cases are either disjunctive or existential, with each way of making them true corresponding to one of their disjuncts or substitution instances.

Let H be a true disjunctive or existential proposition. If E supports H, let's say that E's support for H is *misplaced* just in case E doesn't confirm any true disjunct/substitution instance of H. Notice that there is no contradiction involved in the notion of misplaced support. It is possible that E supports H without confirming any of its true disjuncts/substitution instances. This will be the situation when E supports false disjuncts/substitution instances of H. Then E will support H, but the support will be misplaced. This is precisely the situation exemplified by Gettier's cases.

So my preliminary proposal as to how to deal with the challenge posed by Gettier cases is to add to the definition of inferential knowledge the proviso that H should not be a disjunctive or existential proposition such that E's support for H is misplaced. I think this is a step in the right direction and that it deals adequately with the cases in which the phenomenon that we have identified as the source of the problem is syntactically manifested by the disjunctive or existential form of the proposition in question.

However, not all cases are like this. A mismatch between the way of making a proposition true that actually makes it true and the way of making it true for which the subject has evidence can occur in propositions that are not naturally construed as disjunctive or existential. The point is illustrated by the following case.

Suppose that Jamie reads in the highly reliable local newspaper that the Rolling Stones are in town today for a gig. She believes from the usual sources that Mick Jagger is the lead singer of the Stones, and forms the belief that Jagger is in town. Suppose, though, that unbeknownst to almost everyone, Jagger will be replaced on this gig by an excellent impersonator, since the gig clashes with a doctor's appointment that Jagger cannot miss. However, as luck would have it, the hospital that Jagger is visiting happens to be located in the same town in which the gig will take place.

If E is a true description of Jamie's evidence for the propositions that the Stones are in town and that they are fronted by Mick Jagger, it is hard to avoid the conclusion that E provides adequate support for the proposition that Jagger is in town. There is also no reason why Jamie shouldn't know E and that E supports the proposition that Jagger is in town. Hence our original account of inferential knowledge would yield the result that Jamie knows that Jagger is in town.

However, this verdict seems intuitively wrong. Jamie doesn't know that Jagger is in town, and the reason why she doesn't is the same as in Gettier's original cases: the proposition that Jagger is in town can be made true in several ways, including Jagger being there for a gig with his band and his being there for a doctor's appointment. The problem is, as before, that the way of making it true that actually makes it true is not the same as the way of making it true for which Jamie has evidence.

Unfortunately, the way we've dealt with the problem doesn't cover this case, since the proposition that Jagger is in town doesn't seem disjunctive or existential. One way of accommodating this case would be to abandon the syntactic definition of misplaced support in favour of one in terms of the disparity between the way of making a proposition true that actually makes it true and the way of making it true for which the subject has evidence. One disadvantage of this approach is that our account of evidential support would have to incorporate an explication of the individuation conditions of 'ways of making a proposition true'.

I want to make a tentative proposal that would, if successful, avoid this difficulty. My proposal is to define misplaced support in terms of incremental confirmation. If E supports H and H is true, let's say that E's support for H is *misplaced* just in case there is a true proposition X such that E doesn't confirm H & X.[10]

If we stipulate that inferential knowledge cannot arise from evidence providing misplaced support, using this new construal of the notion, Jamie will no longer have to count as knowing that Jagger is in town, since E doesn't confirm the proposition that Jagger is in town for a hospital visit without his band. Notice, in addition, that the new construal of misplaced support can also be used to handle disjunctive and existential

---

[10] Notice the difference between this proposal and defeasibility approaches to the problem (see, e.g., (Lehrer and Paxson 1969)). A condition along the lines of the defeasibility approach would dictate that S can't know H inferentially on the basis of the evidence provided by E if there is a true proposition X such that E & X does not confirm H, whereas on my account what would make inferential knowledge impossible is a true proposition X such that E doesn't confirm H & X. My account is immune to the standard objections to defeasibility views. Take, e.g., Sosa's modification of Skyrms' pyromaniac example (Sosa 1970). The fact that Sure-Fire matches have so far always ignited when struck (TRACKRECORD) provides the pyromaniac with adequate support for the proposition that the match he now holds will ignite when he strikes it (IGNITE). However, unbeknownst to him, temporary sensory paralysis will prevent him from perceiving the ignition when it happens (UNPERCEIVED). We want to say that the pyromaniac knows IGNITE on the basis of TRACKRECORD. However, the defeasibility account outlined above won't yield this result, since TRACKRECORD & UNPERCEIVED might not confirm IGNITE. My proposal, by contrast, yields the result we need, since we can expect TRACKRECORD to increase the probability of IGNITE & UNPERCEIVED to the same degree as the probability of IGNITE. See also Marshall Swain's discussion of defeasibility accounts in (Swain 1974).

cases. Smith doesn't inferentially know that the man who will get the job has ten coins in his pocket because his evidence doesn't confirm the proposition that the man who will get the job has ten coins in his pocket and he is not Jones. In the second case, his evidence doesn't confirm the proposition that either Jones owns a Ford or Brown is in Barcelona but Jones doesn't own a Ford, or the proposition that someone in the office other than Jones owns a Ford. Hence our new construal of misplaced support is the only construal that we need to deal with both kinds of case.[11]

## 5.3 Moorean inferences

In 1939 G. E. Moore provided what he took to be a perfectly rigorous proof of the existence of the external world. It consisted in holding up his hands and saying, as he made a certain gesture with the right hand, 'here is one hand' and adding, as he made a certain gesture with the left, 'and here is another' (Moore 1939).

The thought that scepticism can be refuted in this way has been embraced by some contemporary epistemologists, who extract from it a strategy for dealing with challenges to our knowledge claims based on sceptical possibilities (Pryor 2004). The strategy offers an account of how we can know, contrary to what the sceptic claims, that a sceptical hypothesis doesn't obtain. The proposal is that I can know, for example, that I am not a brain in a vat inferentially, using as evidence any of the everyday propositions that entail this, as, for example, the proposition that I have hands. Let me refer to an inference of this kind as a *Moorean inference*.

The claim that Moorean inferences can be genuine cases of inferential knowledge would seem to follow from the account of knowledge that I am developing. Notice, first, that we can expect that I'll be able to know that I have hands non-inferentially, by virtue of the fact that my belief in this proposition tracks the truth. We can also assume that I know that envatted brains don't have hands, and hence that the proposition that I have hands provides (deductive) support for the proposition that I am not a brain in a

---

[11]   The proposal might seem to have trouble with a slight modification of the last case, due to Keith Lehrer (Lehrer 1974). Suppose that Jones has deliberately provided Smith with misleading evidence for the proposition that he owns a Ford because he knows that someone else in the office owns a Ford and he has a compulsion to try to trick people into believing true propositions by getting them to believe some false propositions. Assuming that Jones is unlikely to believe falsely that someone else in the office owns a Ford, and that he is unlikely to fabricate evidence of Ford ownership unless he has this belief, we would have to say that the evidence that he has supplied for Smith does confirm the proposition that someone in the office other than Jones owns a Ford. Notice, however, that in order to move from this to the result that Smith knows that someone in the office owns a Ford, we would need to assume that Smith knows that the evidence fabricated by Jones provides adequate support for the proposition that someone in the office owns a Ford (call this proposition linking evidence and hypothesis SUPPORT). This assumption is open to question. If Smith knew SUPPORT, he would know it inferentially, on the basis of evidence provided by general facts about human behaviour, linking evidence of car ownership with actual car ownership. However, evidence of this kind would not provide adequate support for SUPPORT. One way to see this is to reflect that these general facts wouldn't be much less likely to obtain if SUPPORT were false than if it were true, since the truth of SUPPORT is a result of Jones's peculiar pathology. Hence the likelihood ratio of this evidence–hypothesis pair can be expected to be low.

vat. There is no reason to think that this support is misplaced. Hence the account of knowledge currently on the table would seem committed to the result that I can know that I am not a brain in a vat inferentially from the evidence provided by the proposition that I have hands.

Is this a good thing? Here we have arguments pulling in opposite directions. On the one hand, having an explanation of how we know that sceptical hypotheses don't obtain is certainly a desirable outcome. And for those who are convinced that no other explanation can work, its appeal will be almost irresistible. On the other hand, our goal in this area cannot be simply to find some hypothesis on the nature of knowledge which, if correct, would explain how we know that sceptical hypotheses don't obtain. We should seek a hypothesis that is as a matter of fact correct—one that provides an accurate representation of how we know the problematic propositions, if we do indeed know them. From this point of view, the proposal is highly counterintuitive. Our intuitions seem to be firmly against the possibility of knowing that I am not a brain in a vat by means of a Moorean inference. However, although intuitions must play an important role in the assessment of a theory of knowledge, other factors must also be taken into consideration, and we should be prepared in principle to accept a theory that yields some counterintuitive results.

The appeal of treating Moorean inferences as cases of knowledge would be drastically reduced if we could find a cogent reason for withholding this treatment from them—a feature exhibited by these cases and not by unproblematic cases of inferential knowledge which can be argued to pose an obstacle to knowledge ascriptions. If, on the contrary, we failed to identify an objectionable feature of Moorean inferences, the claim that they can produce knowledge would be harder to resist.

## 5.4  Transmission principles

A Moorean inference involves no logical circularity—its conclusion is not among its premises. Nevertheless, many have harboured the suspicion that the way in which the conclusion of a Moorean inference is related to its premise can be legitimately characterized as a form of circularity, not logical, but epistemic, and that epistemic circularity poses as serious an obstacle to inferential knowledge as the logical variety. Clearly, the challenge for this approach is to characterize epistemic circularity as a feature that is (a) present in Moorean inferences and absent from unproblematic cases of inferential knowledge and (b) intuitively incompatible with inferential knowledge.

One appealing proposal in this connection is to say that an inference is epistemically circular when the subject's knowledge of the premises requires that she has independent knowledge of the conclusion. In order to provide an adequate formulation of this proposal, it will help to have at our disposal the concept of *warrant*, understood as the property that turns a true belief into knowledge.[12] More precisely, warrant will be a relation between subjects and propositions such that S knows p just in case S believes p, p is true, and S bears to p the warrant relation.[13]

Now one constraint that is widely accepted by contemporary epistemologists is that warrant is not a primitive property—that when a proposition p has warrant for a subject S, there are some different facts in virtue of which p has warrant for S. Let me refer to the facts that play this role as *warrant-constituting facts*. On the assumption that warrant requires warrant-constituting facts, we can provide a formulation of the proposal under consideration. We can say that an inference is epistemically circular when the subject having warrant for the conclusion is among the warrant-constituting facts of her warrant for the premise.[14]

I think it would be hard to deny that if epistemic circularity is characterized in this way, an epistemically circular inference will be incapable of producing knowledge of its conclusion. Inferential knowledge requires knowledge of the premises, but if an inference is epistemically circular, in this sense, the fact that the subject knows the premises will be grounded in the fact that she knows the conclusion. Hence she will be incapable of using the inference to acquire knowledge of the conclusion, as the intended outcome is among the preconditions of this method of knowledge acquisition.

However, even if we accept, as I propose, that epistemically circular inferences cannot produce knowledge of their conclusions, we won't be able to use this circumstance to argue that Moorean inferences cannot produce knowledge unless we can show that Moorean inferences are epistemically circular. The issue here turns on our explanation of how we know the premise of a Moorean inference, and on the account that I am endorsing, the claim that Moorean inferences are epistemically circular has no plausibility. I am proposing that I can know that I have hands non-inferentially, simply by virtue of the fact that my belief tracks the truth. On this account, truth tracking would be the warrant-constituting fact of my belief that I have hands, and truth tracking doesn't include, or require, that I have warrant for the proposition that I'm not a brain in a vat. If my belief that I have hands can obtain the status of knowledge from the fact that it tracks the truth, Moorean inferences are not epistemically circular.[15]

One could try to rescue this approach with a different account of why Moorean inferences are epistemically circular. The idea now would be that what's wrong with a Moorean inference is that the subject's knowledge of the premise presupposes, not that

---

[12] The term is used in this sense in (Plantinga 1993).

[13] Notice that the definition doesn't rule out the possibility that warrant entails belief or truth. Thus, e.g., if warrant is what Nozick calls truth tracking, warrant will entail both.

[14] Crispin Wright (Wright 1985, 2000, 2002) has explored several versions of this diagnosis of the inadequacy of Moorean inferences.

[15] Versions of this point have been made in (Brown 2003) and (Pryor 2004). See also (Zalabardo forthcoming-b).

she has knowledge of the conclusion, but that the conclusion is true. We can pursue this strategy with a new account of epistemic circularity. Now an inference will be epistemically circular when the truth of the conclusion is among the warrant-constituting facts of the subject's warrant for the premise.

Notice that on this characterization of epistemic circularity the standard Moorean inferences can be expected to be epistemically circular. The facts about me and my relationship to my environment that enable my belief that I have hands to track the truth are clearly incompatible with my being a brain in a vat. If I were a brain in a vat my belief that I have hands would not track the truth. Hence the prospects of the proposal turn on the plausibility of claiming that inferences that exhibit epistemic circularity, on this construal, are incapable of producing knowledge of their conclusions.

It has been argued that this claim is incorrect—that there are inferences that exhibit this brand of epistemic circularity but seem perfectly capable of producing knowledge of their conclusions (Pryor 2004: 358–9; Davies 1998: 352). Here I want to argue that there is an additional source of concern for the proposal. The problem on which I want to focus is that the proposal doesn't deal with all the cases of the pathology that afflicts Moore's inference. I am going to present the argument using a process reliabilist account of non-inferential knowledge, but the argument will work in the same way for the tracking account that I shall present in the next chapter.

Consider Fred Dretske's example of a child, call her Molly, who goes to the zoo and upon seeing the animals in the enclosure marked 'zebras' forms the belief that they are zebras (Dretske 1970). According to process reliabilism, Molly's belief has warrant, since it has been formed with a reliable belief-forming process. Hence, if the belief is true, if the animals are actually zebras, it will have the status of knowledge.

Suppose now that Molly knows that the proposition that the animals are zebras (call it ZEBRAS) entails the proposition that they are not mules cleverly disguised by the zoo authorities to look like zebras (call it ~MULES). On our current account of inferential knowledge, it follows from our assumptions that Molly can know ~MULES inferentially on the basis of the evidence provided by ZEBRAS. However, this inference seems to be afflicted by the same pathology as the inference from HANDS to ~BIV. It is plausible to assume that the right verdict of the difficulty that invalidates the latter inference as a case of inferential knowledge will also apply to the former.

However, on the construal of epistemic circularity currently under discussion, the inference from ZEBRAS to ~MULES would not count as epistemically circular. To see this, notice that the reliability of the process involved in the production of Molly's belief in ZEBRAS doesn't require that ~MULES is true, so long as the reliability that is required for knowledge is not perfect reliability. Molly could have formed her belief with highly reliable perceptual devices even if the animals she is looking at are cleverly disguised mules. Of course, the reliability of the relevant perceptual devices requires that this kind of deception is sufficiently rare, but not that it never occurs, or that it is not occurring on this occasion.

I want to treat the fact that the strategy doesn't deal with all the instances of the problem as an indication that its source hasn't been addressed. We haven't identified the feature of the relationship between premise and conclusion of Moorean inferences that explains why they shouldn't be treated as cases of inferential knowledge.

## 5.5  An idea from Nozick

I am going to argue that there is a more appealing explanation of why Moorean inferences shouldn't be treated as cases of knowledge. My proposal is based on the intuition that what's wrong with a Moorean inference has to do with the circumstances under which you would believe its premise. The problem is that you would still believe it if its conclusion were false. You can't have inferential knowledge of ~BIV based on the evidence provided by HANDS because envatted brains believe in HANDS, and Molly can't have inferential knowledge of ~MULES based on the evidence provided by ZEBRAS because people who are looking at cleverly disguised mules believe in ZEBRAS. Nozick formulated a principle based on this intuition, as a condition for when inferring H from E yields knowledge of H (Nozick 1981: 231):

> I:   If q were false, S wouldn't believe p (or S wouldn't infer q from p).

I believe this principle is along the right lines, but instead of the counterfactual formulation used by Nozick, I want to propose a formulation of the thought in terms of conditional probability. My proposal is that what's wrong with these cases is that you wouldn't be less likely to believe your evidence if the hypothesis were false than if it were true. In other words, the problem with a Moorean inference is that the subject's belief in its premise doesn't confirm its conclusion. Hence we can avoid treating Moorean inferences as cases of inferential knowledge by imposing an additional condition on inferential knowledge:

> PI:  S can have inferential knowledge of H based on the evidence provided by E only if S's belief in E confirms H.[16]

This proposal deals easily with the standard cases. I can't know ~BIV inferentially on the basis of the evidence provided by HANDS because the probability of my believing HANDS is not affected by whether I am a brain in a vat. And Molly can't know ~MULES inferentially on the basis of the evidence provided by ZEBRAS because she is no less likely to believe ZEBRAS if she is looking at cleverly disguised mules than if she isn't.

---

[16] A closer analogue of Nozick's principle, taking account the bracketed clause, would require that H is confirmed either by S's belief in E or by her belief in the proposition that E supports H. I shall not take this line here.

# 5.6 Closure and transmission

Before we proceed, we need to make a distinction between two principles that are involved in the issues under discussion. The first is a principle that stipulates sufficient conditions for inferential knowledge in the specific case of deductive inferences:

*Transmission*: If S knows E non-inferentially, S knows that E logically entails H and S believes H, then S knows H inferentially on the basis of evidence provided by E.[17]

The second principle has, in the first instance, nothing to do with inferential knowledge in particular, although it also concerns cases in which E entails H. It stipulates that the following four states of affairs are incompatible: (a) S knowing E, (b) S knowing that E logically entails H, (c) S believing H, and (d) S not knowing H. It is usually formulated as a conditional:

*Closure*: If S knows E non-inferentially, S knows that E logically entails H and S believes H, then S knows H.

In spite of the superficial similarities, there are important differences between these two principles. Notice that Transmission is stronger than Closure. On the one hand, S will know H whenever she knows H inferentially on the basis of evidence provided by E. On the other hand, S could know H in some other way. Hence Closure might be universally valid even if Transmission has counterexamples.

The most important difference between Transmission and Closure for our purposes concerns how they relate to PI. Transmission, on the one hand, is directly incompatible with PI. Whenever S knows E non-inferentially and S knows that E logically entails H, Transmission will require that S knows H inferentially on the basis of evidence provided by E. But these conditions are compatible with S's belief in E failing to confirm H, and when this happens PI will rule out inferential knowledge of H.

Closure, by contrast, is not directly threatened by PI. If S's belief in E doesn't confirm H, then according to PI S won't know H inferentially on the basis of evidence provided by E. But this is compatible with S knowing H, by some other means, and this is all that Closure requires.

Nevertheless, the adoption of PI would also have adverse consequences for Closure. Prior to the introduction of PI, our account of inferential knowledge guaranteed the satisfaction of Transmission and, a fortiori, of Closure. However, with PI in place, our account of inferential knowledge no longer guarantees satisfaction of Closure. If S's belief in E doesn't confirm H, the new account of inferential knowledge won't rule out the possibility that the antecedent of Closure is satisfied but its consequent isn't.

In sum, our account of inferential knowledge is incompatible with Transmission, but compatible both with Closure and with its negation. Hence, our account of inferential

---

[17] The point of restricting the principle to cases in which E is non-inferentially known is to avoid the problems raised by the intransitivity of the support relation. See Section 5.1.

knowledge can be incorporated in a theory of knowledge for which Closure is universally valid. However, this would require introducing Closure as a separate element of
the theory, since the account of inferential knowledge doesn't guarantee its satisfaction.
I am not going to consider at this point whether we should take this step. Clearly PI
will deprive Closure of the support that it might derive from its connection with
Transmission, but the principle might be recommended by independent considerations.

## 5.7 Reflective knowledge

I want to consider next another type of inference that poses similar issues to those that
we have considered in connection with Moorean inferences. Suppose that I read in a
reliable newspaper that the Bulls won the game last night and form as a result the belief
that the Bulls won the game.[18] Supposing that I don't form beliefs on these matters
from unreliable sources of information, my belief will track the truth. Hence on the
account of non-inferential knowledge that I am recommending, if the Bulls did indeed
win, my belief to this effect will have the status of knowledge.

Consider now the proposition that the newspaper report was veridical. As we are
about to see, there is an issue as to how this proposition should be analysed, but on each
plausible analysis it is logically entailed by propositions that I know—the proposition
that the Bulls won and the proposition that the newspaper report says that the Bulls
won. There is also no reason why I shouldn't know this entailment. Assuming that
I do, I will know that the proposition that the report was veridical is a logical
consequence of (and hence supported by) propositions that I know. If this is sufficient
for inferential knowledge, I will know that the report is veridical inferentially, on the
basis of evidence provided by the proposition that the Bulls won the game.

Intuitively this is the wrong result. If the newspaper report is my only source of
information for the match result, I cannot use it as evidence to obtain inferential
knowledge of the veracity of the report. Notice that I am not arguing that it is impossible
to know the veracity of the report or that it is possible to know that the Bulls won without
knowing that the report was veridical. All I am arguing is that if knowledge that the report
was veridical is to be inferential, it cannot be based on evidence provided by the
proposition that the Bulls won the match. In other words, I am arguing that the inference
from the premise that the Bulls won the match to the conclusion that the newspaper
report was veridical should be a counterexample to Transmission. I am not taking sides on
the question whether we can obtain from this case a counterexample to Closure.

I want to argue that PI succeeds in ruling this out as a case of inferential knowledge.
Now, whether this result holds depends on how we analyse the proposition that the
newspaper report is veridical. One natural approach is to analyse it as a truth function of
the proposition that the Bulls won (BULLS) and the proposition that the newspaper

---

[18] Keith DeRose discusses this case in (DeRose 1995: 18).

reported that the Bulls won (REPORT). There are at least two plausible options as to how to do this. The first is to analyse it as the proposition that the newspaper didn't falsely report a Bulls' victory, that is ~(REPORT & ~BULLS). The second is to treat it as the proposition that the newspaper reported a Bulls victory veridically, that is, REPORT & BULLS.

Which of these options we take is going to make a difference to whether the inference contravenes PI. Consider first REPORT & BULLS. My evidence for this proposition will consist of the propositions REPORT and BULLS. Hence, in order to assess the inference from the point of view of PI we need to determine whether p(Bel(REPORT) & Bel (BULLS) | REPORT & BULLS) is greater than p(Bel(REPORT) & Bel(BULLS) | ~(REPORT & BULLS)). I think it's clear that the answer is yes. Notice that ~(REPORT & BULLS) is the same proposition as ~REPORT ∨ (REPORT & ~BULLS). We can assume that p(Bel(REPORT) & Bel(BULLS) | REPORT & ~BULLS) is the same as p(Bel(REPORT) & Bel(BULLS)) | REPORT & BULLS), since the newspaper report is my only source of information about the game result. However, p(Bel(REPORT) & Bel(BULLS) | ~REPORT) can be expected to be much lower, since I am unlikely to believe in a non-existent newspaper report. Hence, to show that p(Bel(REPORT) & Bel(BULLS) | REPORT & BULLS) is greater than p(Bel(REPORT) & Bel (BULLS) | ~(REPORT & BULLS)), it will suffice to show that

p(Bel(REPORT) & Bel(BULLS) | REPORT & ~BULLS)
>
p(Bel(REPORT) & Bel(BULLS) | ~REPORT)

entails

p(Bel(REPORT) & Bel(BULLS) | REPORT & ~BULLS)
>
p(Bel(REPORT) & Bel(BULLS) | ~REPORT ∨ (REPORT & ~BULLS)).

This can be easily shown (Theorem 27).

I want to suggest that the way in which this result is obtained should render the analysis suspect. The reason why PI is satisfied is due entirely to the low probability of my belief in REPORT if REPORT is false. But intuitively this circumstance should not affect the adequacy of a piece of evidence as support for the veridicality claim. It seems that this should be assessed exclusively in terms of how the probability of my belief in the evidence is affected by whether or not the report is veridical. The situation in which the report doesn't exist shouldn't come into play.

Let's consider now the other proposal as to how to analyse the veridicality claim as a truth function of REPORT and BULLS, that is, to take it as ~(REPORT & ~BULLS). Notice first of all that now REPORT is no longer needed as a premise, since ~(REPORT & ~BULLS) follows from BULLS alone. Hence, in order to determine whether the inference satisfies PI on this construal, it will suffice to compare p(Bel (BULLS) | ~(REPORT & ~BULLS)) with p(Bel(BULLS) | REPORT & ~BULLS).

I am going to argue that p(Bel(BULLS) | ~(REPORT & ~BULLS)) is actually smaller than p(Bel(BULLS) | REPORT & ~BULLS), contrary to what PI calls for.

Notice first that on the assumption that I have no source of information about the match result other than the newspaper report, we have that p(Bel(BULLS) | REPORT & ~BULLS) = p(Bel(BULLS) | REPORT & BULLS) = p(Bel(BULLS) | REPORT). Hence it will suffice to show that p(Bel(BULLS) | ~(REPORT & ~BULLS)) is smaller than p(Bel(BULLS) | REPORT & BULLS).

Notice that p(Bel(BULLS) | ~(REPORT & ~BULLS)) can be rewritten as p(Bel (BULLS) | ~REPORT ∨ (REPORT & BULLS)). Now, clearly, p(Bel(BULLS) | ~REPORT) is smaller than p(Bel(BULLS) | REPORT & BULLS), given my propensity to believe the report. Hence, by Theorem 27, we have that p(Bel(BULLS) | ~(REPORT & ~BULLS)) is smaller than p(Bel(BULLS) | REPORT & BULLS), as desired. We can conclude that Bel(BULLS) doesn't confirm ~(REPORT & ~BULLS), and hence that on this construal of the veridicality claim, the inference is ruled out by PI.

I suggested above that this is the outcome that is in line with our intuitions about this kind of case. However, this construal is open to the same objection as the previous one, since we are still taking into account the probability that I believe the evidence if the report doesn't exist. Inspection of the argument shows that p(Bel(BULLS) | ~(REPORT & ~BULLS)) is dragged down by the relatively low value of p(Bel (BULLS) | ~REPORT), that is, by the low probability that I believe that the Bulls have won in the absence of the report. Hence the reason that I have offered for rejecting the previous proposal cannot be used as a reason for preferring this alternative. If the right analysis of the veridicality claim cannot make the admissibility of a piece of evidence depend on what I would believe if the report didn't exist, the second proposal is as inadequate as the first.

I want to try a different approach to the analysis of veridicality claims. My proposal is to analyse the proposition that the newspaper report is veridical as ascribing a predicate (veridical) to an individual picked out by a definite description (the newspaper report of the Bulls' victory). Thus, if V stands for . . . *is veridical*, and R stands for . . . *is a (unique) newspaper report asserting that the Bulls won the match*, the veridicality proposition can be symbolized as V ɿx Rx. Clearly, REPORT and BULLS logically entail V ɿx Rx. Hence on our account of inferential knowledge I will be able to have inferential knowledge of V ɿx Rx on the basis of the evidence provided by REPORT and BULLS unless the case is ruled out by PI.

In order to determine whether this inference satisfies PI, we need to compare p(Bel (REPORT) & Bel(BULLS) | V ɿx Rx) with p(Bel(REPORT) & Bel(BULLS) | ~V ɿx Rx). PI will be satisfied just in case the former is greater than the latter. The issue turns on the familiar ambiguity of scope afflicting ~V ɿx Rx. If we take the definite description to have narrow scope, the proposition will be true if the report is not veridical, or if it doesn't exist (or if it's not unique). If we take it to have wide scope, the proposition will be true just in case the report is not veridical, that is, just in case there exists a (unique) newspaper report asserting that the Bulls won the game and this report is not veridical.

Given the source of our dissatisfaction with previous analyses of veridicality, it should be clear that the wide-scope reading is to be preferred. Adopting the narrow-scope reading would assign a role in the assessment of my evidence for the veridicality proposition to how likely I am to believe the evidence if the report doesn't exist. With the wide-scope reading, however, this factor is completely excluded. Now the assessment of my evidence will depend exclusively on what I am likely to believe if the report is veridical and if it is not veridical, as intuition recommends.

Once the veridicality claim is analysed in this way, it is clear that my evidence for it doesn't satisfy PI. The probability of my believing REPORT and BULLS is unaffected by whether or not the report is veridical. This is the reason why the information that I have obtained from the report cannot be used as evidence of its veridicality.

## 5.8 Not falsely believing

Similar issues are raised by beliefs concerning the truth value of my own (current) beliefs. Take, for example, my belief that I don't falsely believe A, where A is a proposition that I also believe. How could this belief acquire the status of knowledge? This is a question that we will consider in some detail later on. Here I want to discuss only one possible answer—the view that I can know that I don't falsely believe A inferentially on the basis of the evidence provided by A. Clearly A provides adequate support for the proposition that I don't falsely believe A, since the former logically entails the latter. Hence, if we assume that I know this entailment, and that I know A non-inferentially, all our original conditions on inferential knowledge will be satisfied, and whether the inference can produce knowledge of its conclusion will depend on whether PI is satisfied.

I want to suggest that this inference is intuitively objectionable for exactly the same reason as other inferences that we have recently considered. I argued that the inference from HANDS to ~BIV cannot produce knowledge of its conclusion because if the conclusion were false, if I were a brain in a vat, I would still believe the premise. Similarly, I can't know that the newspaper report is veridical inferentially on the basis of the evidence provided by the Bulls' victory because if the conclusion were false—if the report were not veridical—I would still believe the evidence. The inference from A to *I don't falsely believe A* provides an extreme example of this situation: if the conclusion were false—if I falsely believed A, I would, of necessity, still believe the premise, since it's not possible to falsely believe A without believing A. This seems to me to be a powerful intuitive reason for rejecting this inference as a legitimate source of knowledge.

Propositions to the effect that a proposition is not falsely believed do not allow us to concentrate exclusively on knowledge of the truth values of beliefs, since the proposition ~(Bel(A) & ~A) is true not only when A is truly believed, but also when A is not believed. A similar problem afflicts propositions of the form Bel(A) & A, which are false, not only when A is falsely believed, but also when it is not believed.

We face in effect the same situation as in the case of reflective knowledge, and I propose to adopt the same strategy. This involves concentrating on propositions that ascribe a predicate ( . . . *is true*) to an object identified with a definite description ( . . . *is a belief of mine with A as its content*), and assuming that in its negation the description has wide scope. Thus if V stands now for . . . *is true* and B stands for . . . *is a belief of mine with A as its content*, the proposition will be symbolized as V ɿx Bx. The idea of knowing V ɿx Bx inferentially on the basis of evidence provided by A is as unattractive as the idea of knowing in this way that I don't falsely believe A, but since it is in general possible to know A and to know that A entails V ɿx Bx, the inference will be able to produce knowledge, on my account, unless it violates PI. But we can see easily that it does. To see this, we need to compare p(Bel(A) | V ɿx Bx) with p(Bel(A) | ~V ɿx Bx). Satisfying PI would require the former to be greater than the latter, but this is impossible, since p (Bel(A) | ~V ɿx Bx) = 1: I cannot falsely believe that A without believing that A. Notice also that PI doesn't just manage to rule out the case that we want to rule out. It also reflects the source of our intuitive reluctance to accept that knowledge of the truth value of my belief in A can result from an inference from A. The problem is that I wouldn't be less likely to believe the premise if the conclusion were false than if it were true.

## 5.9 Bootstrapping

I want to turn now to another form of inference that has received considerable attention in this connection. In an example that Jonathan Vogel borrows from Michael Williams, Roxanne forms the belief that the petrol tank in her car is full (FULL) whenever she sees that the gauge on the dashboard reads F (GAUGE) (Vogel 2000). Her gauge is highly reliable and, as a reliabilist, I am committed to according to the true beliefs that Roxanne forms in this way the status of knowledge, even though she has no evidence of the reliability of the gauge. Now suppose that when Roxanne sees that the gauge reads F, in addition to coming to believe FULL, she comes to believe GAUGE, that is, that the gauge reads F. Let's assume that Roxanne can come to know GAUGE in this way.

What would an inductive argument for the reliability of the gauge look like? Notice first that the claim that the gauge is reliable can be understood as the claim that the gauge reading F provides adequate evidence for the hypothesis that the tank is full, that is, as the claim that p(FULL | GAUGE) and LR(FULL, GAUGE) are both high. An inductive argument for this conclusion would seek to derive it from premises concerning observed frequencies. Thus, from the premise that in a very high proportion of the observed cases in which the gauge read F the tank was full, the argument would derive the conclusion that p(FULL | GAUGE) is high. And from the premise that the proportion of F readings to be found among the observed cases in which the tank is full is higher than the proportion of F readings to be found among the observed cases in which the tank is not full, the argument would conclude that LR(FULL, GAUGE) is high.

Let's assume that the premises of this argument provide adequate support for their conclusion—that evidence concerning observed frequencies provides, in suitable circumstances, adequate support for conclusions about probabilities—and let's assume that Roxanne knows this. Clearly, Roxanne could also know the premises of the argument. Her true beliefs as to whether or not the gauge reads F can have the status of knowledge, and since the gauge is reliable, the true beliefs about the contents of the tank that she forms with the help of the gauge will have to be treated as knowledge by a reliabilist account of non-inferential knowledge like the one I am defending. It follows that Roxanne will have knowledge of the observed relative frequencies that figure in the premises of the argument. Hence, if knowing the premises and knowing that the premises support the conclusion is all that's required for inferential knowledge, we will have to conclude that Roxanne knows that the gauge is reliable.

This is a highly counterintuitive outcome. Roxanne cannot use this inference to gain knowledge of the reliability of the gauge. The problem with her procedure doesn't concern the argument itself, or the epistemic status of Roxanne's belief in the premises or in the connection between premises and conclusion. Hence accommodating our intuitive rejection of this form of knowledge acquisition would require arguing that even though Roxanne knows the premises of the argument and she knows that the premises support the conclusion, there is another condition on inferential knowledge that she fails to meet.

Much of the recent literature on this topic assumes that we could avoid counting Roxanne as coming to know with her inductive argument that the gauge is reliable only if we invoked a principle that treats knowledge of the reliability of the gauge as a pre-condition for obtaining from the gauge knowledge of the contents of the tank (Cohen 2002; Van Cleve 2003). But principles along these lines have been accused of leading directly to scepticism and of being incompatible with reliabilist theories of knowledge. I have argued elsewhere that the problems faced by these principles are not as serious as they might seem at first (Zalabardo 2005). But here I want to present a different strategy for ruling out Roxanne's inference as a case of inferential knowledge.

It seems to me that the most intuitive explanation of the inadequacy of Roxanne's inference focuses on the fact that the gauge is the only method at her disposal for ascertaining whether the tank is full. This circumstance should pose no obstacle to her beliefs about the contents of the tank having the status of knowledge, but it should rule out these beliefs as premises in an inference for the reliability of the gauge. I want to argue that the reason why this feature of Roxanne's situation poses a problem is that it severs the connection between Roxanne's belief in the premises and the truth value of the conclusion. The problem is, once more, that PI is not satisfied: Roxanne is no less likely to believe the premises of the argument if the conclusion is false than if it's true. Given Roxanne's state of information, the probability that she will believe the premises of her inductive argument for the reliability of the gauge is not affected by the values of p(FULL | GAUGE) or LR(FULL, GAUGE). She will be just as likely to believe that the observed cases in which the gauge reads F are precisely the cases in which the tank is full if these values are low as if they are high.

On Vogel's construal, Roxanne's inductive argument for the reliability of the gauge involves, for every time t at which she forms belief in GAUGE and FULL in the way described, a lemma to the effect that the gauge is reading accurately on that occasion (ACCURATE). Vogel suggests that the epistemic status of Roxanne's belief in ACCURATE is already problematic, but since she has validly inferred ACCURATE from GAUGE and FULL, he thinks that any shortcoming of the epistemic status of her belief in ACCURATE would also have to affect her belief in FULL (assuming that her knowledge of GAUGE is above suspicion). I share Vogel's misgivings about the epistemic status of Roxanne's belief in ACCURATE. I don't think she can know this proposition inferentially on the basis of the evidence provided by GAUGE and FULL. But my proposal has the resources for securing this result without withholding from Roxanne's belief in FULL the status of knowledge.

We can use the ideas that we presented in our discussion of reflective knowledge to explain why this inference should be ruled out as a case of inferential knowledge. Notice that ACCURATE can be construed as an instance of the veridicality propositions that we considered there. If R denotes a plausible description of the reading, and V is the predicate that ascribes accuracy to it, ACCURATE can be analysed as V ɿx Rx. Hence, in order to determine whether Roxanne's inference gives her inferential knowledge of ACCURATE, we need to compare p(Bel(GAUGE) & Bel(FULL) | V ɿx Rx) with p(Bel(GAUGE) & Bel(FULL) | ~V ɿx Rx). As I argued in Section 5.7, the description in ~V ɿx Rx should be understood as having wide scope. Hence the question that we need to ask is whether Roxanne is less likely to believe GAUGE and FULL if the gauge is reading inaccurately (i.e. GAUGE & ~FULL) than if it is reading accurately (i.e. GAUGE & FULL). And this question should be answered in the negative. So long as GAUGE is true, the probability that Roxanne believes GAUGE and FULL will be high, and unaffected by the truth value of FULL.

Contrast this situation with one in which Roxanne can ascertain whether or not the tank is full independently of the gauge, say, using a dipstick. Intuitively this would make all the difference to Roxanne's ability to gain knowledge of the reliability of the gauge from the argument. And PI registers this difference. In this new scenario, a low value for p(FULL | GAUGE) will decrease the probability that Roxanne believes that in most observed cases in which the gauge reads F the tank is full. If p(FULL | GAUGE) is low, it is likely that there are many observed cases in which the gauge reads F but the tank isn't full, and her dipstick will enable Roxanne to spot them. Similarly, a low value for LR(FULL, GAUGE) will decrease the probability that she believes that the gauge reads F more often in the cases in which the tank is full than in those in which it isn't full. If LR(FULL, GAUGE) is low, that is, if p(GAUGE | FULL) is not much higher than p(GAUGE | ~FULL), it is likely that there will be nearly as many observed cases in which the gauge reads F among the cases in which the tank is not full as among those in which it is full, and Roxanne, with her dipstick, will be able to detect this. These points about her inference for the reliability of the gauge can also be applied to her inference for the proposition that the gauge is reading accurately on a given occasion. Armed with her dipstick, Roxanne will be more likely to believe GAUGE and FULL if the gauge is reading accurately than if it isn't.[19]

## 5.10 Roush on inferential knowledge

In the picture that I have presented in this chapter, knowledge will have a recursive structure, with non-inferential knowledge at the base and inferential knowledge providing the inductive clause. A position with this general structure has been recently defended by Sherrilyn Roush (2005). Roush has used for her account the label *recursive tracking*. I'd like to close this chapter by considering how the account of inferential knowledge that I am advocating relates to Roush's view.

Roush presents the aspect of her position on which I want to concentrate in the following passage, where she uses the term *Nozick-knows* to refer to the knowledge that results from truth tracking:

[ . . . ] on the new view Nozick-knowing is not the only way to know. From what we Nozick-know we can get by known implication to other beliefs that are also knowledge. Thus, to analyze the concept of knowledge I combine the notion of Nozick-knowing with a recursion clause: For subject S and proposition p, S *knows* that p if and only if:

S Nozick-knows that p

or

p is true, S believes p, and there is a q not equivalent to p such that q implies p, S knows that q implies p, and S knows that q.

According to this analysis, anything that you derive from something you Nozick-know by n steps of deduction, for some finite n, is also something you know. (Roush 2005: 42–3)

This is only a preliminary formulation of Roush's highly sophisticated proposal, but it adequately highlights the features on which I want to focus.

The first major difference between Roush's position and mine that I'd like to discuss is that her inductive clause contemplates inferential knowledge involving only *deductive*

---

[19] PI will not rule out some inferences that appear illegitimate. Consider, e.g., the inference from HANDS to the proposition that I believe I have hands (Bel(HANDS)) and I'm not a brain in a vat. Suppose that the correlation between HANDS and Bel(HANDS) if I'm not a brain in a vat is such that HANDS provides adequate support for Bel(HANDS) & ~BIV. The inference will satisfy PI so long as p(Bel(HANDS) | Bel(HANDS) & ~BIV) is greater than p(Bel(HANDS) | ~(Bel(HANDS) & ~BIV)), but p(Bel(HANDS) | Bel(HANDS) & ~BIV) equals one, and p(Bel(HANDS) | ~(Bel(HANDS) & ~BIV)) will be less than that. Notice, however, that we cannot know ~BIV inferentially on the basis of the evidence provided by Bel(HANDS) & ~BIV, since the inference doesn't satisfy PI. I am no less likely to believe this evidence if I am a brain in a vat than if I'm not. See, in this connection, Nozick's discussion of the possibility of knowing a conjunction without knowing each of its conjuncts (Nozick 1981: 228).

inference, whereas my inductive clause includes both deductive and non-deductive inference. Notice that this feature of Roush's account doesn't entail that knowledge cannot be acquired by non-deductive inference. What it does entail is that this will be possible only when as a result of the inferential process the subject's belief in the conclusion comes to track the truth. Roush is explicit about this: 'it is clear that on this view all inductive routes to knowledge must be such that through them we satisfy the tracking conditions' (Roush 2005: 52). On my account, by contrast, non-deductive evidence can in principle confer on one of your true beliefs the status of knowledge even in cases in which the belief doesn't track its truth.[20]

As I argued in Chapter 3, I regard this as a desirable feature of an account of inferential knowledge. An important role for evidence to play in our cognitive economy is to enable us to overcome the epistemic handicap posed by the kind of doxastic bias that prevents a belief from tracking the truth. Evidence should enable us to overcome this handicap even in cases in which the bias persists and the belief fails to track the truth. In the example that I used there, the interrogator who has obtained adequate evidence that the suspect is lying should count as having inferential knowledge of this proposition even though her belief in it is rendered insensitive by her bias.

The second respect in which my account of inferential knowledge differs from Roush's inductive clause is that, whereas she is prepared to accept as knowledge all cases in which I know that a proposition I believe is deductively entailed by known evidence, my account excludes cases in which PI is not satisfied. As we have seen, the main consequence of this restriction is to rule out three types of case: Moorean inferences, inferences from a belief to the veridicality of its source (or to the truth of the belief), and inductive bootstrapping arguments. Roush discusses all these cases in some detail.

Concerning Moorean inferences, there can be no question that it follows from Roush's recursive tracking account of knowledge that if my belief in HANDS tracks the truth, and I know that HANDS entails ~BIV, then I know ~BIV. Furthermore, on her account, knowledge of ~BIV would be 'gained via known implication from beliefs that are already knowledge' (Roush 2005: 51).

Nevertheless, Roush seems reluctant to accept this consequence of her view. She writes:

---

[20] This feature of my view sustains a strategy for dealing with some counterexamples to Roush's account presented by Alvin Goldman. Here's one of Goldman's cases, where p is the proposition 'there is a sphere in front of me': 'Suppose p is true and S comes to know it by running his hand around the object (with his eyes closed). If there weren't such a sphere there, however, S would use vision rather than touch to try to detect objects in front of him. (We can easily elaborate the story to make this plausible.) Further suppose that S's vision is poor, and he is prone to see spherical things when they aren't there.' (Goldman 2009: 226). As Goldman argues, S's belief doesn't track the truth, and there is no other proposition that S knows from which S's belief could obtain the status of knowledge by deductive inference. However, there is no problem, in my account, with explaining this as a case of inferential knowledge, based on the evidence that the object feels to the touch like a sphere. This evidence provides adequate non-deductive support for p, it is unproblematically known, and, as we shall see in Chapter 6, my account has the resources for explaining how S can know that the support relation obtains.

According to this view of knowledge I may know that there is a table in front of me, in which case I also know that I am not a brain in a vat (by known implication), or I may not know that there is a table in front of me, because I do not know that I am not a brain in a vat. Recursive tracking does not determine which of these positions one must adopt [ ... ]. (Roush 2005: 55)

Her choice of everyday proposition in this passage is unfortunate, since the proposition that there is a table in front of me does not entail ~BIV, but let's assume for the sake of the argument that the entailment holds. My main point about this passage is that if I believe that my belief that there is a table in front of me tracks the truth, then, contrary to what Roush suggests, recursive tracking does tell me which of these propositions to adopt: I have to believe that I also know ~BIV (by known implication). If Closure is treated as an independent constraint on our knowledge ascriptions, then it is indeed neutral as between the two options that Roush describes. But the same cannot be claimed for recursive tracking. If I believe that my belief in HANDS tracks the truth, and that I know that HANDS entails ~BIV, then recursive tracking doesn't leave me the option of saying that I don't know HANDS because I don't know ~BIV. It forces me to say that I know HANDS (by tracking) and ~BIV (by known implication).

Roush's discussion of Moorean inferences reveals another important difference between her approach and mine. In my view, whenever a proposition p is known inferentially, the evidence on which this knowledge is based will provide the subject with adequate reasons or justification for p. Roush, by contrast, doesn't expect her inductive clause to throw any light in general on the justificatory status of beliefs. She writes:

[ ... ] though we may, and ordinarily think we do, have knowledge that we are not brains in vats, we lack, and will always lack, the ability to offer justification for such claims. This would mean that there can be knowledge without justification, a view that I hold on other grounds [ ... ]. (Roush 2005: 56)

In her view, knowledge of ~BIV is gained by known implication from HANDS, even though HANDS provides no justification for ~BIV. In my view, by contrast, knowledge can be gained by known implication only from propositions that provide me with justification. My view, like Roush's, accepts that there can be knowledge without justification, but restricts this possibility to propositions that are known but not known inferentially. In her view, by contrast, knowledge without justification can also be found in cases of knowledge by known implication.

Concerning reflective knowledge, once again, it seems hard to deny that recursive tracking dictates that, if my belief that p tracks the truth, and I know that p entails that my belief that p is true, I will count as knowing that my belief that p is true by known implication. Roush accepts that I can come to know that my belief that p is true in this way for any p that I know, but once again she seems reluctant to accept this consequence of her view. This reluctance is manifested in her discussion of someone's belief that there is no motion of the earth relative to the ether. Assume that this belief is knowledge and that the subject believes that it is not false. Roush writes:

Still, though it does seem possible that her reflective belief is knowledge we seem to need to know more than that she knows p in order to see her as knowing that she does not falsely believe p, even when she believes the latter. [ . . . ] I conclude that it ought to follow from a view of knowledge that there are ways of acquiring the reflective knowledge in question but that it is not automatic, and less effort may be needed for this in the case of easily known statements like 'I have hands' than is required for more elaborate beliefs whose status as knowledge itself required much more deliberate effort (on the part of someone, not necessarily the subject). (Roush 2005: 60)

I agree that it ought to follow from a view of knowledge that the acquisition of reflective knowledge should not be automatic. However it is clear that Roush's view does not satisfy this requirement. It follows from her view that if I know p, and I believe that my belief that p is true (or not false), the reflective belief will have the status of knowledge so long as I know that p entails the corresponding reflective belief. It seems to me that knowledge of this entailment is a sufficiently weak requirement for the resulting reflective knowledge to count as automatic, since knowledge of the entailment would seem to be required for possessing the concept of true belief, which is required, in turn, for having reflective beliefs. At any rate, knowledge of the entailment won't be harder in cases in which knowledge of p requires deliberate efforts than in cases in which p is easily known, as Roush thinks it should be.

In my view, by contrast, this route to automatic reflective knowledge is blocked by PI. Knowing p and knowing that p entails that my belief that p is true is not sufficient for inferential knowledge of the reflective proposition, since, as we have seen, p does not provide me with adequate evidence for the proposition that my belief that p is true.

Let's turn now to bootstrapping inferences for reliability claims. As Roush explains, recursive tracking is not committed to the view that these inferences confer the status of knowledge on their conclusions. Roxanne's belief that the petrol gauge in her car is reliable doesn't come to track the truth as a result of her inference, and it doesn't acquire the status of knowledge by known implication either, since as Roush points out, the inference involves non-deductive steps.

Notice, however, that recursive tracking *is* committed to conferring the status of knowledge on Roxanne's beliefs to the effect that the gauge is reading accurately on particular occasions. As she puts it,

The steps of S's procedure that are deductive—conjunction and the inference from 'F and the gauge says "F"' to 'the gauge was accurate this time'—cannot be objectionable to recursive tracking, which allows that knowledge is preserved by deduction. (Roush 2005: 120)

I have argued above that this outcome is in conflict with our intuitions. Roxanne might know these propositions, and knowing them might be required for gaining knowledge from the gauge about the contents of the tank. What I find implausible is the idea that Roxanne can come to know that the gauge is reading accurately by virtue of the fact that she knows this proposition to be entailed by the propositions that the gauge is reading F and the tank is full, which she also knows. On my account, PI explains why this account of how Roxanne knows that the gauge is reading accurately cannot be right. Recursive tracking, by contrast, treats it as the right account.

# 6

# Knowledge Without Evidence

## 6.1 Tracking and probability

In Chapter 3 I argued that our account of knowledge has to respect the fundamental distinction between inferential and non-inferential knowledge. In Chapters 4 and 5 I provided an account of inferential knowledge. In the present chapter I turn to non-inferential knowledge. I am going to articulate and defend a proposal as to how non-inferential knowledge should be analysed. I am going to argue that there are two ways in which we can come to count as knowing propositions for which we have no adequate evidence.

The first source of non-inferential knowledge that I want to contemplate is truth tracking—I know that p if my (true) belief that p tracks the truth. As we saw in Chapter 3, Nozick construed truth tracking in terms of counterfactuals, but Roush has shown that Nozick's tracking counterfactuals have straightforward translations into the language of conditional probability. Thus sensitivity can be rendered as the condition that you are unlikely to believe A if A is false, that is, that $p(Bel(A) \mid \sim A)$ is low (or, equivalently, that $p(\sim Bel(A) \mid \sim A)$ is high). Similarly, adherence can be rendered as the condition that you are very likely to believe A if A is true, that is, that $p(Bel(A) \mid A)$ is high.

I am going to follow Roush in construing truth tracking in terms of conditional probabilities. As a modelling tool, conditional probabilities have many advantages over counterfactuals. I will mention two. One is the possibility of using the probability calculus to study the consequences of tracking claims. Another is the replacement of the problematic notion of the distance of a possible world from the actual world with the comparatively clearer notion of the probability of a state of affairs conditional on another.

We can see both these factors at work if we consider in some detail an important difference between Nozick's counterfactuals and Roush's probabilistic translations. Let's focus on sensitivity. As we construed Nozick's third condition in Chapter 3, the sensitivity of S's belief that p is determined by what happens in a specific range of possible worlds—those not-p-worlds whose distance to the actual world exceeds the distance to the actual world of the nearest not-p-world by no more than a fixed magnitude d. On this picture, the relevance of a possible world for the sensitivity of a belief is not a matter of degree. All the worlds in the range we described count the same; any world outside the range doesn't count at all.

Once we translate sensitivity to the probabilistic idiom, the situation is very different. Now all the alternatives to A will have an influence on the sensitivity of S's belief in A, but this influence will be proportional to the probability of each alternative: the more probable an alternative is, the more it will influence whether the belief is sensitive. To see this, let $B_1, \ldots, B_n$ be pairwise inconsistent propositions such that $B_1 \vee \ldots \vee B_n$ is logically true. Then the sensitivity of S's belief that A will depend on the probability of S believing A conditional on each of $B_1, \ldots, B_n$. But it is easy to show that the following equation holds (see Theorem 28, in the Appendix):

(Distribution)

$$p(\sim\!\text{Bel}(A) \mid \sim\!A) =$$
$$p(\sim\!\text{Bel}(A) \mid \sim\!A \,\&\, B_1) \cdot p(B_1 \mid \sim\!A) + \ldots + p(\sim\!\text{Bel}(A) \mid \sim\!A \,\&\, B_n) \cdot p(B_n \mid \sim\!A)$$

Notice that, according to Distribution, the probability that S believes that A if A is false and $B_i$ is true will always have some influence on the sensitivity of S's belief (unless the probability of $B_i$ given $\sim\!A$ is 0), but this influence will be proportional to the probability of $B_i$ given $\sim\!A$.

An example might help appreciate this difference. It is a familiar point about the consequences of Nozick's account for Cartesian scepticism that the sensitivity of my belief that I have hands is determined by what I believe in a situation in which, say, my hands have been amputated, and everything else is as far as possible the same, and not by what I believe in a situation in which I am a brain in a vat. The first situation (amputation) is within the relevant range of worlds, but the second (envatment) is not.

On the probabilistic rendering of sensitivity the picture is slightly different. Notice first that the contrast between amputation and envatment is characterized in a different way in each version of sensitivity. On the counterfactual version, it is done in terms of the difference between the distances from the actual world of both situations. On the probabilistic version, by contrast, this is done in terms of the difference between the probabilities of amputation and envatment conditional on my not having hands. On the probabilistic version, the difference between these probabilities means that how likely I am to believe that I have hands in the amputation scenario will have a much bigger influence on the sensitivity of my belief than the probability that I believe it in the envatment situation. However, so long as there is a non-zero probability that I am an envatted brain (if I don't have hands), what I believe in that situation will have some influence, albeit small, on the sensitivity of my belief.

Amputation and envatment lie at opposite ends of a spectrum, from the most probable alternative to having hands to the least probable. For them, the difference between the counterfactual and probabilistic versions of sensitivity is only marginal. The difference becomes more pronounced as we move towards the middle of the spectrum. Here we find alternatives to HANDS which will have a moderate but substantial influence on the sensitivity of my belief, on the probabilistic construal, whereas on the counterfactual construal they would have either as much influence as the amputation scenario or no influence at all. As we are about to see, this feature holds the key to the solution of many problems faced by counterfactual accounts of tracking.

## 6.2 Probabilistic tracking

Roush's probabilistic account of truth tracking is a straight translation of Nozick's account to the probabilistic framework: S's belief that A will track the truth just in case p(Bel(A) | A) and p(~Bel(A) | ~A) are both high.[1] The only major difference with Nozick's account is that Roush shuns relativization to methods. I am going to defend an account of truth tracking that uses Roush's central ideas. Like her, I propose to construe truth tracking in probabilistic terms and, as I argued in Chapter 3, I don't think we should follow Nozick in relativizing truth tracking to methods. However, my proposal is going to differ from Roush's in two important respects.

The first difference between my account of truth tracking and Roush's is that, whereas she imposes absolute lower bounds on p(Bel(A) | A) and p(~Bel(A) | ~A), I am going to propose that what matters for truth tracking is not that p(Bel(A) | A) should be high and p(Bel(A) | ~A) low, in absolute terms, but that the latter should be lower than the former, that is, that the ratio of p(Bel(A) | A) to p(Bel(A) | ~A) should be high. In other words, in order for S's belief that p to track the truth, LR(A, Bel(A)) will have to be high. I shall refer to LR(A, Bel(A)) as the *tracking ratio* of the belief.

In order to explore the differences between the two approaches, let's assume that we set our lower bound for LR(A, Bel(A)) at 19, since this is the value that would result from Roush's lower bound for p(Bel(A) | A) and p(~Bel(A) | ~A), that is, 0.95. Let's consider now the consequences of adopting LR(A, Bel(A)) as our measure of truth tracking for the relationship between truth tracking, on the one hand, and sensitivity and adherence, on the other. Here we find an important asymmetry. Whereas, on the one hand, inadherence of any degree can be compensated for by increased sensitivity, on the other hand, there is only a very small margin for compensating for insensitivity with increased adherence.

The first point holds because, for any value of p(Bel(A) | A), there will be values of p(Bel(A) | ~A) for which LR(A, Bel(A)) comes out higher than 19, that is, all values of p(Bel(A) | ~A) lower than p(Bel(A) | A)/19. This means that on my proposal truth tracking is in principle compatible with any level of inadherence. Adherence is only required, in effect, to compensate for relatively low levels of sensitivity.

Concerning sensitivity the situation is very different. Since p(Bel(A) | A) cannot be higher than 1, LR(A, Bel(A)) cannot be higher than 19 unless p(Bel(A) | ~A) is lower than 1/19 (≈ 0.053). This is only marginally more permissive than Roush's lower bound for sensitivity. Hence on the account of truth tracking that I am putting

---

[1] She also requires that p(Bel(~A) | A) should be low, in order to avoid counting S's belief that A as tracking the truth when she is likely to believe both A and ~A if A is true (Roush 2005: 45–6). I shall ignore this complication.

forward, truth tracking cannot be secured without almost as much sensitivity as Roush's account calls for. On the other hand, there is no upper limit to how much sensitivity will be required for truth tracking in cases of inadherent belief.

Notice that this contrast corresponds to the asymmetry between adherence and sensitivity for which I argued in Chapter 3. On the account that I'm putting forward, truth tracking requires an absolutely high level of sensitivity, but is compatible with arbitrarily low levels of adherence. Adherence can be seen as a calibration parameter for sensitivity—it dictates how much sensitivity is required for truth tracking.

One way to appreciate this difference between Roush's account and my proposal is to compare a subject S1 whose belief that A meets Roush's thresholds of adherence and sensitivity with another subject S2 whose belief that A is, say, ten times less adherent than S1's but ten times more sensitive. On Roush's account, S1's belief that A will track the truth, but S2's won't, as it fails the adherence condition. On my proposal, by contrast, S2's belief will track the truth if S1's does, as it will on our assumption that the lower bound for LR(A, Bel(A)) should be set at 19. I want to argue that the verdict of my proposal on this kind of scenario is preferable to Roush's.

Notice that if S2's belief that A is ten times less adherent but ten times more sensitive than S1's, it follows that S2 is ten times less likely to believe A (see Theorem 29). We can think of S2 as a more reluctant A-believer than S1. Nevertheless, when S2 does form a belief that A, the probability that it is true (/false) is just as high (/low) as the corresponding probability for S1's belief that A (see Theorem 30). I think that in this situation it would be natural to say that if S1's belief that A tracks the truth then so does S2's. And, other things being equal, if S1's belief counts as knowledge, S2's belief should also count as knowledge. This is the verdict that we obtain from my proposal.

Let's consider an illustration of this situation. Consider two art experts, Smith and Jones, who have independently formed the (true) belief that a recently found painting is a Rembrandt (REMBRANDT). Suppose that the probability that Smith believes REMBRANDT is ten times higher than the probability that Jones does, but the probability that REMBRANDT is true (/false) if Jones believes it is as high (/low) as if Smith believes it. I want to suggest that from the point of view of the level to which they track the truth, both beliefs should be on the same footing, as my proposal dictates. Roush's account, by contrast, doesn't secure this verdict. If Smith's belief meets Roush's adherence and sensitivity thresholds, Roush will count it as tracking the truth, but unless Smith's belief is substantially above the adherence threshold, Jones's belief will be below this threshold, and won't count as tracking the truth.[2]

---

[2] By setting a threshold for the tracking ratio, instead of the absolute values for adherence and sensitivity, we also circumvent some of the problems that Roush invokes to motivate the introduction of her *rules of application* for the tracking conditions. The first problem is that there are many cases in which the probability of S believing p given p is extremely small simply because the probability that S will form a belief on whether or not p is extremely small. Roush illustrates the point by taking S to be a palaeontologist and p the proposition that dinosaur Bob, which S has been studying, was a vegetarian.

## 6.3 Safety

Safety is another property that can receive a probabilistic makeover. On one construal of safety in terms of possible worlds, your belief that A is safe when there are no nearby possible worlds in which you falsely believe A (Williamson 2000: 123–5). On a natural probabilistic rendition of this notion, your belief that A is safe just in case A is likely to be true (unlikely to be false) if you believe it, that is, just in case $p(A \mid Bel(A))$ is high. In what follows I shall use *safety* to refer to this property.

I think it is unquestionable that safety, thus construed, is a desirable feature for a belief to have (Roush 2005: 123). In order to assess the relevance of this point for the enterprise of analysing truth tracking we need to start by asking whether a high tracking ratio is compatible with a low level of safety.[3] If this question is answered in the negative, an account of truth tracking in terms of the tracking ratio will accommodate the desirability of safety. If, on the contrary, the question receives an affirmative answer, we will need to ask whether a belief with a high tracking ratio but a low sensitivity level should count as tracking the truth and obtain the status of knowledge as a result. If this question is answered in the negative, then once again there will be no need to revise our account of truth tracking in terms of tracking ratios. However, if it receives a positive answer, our account of truth tracking will have to be revised in order to ensure that only safe beliefs count as tracking the truth.

In order to answer the first question, it will help to consider that, by Bayes's Theorem, the safety level of Bel(A) can be expressed as:

$$\frac{p(Bel(A) \mid A) \cdot p(A)}{p(Bel(A))}$$

And, by mixing, this equals:

Under the right circumstances, we would want to say that S knows p. However, S's belief that p will have a very low level of adherence:

From the point of view of a world where there was a male vegetarian dinosaur at the appropriate time and other things are constrained to be as they have been since only insofar as p's truth and the way things generally work constrain that, S cannot be said to be likely to form any belief at all about Bob. She might have been a carpenter or taxicab driver or any number of other things instead of a palaeontologist. In fact, S might not have existed at all, or might have existed but died in the car crash she narrowly escaped ten years ago, all of which says that condition IV [adherence] is not fulfilled. (Roush 2005: 78)

This particular example could also be handled on my account, by treating S's belief in p as a case of inferential knowledge, but we could easily describe similar cases of inadherent belief in which S would not know unless her belief tracked the truth. Roush solves this problem by stipulating 'that the probability functions used to evaluate IV assign probability 1 to the claim that either S believes p or S believes –p' (Roush 2005: 79). Shifting to the tracking ratio, as I am recommending, renders this stipulation unnecessary. The possibility that S might have been a carpenter, died in a car crash, etc. doesn't affect the tracking ratio of her belief, since it has the same deflating effect on its denominator as on its numerator.

The same goes for the worry that 'there could be an overwhelming number of scenarios considered in which our subject was not even present and so would have a 50–50 chance of forming either belief on the assumption that she formed one or the other belief' (Roush 2005: 79). The swamping effect of these scenarios can be expected to affect the denominator of the tracking ratio as much as its numerator.

[3] See, in this connection, Roush's discussion of the relationship between safety and sensitivity (Roush 2005: 123–6).

$$\frac{p(\text{Bel}(A)\,|\,A)\,.\,p(A)}{p(\text{Bel}(A)\,|\,A)\,.\,p(A) + p(\text{Bel}(A)\,|\,\sim A)\,.\,p(\sim A)}$$

It is clear from this that the safety level of a belief is determined exclusively by its levels of sensitivity and adherence and the probability of the proposition believed. In fact we can show (see Theorem 31) that it is determined by its tracking ratio and the probability of the proposition believed. It follows that, for a given tracking ratio, the safety level of a belief is determined exclusively by the probability of the proposition believed: the safety level will increase with the probability of the proposition believed.

Our question was whether a belief with a high tracking ratio will also exhibit a high level of safety. We can see now that the answer depends on the probability of the proposition believed. For highly probable propositions, the answer is 'yes': a belief with a high tracking ratio will also be safe. For highly improbable propositions, however, the answer is 'no': A belief in an improbable proposition will be unsafe even if it has a high tracking ratio.[4]

In order to illustrate this phenomenon, let's assume the tracking ratio of Bel(A) is 19. It can be easily verified that if the probability of A is 0.5, then the safety level of Bel(A) will be 0.95, but if the probability of A is less than 0.05 the safety level of Bel(A) will be less than 0.5: if S believes A, A will be more likely to be false than true.

One way of looking at the situation is to say that the tracking ratio required for securing a given level of safety increases as the probability of the proposition believed decreases. Thus, for example, as we have just seen, if $p(A) = 0.5$, a safety level of 0.95 for Bel(A) will be achieved with a tracking ratio of 19, but if $p(A) = 0.05$, the same safety level will require a tracking ratio of 361. Hence the question that we need to ask is whether the threshold for the tracking ratio that confers on a true belief the status of knowledge should be fixed, or whether it should increase as the probability of the proposition believed decreases, in order to secure a high level of safety.

An illustration might help us address the question. Suppose that during a basic seamanship exam held on a boat, a candidate is asked whether the wind is coming from port or starboard, and she forms the (true) belief that it is coming from starboard. Suppose that both options have equal probability and that the candidate's belief has the safety and adherence levels required by Roush's account, that is, $p(\text{Bel}(A) \mid A) = p(\sim\text{Bel}(A) \mid \sim A) = 0.95$. On my account, as well as Roush's, the candidate knows that the wind is coming from starboard. The desirability of safety poses no obstacle to this verdict, since, as we have seen, the safety level of the candidate's belief is 0.95.

Suppose now that in the advanced seamanship exam a harder wind-awareness question is asked. The compass is divided into twenty equal sectors, and the candidate

---

[4] This is the probabilistic correlate of a familiar phenomenon concerning the counterfactual rendition of safety and sensitivity. If p is false in very close possible worlds, then S's belief that p can be sensitive without being safe. If it is sensitive, S won't believe p in the nearest ~p worlds. However there might still be nearby worlds (not the closest ~p worlds) in which S falsely believes p. Then S's belief will be sensitive but not safe.

is asked to indicate which of these sectors the wind is coming from. Suppose that she forms the (true) belief that the wind is coming from the 180°–198° sector. Assume, as before, that all wind directions have equal probability, and that the candidate's belief has the sensitivity and adherence levels required by Roush's account. On Roush's account, the candidate's belief has the status of knowledge. Notice, though, that the situation with respect to safety is very different now. In spite of the high levels of sensitivity and adherence, the candidate's belief is as likely to be false as true—$p(A \mid Bel(A)) = p(\sim A \mid Bel(A)) = 0.5$. It seems to me that in these circumstances it would be wrong to say that the candidate knows that the wind is coming from the 180°–198° sector. The low level of safety of her belief is intuitively incompatible with knowledge, in spite of the high levels of adherence and sensitivity. Equivalently, knowledge by truth tracking in this case would require a higher tracking ratio than in the port/starboard case. I conclude that, in order for a belief to acquire the status of knowledge by virtue of the fact that it tracks the truth, in addition to a high tracking ratio it will need to exhibit a high level of safety.[5] Hence, if we define truth tracking as high values for $LR(A, Bel(A))$ and $p(A \mid Bel(A))$, S will count as knowing (true) A if her belief that A tracks the truth.

Supporters of safety accounts may wonder whether a high level of safety wouldn't by itself constitute a suitable account of truth tracking, obviating the need to appeal to tracking ratios. However, this proposal faces an obstacle that mirrors the argument that we have offered for the introduction of safety in our account of truth tracking.

It follows from what we have said that when the proposition believed is highly improbable a high level of safety brings with it a (very) high tracking ratio. Hence, in these cases, the tracking-ratio requirement is redundant. However, when the proposition believed is very probable the converse situation obtains. Now high levels of safety are accompanied by low tracking ratios.[6] To illustrate this point, notice that if $p(A) = p(A \mid Bel(A)) = 0.95$, $Bel(A)$ will have a tracking ratio of 1. The belief will be just as probable if A is false as if it is true. I think it is clear that it would be wrong to say that these values secure for a belief the status of knowledge. This can be easily appreciated if we take A to be the proposition that my ticket hasn't won a 20-ticket lottery, where my belief is stochastically independent of the outcome of the lottery. I conclude that a high tracking ratio has to be kept alongside a high level of safety in a plausible account of truth tracking. I shall treat them as individually necessary and jointly sufficient conditions for a belief to track the truth.[7]

[5] Another option would be to set a threshold for the tracking ratio that varies with the probability of the proposition believed, e.g. $n/p(A)$ or $n \cdot p(\sim A)$. I shall not explore these possibilities here.

[6] This is the probabilistic version of a phenomenon that is often presented as a selling point of safety accounts of knowledge, construed in counterfactual terms. When p is false only in remote worlds, S's belief that p can be safe even if it isn't sensitive, since the $\sim p$ worlds in which S believes that p to render her belief insensitive are too far away to render the belief unsafe. Hence if safety is sufficient for knowledge, even in the absence of sensitivity, we have an explanation of how I can know that I am not a brain in a vat (Sosa 1999).

[7] In Chapter 4 (footnote 24) I suggested that necessary truths should be taken as supported to an infinite degree by any proposition that's not necessarily false. If we apply this approach to tracking ratios, it will follow that any belief in a necessarily true proposition tracks the truth to an infinite degree. It follows that truth tracking can be treated as a sufficient condition for knowledge only of contingent propositions.

In the resulting account, tracking ratio and safety level work in conjunction, with one or the other acquiring increasing prominence as the proposition believed becomes more or less probable. For highly improbable propositions, beliefs will be treated as failing to track the truth even though they have a sufficiently high tracking ratio, because their safety level is not high enough. For highly probable propositions, beliefs will be treated as failing to track the truth even though they have a high level of safety, because their tracking ratio is not sufficiently high.

In this way the account achieves a reconciliation between the two main lines in counterfactual accounts of knowledge—sensitivity accounts and safety accounts. These have often been seen as mutually exclusive, but my proposal combines both approaches. Sensitivity, calibrated by adherence, is a necessary condition for truth-tracking knowledge, but so is safety. A belief has to be both sensitive and safe in order to track the truth.

## 6.4 Inferential and non-inferential knowledge

In Chapter 3 I argued that inferential and non-inferential knowledge should receive separate accounts, and that the resulting view should allow for cases of inferential knowledge in which the belief doesn't track the truth. The account of knowledge provided so far exhibits this pattern. A belief that doesn't track the truth can nevertheless acquire the status of knowledge as a result, not only of deductive inference, as Roush allows, but also of non-deductive inference.

However, although we have maintained the division between truth-tracking knowledge and inferential knowledge, the reader will have observed a remarkable similarity between my proposals as to how to construe each of these notions. On the one hand, inferential knowledge of H requires being suitably related to evidence E that provides adequate support for H, and adequate support has been construed as high values for $LR(H, E)$ and $p(H \mid E)$. On the other hand, truth tracking has been construed as high values for $LR(A, Bel(A))$ and $p(A \mid Bel(A))$. In other words, a belief tracks the truth when it provides adequate support for its truth.

This outcome vindicates yet another important intuition of Nozick's. Concerning the conditions in terms of which he proposed to construe the evidential connection he wrote:

[ . . . ] they specify that evidence *e* stands in the same relationship to the hypothesis as belief does to the truth when belief tracks the truth. (Nozick 1981: 249)

It shouldn't come as a surprise that evidence and truth tracking are related in this way. By virtue of this connection, if S's belief that p tracks the truth, someone can know p inferentially on the basis of the evidence provided by the fact that S believes that p, so long as they are suitably related to this fact and to its connection with p. This, I take it, is a highly intuitive outcome.

The connection can also be seen as a *sui generis* vindication of the connection between knowledge and evidence. As we saw in Chapters 1 and 2, one of the central tenets of externalist accounts of knowledge is the contention that knowing p doesn't require being in possession of adequate evidence for p. My account of knowledge is firmly committed to this view. Adequate evidence is required for inferential knowledge, but inferential knowledge is not the only kind of knowledge there is. Nevertheless, on the account of non-inferential knowledge that has emerged, knowing p non-inferentially requires that your belief provides adequate evidence for p. Hence evidence is somehow involved in non-inferential as well as in inferential knowledge. To know that p requires either possessing or 'embodying' adequate evidence for p. You can know the temperature of the room either by having a reliable thermometer or by *being* one—that is by having your doxastic inclinations regarding the temperature of the room regulated by a reliable sub-personal heat-measuring device. My account differs from evidentialist positions only in countenancing this second, more direct involvement of evidence in the generation of knowledge.

## 6.5 Problem cases I: positive misclassifications?

Nozick's account of knowledge has been accused of producing counterintuitive verdicts as to who knows what in a wide variety of cases. In this section and the next I want to argue that my proposal has the resources for dealing with these cases. The strategies that I will deploy mirror closely Roush's defence of her own account in her excellent discussion of purported counterexamples to tracking accounts. In this section I shall consider cases in which tracking accounts seem committed to treating as knowledge beliefs that intuitively lack this status. In the next section I shall deal with intuitive cases of knowledge to which tracking accounts seem incapable of according this status.

The first case that I want to consider is due to Alvin Goldman:

Suppose Sam spots Judy across the street and correctly believes that it is Judy. If it were Judy's twin sister, Trudy, he would mistake her for Judy. Does Sam know that it is Judy? As long as there is a serious possibility that the person across the street might have been Trudy rather than Judy (even if Sam does not realize this), we would deny that Sam knows. (Goldman 1986: 46).

As Goldman argues, Nozick's account might not deliver this verdict. We may suppose that if Judy hadn't been there, no one would have been there, or someone else, not Trudy, would have been there, and then Sam wouldn't have formed the belief that Judy is across the street. It follows that Sam's belief satisfies Nozick's sensitivity condition. Since it would also be expected to satisfy adherence, Nozick is committed to treating Sam's belief as knowledge.

Notice that Nozick's account will face this problem whenever the alternative possibility that Trudy is across the street is not the closest alternative to Judy being there, or, at any rate, not close enough to affect the truth value of the sensitivity subjunctive. But although the possibility that Trudy was there is not close enough to be relevant for the sensitivity subjunctive, it is its proximity that produces our intuition that Sam doesn't know. As Roush observes, '[i]t is essential to maintaining the intuition that Sam does not know it is Judy that we suppose that the possibility that it was Trudy rather than Judy is what Goldman called "serious"' (Roush 2005: 99).

This suggests that the problem with Nozick's account is that the truth value of the sensitivity counterfactual is determined by what happens in an overly restricted range of alternatives to Judy being there—one that doesn't include Trudy being there instead. If this is correct, then the problem will not arise for construals of truth tracking that can take into account what happens in a wide range of alternatives. This is how Roush argues that her proposal is not subject to Goldman's objection. I am going to argue that my own proposal can be vindicated in the same way.

On my account, Sam's belief in the proposition that Judy is across the street (JUDY) will track the truth just in case its tracking ratio and safety level are sufficiently high. We assume that if it weren't for the possibility that Trudy is across the street if Judy isn't there, the tracking ratio and safety level of Sam's belief would be sufficiently high. Our question is whether this possibility can be expected to have a significant deflating effect on these values. Notice that we don't need to consider tracking ratio and safety level separately. As we saw in the previous section, a decrease in the tracking ratio of a belief in TRUDY will always be accompanied by a decrease in its safety level, and vice versa. Hence we can concentrate, without loss of generality, on whether the possibility that Trudy is across the street if Judy isn't will significantly reduce the tracking ratio of Sam's belief.

Since Goldman's case has no obvious bearing on the level of adherence of Sam's belief, the crucial question for us is whether the possibility that Trudy was across the street (TRUDY) can be expected to bring about a significant reduction in the sensitivity of the belief, and hence a significant increase in the denominator of the tracking ratio. We can answer this question by appeal to the Distribution principle. If we apply the principle to Sam's belief, it yields the following equation:

$$p(\sim Bel(JUDY) \mid \sim JUDY)$$
$$=$$
$$p(\sim Bel(JUDY) \mid \sim JUDY \,\&\, \sim TRUDY) \cdot p(\sim TRUDY \mid \sim JUDY)$$
$$+$$
$$p(\sim Bel(JUDY) \mid \sim JUDY \,\&\, TRUDY) \cdot p(TRUDY \mid \sim JUDY)$$

Notice that it is common ground that $p(\sim Bel(JUDY) \mid \sim JUDY \,\&\, \sim TRUDY)$ is very high: if neither Judy nor Trudy were across the street, Sam would be very unlikely to believe that Judy was across the street. It is also common ground that $p(\sim Bel(JUDY) \mid \sim JUDY \,\&\, TRUDY)$ is very low, since if Trudy were across the street, Sam would be very likely to mistake her for Judy. It follows that the extent to which Trudy's existence will lower the sensitivity of Sam's belief is determined by the probability that Trudy was across the street instead of Judy.

On the one hand, as $p(TRUDY \mid \sim JUDY)$ approaches 0 and $p(\sim TRUDY \mid \sim JUDY)$ approaches 1, the value of $p(\sim Bel(JUDY) \mid \sim JUDY)$ will come closer and closer to the (high) value of $p(\sim Bel(JUDY) \mid \sim JUDY \,\&\, \sim TRUDY)$. Hence Trudy's existence will have less and less of a deflating effect on the sensitivity of Sam's belief and, a fortiori, on its tracking ratio. On the other hand, as p(TRUDY | ~JUDY) approaches 1 and p(~TRUDY | ~JUDY) approaches 0, the value of p(~Bel(JUDY) | ~JUDY) will come closer and closer to the (low) value of p(~Bel(JUDY) | ~JUDY & TRUDY). This will amplify the deflating effect of Trudy's existence on the sensitivity of Sam's belief and, a fortiori, on its tracking ratio.

This is precisely the result that we want. If, on the one hand, there is a serious possibility that the person across the street might have been Trudy (i.e. if p(TRUDY | ~JUDY) is high), the sensitivity and tracking ratio of Sam's belief will be reduced, and Sam won't count as knowing that Judy is across the street. If, on the other hand, the possibility is not serious (i.e. if p(TRUDY | ~JUDY) is low), say, because she lives in a different continent, the epistemic status of Sam's belief will be unaffected by her existence. I conclude that the verdicts that my account of tracking delivers for this case are in line with our intuitions. Notice that the feature of the account that addresses the problem is the fact, expressed by Distribution, that the sensitivity level of a belief is affected by what the subject believes in all the alternatives to the belief being true. This is in sharp contrast to Nozick's construal of the notion, which made sensitivity depend exclusively on what happens in a narrow range of alternatives. This will be the key to dealing with all the remaining cases that I am going to consider in which Nozick's account appears committed to intuitively unacceptable knowledge ascriptions.

The next case that I want to consider is the modification, due to Saul Kripke, of the fake-barn case. In the standard barn case (Goldman 1976), I am driving through an area which, in addition to some real barns, contains, unbeknownst to me, numerous barn facades that look from the road exactly like real barns. Suppose that when I happen to be looking at one of the few real barns, I form the true belief that it's a barn (BARN). Intuitively we wouldn't want to count this true belief as knowledge and my tracking account delivers this verdict.

Once again we can focus on the tracking ratio of my belief. Its adherence level can be expected to be sufficiently high. Hence we can hope to avoid treating it as knowledge only if its sensitivity level can be expected to be low on account of the (unactualized) possibility that the structure I'm looking at is a barn facade (FACADE). Distribution tells us that:

$$p(\sim Bel(BARN) \mid \sim BARN)$$
$$=$$
$$p(\sim Bel(BARN) \mid \sim BARN \,\&\, \sim FACADE) \cdot p(\sim FACADE \mid \sim BARN)$$
$$+$$
$$p(\sim Bel(BARN) \mid \sim BARN \,\&\, FACADE) \cdot p(FACADE \mid \sim BARN)$$

We can assume that p(~Bel(BARN) | ~BARN & ~FACADE) is high, as I am unlikely to believe of anything other than a barn or a barn facade that it is a barn. We can also assume that p(~Bel(BARN) | ~BARN & FACADE) is low, since I am likely to be fooled by barn facades. p(~Bel(BARN) | ~BARN) will approach the (high) value of p(~Bel(BARN) | ~BARN & ~FACADE) as p(FACADE | ~BARN) decreases, and the (low) value of p(~Bel(BARN) | ~BARN & FACADE) as p(FACADE | ~BARN) increases. This suggests that the sensitivity of my belief will depend on the probability that I am looking at a barn facade instead of a barn, and given the high number of barn facades in the area, this probability can be expected to be high. This will decrease the sensitivity of my belief, as required by intuition.[8]

In Kripke's modification of the case in unpublished work, the area I'm driving through contains red barns, blue barns, and red barn facades, but no blue barn facades. Looking at a blue barn, I form the true belief that that's a blue barn (BLUEBARN). Once again, intuition dictates that I don't know that the structure I'm looking at is a blue barn, but since there are no blue barn facades in the area, tracking accounts might seem committed to treating my belief as knowledge. Now Distribution yields the following equation, in which BLUEFACADE denotes the proposition that the structure I'm looking at is a blue barn facade:

p(~Bel(BLUEBARN) | ~BLUEBARN)

=

p(~Bel(BLUEBARN) | ~BLUEBARN & ~BLUEFACADE) · p(~BLUEFACADE | ~BLUEBARN)

+

p(~Bel(BLUEBARN) | ~BLUEBARN & BLUEFACADE) · p(BLUEFACADE | ~BLUEBARN)

In the unmodified barn case, I argued that my belief in BARN is not sensitive because of the high value of p(FACADE | ~BARN), which follows in turn from the abundance of barn facades in the area. Here, once more, we would be able to say that my belief in BLUEBARN is insensitive if we could argue that the value of p(BLUE-FACADE | ~BLUEBARN) is high. One obstacle to saying this—the reason why this case is supposed to be harder for tracking accounts than the unmodified barn case—is that there aren't any blue barn facades in the area. This means that we cannot argue that p(BLUEFACADE | ~BLUEBARN) is high with the argument that we used for p(FACADE | ~BARN). Nevertheless we can make a different case for the same conclusion. I want to suggest that the reason why the existence of red barn facades generates the intuition that I don't know BLUEBARN is that the existence of red barn facades increases the probability of the existence of barn facades of any colour. This, in turn, increases the value of p(BLUEFACADE | ~BLUEBARN).

This point is perfectly compatible with the non-existence of blue barn facades. The proposition that there are blue barn facades in the area (BLUEFAKES) is false but its probability is increased by the presence of red barn facades in the area. Since p(BLUE-

---

[8] The same result can be reached by concentrating on safety instead. It is clear that the value of p(BARN | Bel(BARN)) will decrease as the number of convincing barn replicas increases.

FAKES) is high, and ~BLUEBARN doesn't disconfirm BLUEFAKES, it follows that p(BLUEFAKES | ~BLUEBARN) is also high. This gives us what we want. By another application of Theorem 28, we have that:

p(BLUEFACADE | ~BLUEBARN)

=

p(BLUEFACADE | ~BLUEBARN & ~BLUEFAKES) · p(~BLUEFAKES | ~BLUEBARN)

+

p(BLUEFACADE | ~BLUEBARN & BLUEFAKES) · p(BLUEFAKES | ~BLUE-BARN)

p(BLUEFACADE | ~BLUEBARN & ~BLUEFAKES) is very low, but p(BLUE-FACADE | ~BLUEBARN & BLUEFAKES) is high. Since, as I have argued, p(BLUEFAKES | ~BLUEBARN) is also high, it follows that p(BLUEFACADE | ~BLUEBARN) is also high, as desired. Even though there are no blue barn facades around, the presence of red barn facades decreases the sensitivity, and the tracking ratio, of my belief that I'm looking at a blue barn. My account of truth tracking can accommodate the intuition that I don't know this proposition.

I want to consider next another purported counterexample to Nozick's account due to Raymond Martin (Martin 1983). In Martin's case, S goes to the races and places a bet that will pay 10 dollars if Gumshoe wins the first race or Tagalong wins the second or both win their races, and pays nothing otherwise. Payments at the track are automated: after the relevant race, you insert the ticket in the machine and you get your money if you won, and nothing if you didn't, with no further information about race results. S has a peculiar disposition to form beliefs on the outcome of the races: he will believe that Gumshoe won the first race if and only if the machine pays him 10 dollars. In the event, Gumshoe wins the first race and Tagalong comes last in the second. These two events are causally independent: Tagalong would still have come last if Gumshoe hadn't won. S presents his ticket to the machine, gets his 10 dollars, and forms the true belief that Gumshoe won the first race.

As Martin argues, S's belief satisfies Nozick's tracking conditions. Crucially, his belief is sensitive: if Gumshoe hadn't won, then neither horse would have won, the machine wouldn't have paid and S wouldn't have formed the belief that Gumshoe won. But this result is highly counterintuitive. Given his belief-forming dispositions, S doesn't know that Gumshoe won.

Notice that it is crucial to securing this result that worlds in which Tagalong wins the second race are not taken into consideration for determining the truth value of the sensitivity counterfactual, as they are more distant from the actual world than worlds in which neither horse wins. If they were taken into account, the result would no longer follow, since in those worlds S believes that Gumshoe won, contrary to what's required by the sensitivity counterfactual. And this is the source of the problem, since our intuition that S doesn't know is generated by what happens in these worlds. As Roush puts it:

It is obvious, I think, that it is precisely because S's belief isn't good against that scenario, in which Gumshoe doesn't win and Tagalong does, that we don't think S knows about Gumshoe even though her belief is true. (Roush 2005: 97)

This suggests that the strategy that we have deployed in the previous two cases will enable us to show once more that the suspect belief doesn't satisfy my account of truth tracking. Once again we concentrate on the tracking ratio of the belief and specifically on its sensitivity level, since its adherence level is not affected by the case. Applying Distribution we obtain the following equation for the sensitivity of S's belief.

p(~Bel(GUMSHOE) | ~GUMSHOE)

=

p(~Bel(GUMSHOE) | ~GUMSHOE & ~TAGALONG) · p(~TAGALONG | ~GUMSHOE)

+

p(~Bel(GUMSHOE) | ~GUMSHOE & TAGALONG) · p(TAGALONG | ~GUM-SHOE)

The pattern of the argument now is the same as in the previous cases. p(~Bel(GUM-SHOE) | ~GUMSHOE & ~TAGALONG) is high, since if neither horse won, the machine wouldn't pay out. However, p(~Bel(GUMSHOE) | ~GUMSHOE & TAG-ALONG) is low, since if Tagalong wins the machine will pay, even if Gumshoe doesn't win. It follows that the sensitivity of S's belief will depend on the value of p(TAGALONG | ~GUMSHOE). Given Martin's description of the case, we can assume that GUMSHOE and TAGALONG are stochastically independent, that is, that p(TAGALONG | ~GUMSHOE) = p(TAGALONG). Hence the sensitivity of S's belief will be determined by the probability that Tagalong wins the second race: the more probable this is, the less sensitive the belief will be. Hence, if Tagalong has a significant chance of winning the second race, S's belief can be expected to fall short of the sensitivity level that would secure the requisite tracking ratio. This is why it doesn't track the truth.

A similar reasoning would establish that S doesn't know that Gumshoe won inferentially, on the basis of the evidence provided by the machine's pay-out. Our argument for the claim that the tracking ratio of S's belief is low can be easily adapted to establish the conclusion that the hypothesis that Gumshoe won is not adequately supported by the evidence of the machine payout, since the relevant likelihood ratio is not sufficiently high.

Let me turn now to the last case that I want to consider in this section, also discussed by Alvin Goldman (Goldman 1986). A mother takes her child's temperature with a thermometer. The thermometer is working properly, and it says, correctly, that the child's temperature is normal. The mother forms the belief that it is. Under normal circumstances, we would want to say that the mother knows that the child's temperature is normal, and Nozick's account accommodates this intuition, since the belief satisfies his tracking counterfactuals.

However, suppose now that the thermometer was taken at random from a box containing hundreds of thermometers, but the one that was taken happens to be the only one that works. All the others are stuck at 'normal'. When we add this information about the case, it seems natural to say that the mother doesn't know. However, Nozick's account delivers the opposite result. On the natural assumption that the method by which the belief was formed is using the (working) thermometer that was actually picked, the mother's true belief is method sensitive and method adherent.

Clearly the reason why Nozick faces a problem here is that, as a result of his relativization of tracking to method, what the mother would believe if she used any of the other thermometers has no influence on whether her actual belief satisfies the tracking counterfactuals. Hence the problem doesn't arise for my account, since I am not making truth tracking relative to the method employed.

We can use Distribution once more to see how the possibility that other thermometers are picked would affect the sensitivity of the mother's belief (NORMAL stands for the proposition that the child's temperature is normal and WORKING for the proposition that the child's temperature was taken with a functioning thermometer):

$p(\sim Bel(NORMAL) \mid \sim NORMAL)$
=
$p(\sim Bel(NORMAL) \mid \sim NORMAL \& WORKING) \cdot p(WORKING \mid \sim NORMAL)$
+
$p(\sim Bel(NORMAL) \mid \sim NORMAL \& \sim WORKING) \cdot p(\sim WORKING \mid \sim NORMAL)$

We can argue in the same way as in the previous cases that the mother's belief will have a low level of sensitivity. Although $p(\sim Bel(NORMAL) \mid \sim NORMAL \& WORKING)$ will be high, $p(\sim Bel(NORMAL) \mid \sim NORMAL \& \sim WORKING)$ is clearly low. Hence, if $p(\sim WORKING \mid \sim NORMAL)$ takes a high value $p(\sim Bel(NORMAL) \mid \sim NORMAL)$ will be low. On the assumption that there is no probabilistic connection between the child's actual temperature and which thermometer the mother picks, we have that $p(\sim WORKING \mid \sim NORMAL) = p(\sim WORKING)$. And if the thermometer was picked at random, $p(\sim WORKING)$ will be very high, that is $1-1/n$, where n is the number of thermometers in the box. Therefore the mother's belief is highly insensitive.

We can also show that the mother doesn't know that the child's temperature is normal inferentially either. Here we have three possibilities, depending on how we choose to construe the evidence at her disposal. First, we can think of her evidence as represented by the proposition E1 that a thermometer she picked from the box says that the child's temperature is normal. Clearly this evidence won't provide adequate support for NORMAL, since the probability of E1 conditional on ~NORMAL is very high, and consequently LR(NORMAL, E1) is very low. Second, we can represent her evidence with the proposition E2 that the thermometer she actually picked says that the child's temperature is normal. Since that thermometer works properly, we can expect that E2 will provide adequate evidence for NORMAL. The problem now is that the mother won't know this, as required for inferential knowledge. We can start to see why she doesn't if we consider that her belief that E2 provides adequate support for NORMAL doesn't track the truth, since the probability that she believes that the thermometer is working properly wouldn't be significantly decreased if it wasn't. Finally, we could represent her evidence with the proposition E3 that a working thermometer says that the child's temperature is normal. Now the problem is with knowing E3, since this would require that the thermometer that she is using is working properly and we have just seen that the mother doesn't know this.

## 6.6  Problem cases II: negative misclassifications?

In this section I want to consider cases in which tracking accounts have been claimed to have trouble ascribing the status of knowledge in cases in which we intuitively know. I want to start by revisiting Nozick's grandmother case, already discussed in Chapter 3. In this case, a grandmother forms the (true) belief that her grandson is well when he comes to visit, but if he was ill others would ensure that she doesn't find out and continues to believe that he is well. As we saw, Nozick uses this case to motivate the relativization to methods of his tracking clauses. Before this feature of the account is introduced, Nozick can't count the grandmother as knowing that her grandson is well, since her belief is insensitive: if her grandson weren't well, she would still believe that he is well. But this is in conflict with our intuition that the grandmother knows.

Nozick addresses the problem with his method-relative construal of sensitivity, but the strategy is not open to me, since I have rejected this feature of Nozick's account. I suggested in Chapter 3 that the way to deal with this case is to accept that the grandmother's belief doesn't track the truth and to treat it instead as a case of inferential knowledge, after recognizing that it is possible to inferentially know that p without tracking the truth of p. In light of our subsequent account of inferential knowledge, this requires finding a proposition that represents the grandmother's evidence and satisfies the objective and subjective conditions in terms of which I have construed inferential knowledge. A proposition E describing the grandson's visit and his appearance on that occasion will do the job. E will provide adequate support for the proposition that the grandson is well (WELL), since both LR(WELL, E), p(WELL | E) can be expected to be high. In addition, the grandmother can be expected to know E, as well as the evidential connection between E and WELL—she knows that looking as he did denotes good health. Finally, E's support for WELL is clearly not misplaced, and it doesn't violate PI: she is more likely to believe E if her grandson is well than if he isn't. The grandmother's belief is a case of inferential knowledge that doesn't track the truth. We are going to see that we can apply the same strategy to other problematic cases.

I want to consider next Goldman's case in which Oscar, who sees Dack the dachshund in front of him, forms the belief that there is a dog before him (DOG) (Goldman 1983). Intuitively this is a clear case of knowledge: Oscar knows that there is a dog before him. However, Nozick's account might not be able to deliver this result. Suppose that if there hadn't been a dog in front of Oscar, there would have been a hyena, and that Oscar always mistakes hyenas for dogs. In this situation, Oscar's belief that there is a dog in front of him is not sensitive, as he would have it if it were false. On Nozick's construal of truth tracking, Oscar's belief doesn't track the truth. The same situation obtains on my construal, since Oscar's tendency to mistake hyenas for dogs, and the probability that there is a hyena in front of him if there isn't a dog, will clearly reduce the sensitivity and the tracking ratio of his belief: the probability that he believes DOG if DOG is false will be unacceptably high.

However, as we have seen, my proposal, unlike Nozick's, has the resources for ascribing the status of knowledge to beliefs that don't track the truth. We will be able to do this whenever we can describe the belief in question as a case of inferential knowledge. This is the strategy that I am going to adopt for this case. I want to argue that Oscar knows DOG inferentially, on the basis of evidence provided by another proposition whose truth he does track. Clearly the proposition that there is a dachshund before him would do the job, provided that Oscar believes it. But presumably Oscar can know DOG even if he doesn't have the concept of a dachshund. What Oscar is bound to have is a perceptual concept composed of the ostensible properties that have led him to believe that there is a dog before him. These properties can be expected to include, as Roush suggests, being 'a four-legged, floppy-eared, friendly animal with short fur, short legs, disproportionately long body, wagging tail, etc., etc.' (Roush 2005: 58). Let me abbreviate the proposition that a creature with these features is before Oscar as DACHSHUNDLIKE. The proposal is that Oscar knows DOG inferentially on the basis of evidence provided by DACHSHUNDLIKE, which he knows, in turn, by truth tracking.

We can easily check that the case satisfies all the conditions entailed by this knowledge claim. Notice first that Oscar's belief in DACHSHUNDLIKE can be expected to track the truth. The properties that the proposition ascribes to the creature in front of him are properties whose presence or absence he can detect by visual inspection. Hence he will be very unlikely to believe the proposition if it is false, and very likely to believe it if it is true. The evidential link between DACHSHUNDLIKE and DOG can also be easily verified. One apparent obstacle here is the high probability that the animal in front of Oscar doesn't look like a dachshund if it is a dog, but the extremely low probability that something other than a dog looks like a dachshund can be expected to compensate for this. Notice, in this connection, that the probability that a non-dog looks like a dachshund can be expected to be proportionally smaller than the probability that a non-dog looks like a dog. Furthermore, the probability that something is a dog if it looks like a dachshund can be expected to be very high. Oscar can also be expected to know that DACHSHUNDLIKE provides adequate support for DOG. Finally, this support is not misplaced and it doesn't violate PI. I conclude that Oscar can know DOG on the basis of the evidence provided by DACHSHUND-LIKE.

My treatment of this case is very similar to Roush's, but there is an important difference. On her recursive-tracking view, the strategy only works if DACHS-HUNDLIKE logically entails DOG. In light of the 'phenomenological' nature of the properties ascribed in DACHSHUNDLIKE, this requires adopting a construal of DOG on which it also ascribes a collection of superficial properties (Roush 2005: 58, fn. 24). Thus it seems that, on Roush's position, Oscar is incapable of knowing by visual inspection that Dack is a member of the dog species, construed in terms of genetics. This result has to come as a disappointment for a fallibilist like Roush. If there is a sufficiently tight probabilistic connection between surface properties and genetics, it should be possible to acquire knowledge about the genetics from the looks. This should be possible, in particular, in Oscar's case. On my view, by contrast, there is no difficulty here, since inferential knowledge can arise from non-deductive evidence. Oscar can know inferentially that Dack is a dog, not merely that he looks like one.

I want to consider next a similar case put forward by Tim Williamson (Williamson 2000: 159–61). Suppose that I tend to underestimate distances. When I see a distance of twenty-one metres, I judge it to be less than twenty metres. I see a mark on the side of a ship that is one metre above the waterline, and I form the belief that it is less than twenty metres above the waterline (LESSTHANTWENTY). Clearly this belief should count as knowledge. My slight tendency to underestimate distances should not be an obstacle to this. And yet, assuming that the mark would have been less than twenty-one metres above the waterline if it hadn't been less than twenty metres above the waterline, we have to conclude that my belief is insensitive: if LESSTHAN-TWENTY were false I would believe it. On my construal of truth tracking the same result ensues since I will be very likely to believe LESSTHANTWENTY if it is false, provided that there is a significant probability that the mark is between twenty and twenty-one metres above the waterline.

Once again I propose to deal with the problem by construing my knowledge that the mark is less than twenty metres above the waterline as inferential. On this approach, I will know LESSTHANTWENTY on the basis of the evidence provided by another proposition whose truth I track. Williamson considers a similar suggestion, taking as the evidence the proposition that the mark is less than two metres above the waterline, but he raises two objections against this proposal. He argues, first, that

I can know p [LESSTHANTWENTY] even if I do not derive p from anything like the proposition that the mark is less than two metres above the waterline; p may be the only proposition that I entertain about the distance in metres. (Williamson 2000: 160)

His second objection to the proposal is that even if I believe that the mark is less than two metres above the waterline, this belief might be insensitive:

I have a general tendency to underestimate distances; if the mark were not less than two metres above the waterline, it might be only slightly more than two metres above, and I would still judge it to be less than two metres above the waterline. Even so, I can know that it is less than twenty metres above. (Williamson 2000: 160)

The first of Williamson's objections doesn't really affect my proposal, since knowing p inferentially doesn't require engaging in an actual process of derivation of p from the evidence, and believing the evidential proposition does not require entertaining it (Roush 2005: 72). The second objection relies on choosing as evidence a precise proposition about the height of the mark. Suppose that we use instead the proposition that the mark is *roughly* one metre above the waterline, where the borders of the concept are determined by my discriminatory propensities, taking into account my tendency to underestimate distances: a distance is roughly one metre just in case I would judge it to be one metre. This is a proposition that I can be expected to believe, even if I haven't entertained it in consciousness, since my behavioural dispositions will manifest a commitment to its truth. When we use this proposition as evidence, Williamson's second objection no longer applies: if the mark weren't roughly one metre above the waterline, I would be very unlikely to believe that it is roughly one metre above the waterline. Hence my belief in the evidence is highly sensitive. Since adherence and safety don't pose a problem in this case, I can conclude that my belief in the evidence tracks the truth. Furthermore, this evidence will provide adequate (deductive) support for LESSTHANTWENTY, and I can be expected to know this. I conclude that in the situation that Williamson describes I know LESSTHANTWENTY inferentially.

The last family of cases that I want to consider in this section concerns propositions to the effect that a very unlikely occurrence has not taken place. Intuition dictates that it is possible to know these propositions, but tracking accounts appear to have problems delivering this result. I am going to concentrate on Jonathan Vogel's excellent discussion of the issue. Vogel introduces the problem with the following case:

Imagine it's a hot day in August, say 95 degrees in the shade. Several hours ago, you left some ice cubes in a glass out in the direct sun, and since that time you've gone inside to get out of the heat. You think about the ice cubes, and it occurs to you that the ice you left outside must have melted by now. Despite the fact that you are not, at that moment, perceiving the shallow layer of water at the bottom of the glass, you know that the ice has melted. (Vogel 1987: 206)[9]

As Vogel argues, Nozick's account seems to have trouble delivering the intuitive result. The problem is that the subject's belief in the proposition that the ice cubes have melted (MELTED) doesn't seem to satisfy Nozick's sensitivity counterfactual: if the ice cubes hadn't melted he would believe that they had melted, as the subject is not in a position to detect their failure to melt.

---

[9] Ernest Sosa's garbage-chute case has a similar structure (Sosa 1999: 145–6).

Vogel considers a strategy for avoiding this outcome to which Nozick alludes in a footnote (Nozick 1981: 223n). The strategy consists in arguing that the belief in MELTED does satisfy the sensitivity counterfactual because the following conditional is true:

(6) If the ice hadn't melted, it would have been the case that your previous experience was different in ways that would have led you not to expect that the ice would melt under the circumstances. (Vogel 1987: 207–08)

Vogel objects to this strategy on the grounds that (6) is, at best, indeterminate. It would be true if in the nearest ~MELT-world there are lots of other exceptions to the usual laws about the behaviour of ice, but it would be false if in that world the failure of these ice cubes to melt is a unique exception, with everything else remaining the same. According to Vogel, there is no reason to favour one story over the other.

I agree with Vogel that this attempt to ensure that Nozick's counterfactual delivers the intuitive verdict faces formidable difficulties, cogently mapped out in his subsequent discussion of the proposal. I want to argue, however, that when we consider the issue in the context of my account of truth tracking and inferential knowledge in probabilistic terms, a similar strategy does enable us to treat my belief in MELT as knowledge.

I propose to consider in the first instance how my belief fares as a case of inferential knowledge. Clearly I don't have direct evidence of the melting of the ice, what I do have is beliefs in the general behaviour of ice in hot environments that render MELT extremely probable. As Vogel points out:

If, in the situation described, the ice cubes hadn't melted, there would have been a violation of the law that ice melts at temperatures above 32 degrees F. (Vogel 1987: 209)

I want to argue that I know MELT inferentially, on the basis of the evidence provided by this law (call it LAW).[10] I think we can assume that I know LAW, typically on the basis of the inductive evidence provided by my past experience of what happens to ice when the temperature rises. Hence, in order to establish that I know MELT, it would suffice to show that LAW provides adequate support for MELT. Showing this would require ascertaining that $p(\text{MELT} \mid \text{LAW})$ and $\text{LR}(\text{MELT}, \text{LAW})$ have sufficiently high values.

$p(\text{MELT} \mid \text{LAW})$ is obviously not a problem. If we think of LAW as an exceptionless generalization, it will have MELT as a logical consequence, and $p(\text{MELT} \mid \text{LAW})$ will equal one. But even if we think of LAW as a statistical generalization, the probability of MELT given LAW can be expected to be extremely high.

We can also show that $\text{LR}(\text{MELT}, \text{LAW})$ will take a very high value. Notice, first, that its denominator, $p(\text{LAW} \mid \sim\text{MELT})$, will be very small. If LAW is a strict

---

[10] A more rudimentary generalization would also do the job, as, e.g., that ice left in the sun on a hot day doesn't take long to melt.

generalization, ~MELT will entail ~LAW, and p(LAW | ~MELT) will be zero, but even if we take as a statistical generalization the probability of LAW given ~MELT can be assumed to be very low. This is simply a reformulation of the uncontroversial point that laws are confuted by their counter-instances.

The claim that LR(MELT, LAW) is high might seem to come under threat when we consider its numerator: we can't expect p(LAW | MELT) to be particularly high. The reason is that, although MELT can be assumed to provide *some* confirmation for LAW, we can expect this level of confirmation to be very small. This means that p(LAW | MELT) will be greater than p(LAW), but only marginally so.[11] Hence, unless the prior probability of LAW is very high, p(LAW | MELT) won't take a very high value.

However, this point won't affect the value of LR(MELT, LAW). The reason is that if LAW has a low prior probability, this can be expected to affect the value of p(LAW | ~MELT) to the same extent as the value of p(LAW | MELT). The claim that ~MELT disconfirms LAW to a high degree entails that p(LAW | ~MELT) is much lower than p(LAW). For a given degree of disconfirmation, p(LAW | ~MELT) will decrease with p(LAW). Therefore the ratio of p(LAW | MELT) to p(LAW | ~MELT) won't be affected by the value of p(LAW | MELT).

Notice, finally, that PI is not an obstacle to my inferential-knowledge claim. I have just argued that p(LAW | ~MELT) will be much smaller than p(LAW | MELT). Furthermore, the probability of the evidence on which I ground my belief in LAW will be drastically reduced if LAW is false. It follows that p(Bel(LAW) | ~MELT) is much smaller than p(Bel(LAW) | MELT), as required by PI. I conclude that LAW provides me with adequate support for MELT. Since I know LAW, I also know MELT.

So far, my argument concerning this case has followed the same pattern as my treatment of the cases previously considered in this section. Nevertheless there is an important difference. In the previous cases I argued that we had to concede that the subject doesn't track the truth of the proposition that he knows inferentially. In this case, by contrast, there is no reason to make this concession. As I have just argued, my belief in LAW provides adequate support for MELT. We can also see that my belief in MELT provides adequate support for my belief in LAW: I'm much more likely to believe MELT if I believe LAW than if I don't. Hence, so long as the values of LR in these cases are sufficiently high to sustain an instance of transitivity, we can conclude that my belief in MELT has a sufficiently high tracking ratio. We can also argue that the belief has a high safety level, assuming that I'm unlikely to believe MELT without adequate evidence. It follows that my belief in MELT tracks the truth.

---

[11] Here, and in the next paragraph, I am assuming that measuring confirmation with the probability measures yields similar results as using LR.

Roush deploys a similar strategy for handling this case, but once again differences arise from the fact that the recursion clause of her account of knowledge contemplates only deductive inferences. This means that on her account I cannot know that the ice cubes have melted, only that they have *very probably* melted. Here is her explanation of why she feels forced to take this line in this and other similar cases:

That is as far as the recursion clause can take us because the generalisations I know from which the instances follow deductively are not strict. Their truth is consistent with the existence of exceptional cases [ . . . ]. (Roush 2005: 66)

This seems to me to be in conflict with intuition. The intuitive verdict, as Vogel's discussion assumes, is that I know that the ice cubes have melted, not merely that they have very probably melted.[12] Hence I take this difference between our accounts to count in favour of mine.

Roush does offer an argument in favour of her more modest knowledge claim. This highlights another difference between her position and mine. She writes:

Notice that if we attributed knowledge that the ice cubes melted, and not merely that they probably melted, to the person in the house, then by Closure our subject would, if he or she were sufficiently reflective, thereby have knowledge that this instance was not one of the exceptional cases. This is because this follows deductively from the generalization and the instance, both of which the subject knows. (Roush 2005: 66)

I agree with Roush that there would be something wrong in ascribing to the subject knowledge that this instance was not one of the exceptional cases. However, the account of inferential knowledge that I am putting forward would not license this knowledge ascription. The reason is that the inference from LAW and MELT to the conclusion that this instance was not one of the exceptional cases violates PI: I am as likely to believe the premises if the conclusion is false as if it is true. Hence, on my account, the inference that Roush describes would not produce knowledge of its conclusion.

My treatment of Vogel's case might seem to create trouble elsewhere. I have in mind the epistemic status of my belief that I haven't won the lottery provided that it is a fair lottery for which I hold only one of, say, ten million tickets whose result hasn't been announced yet. It is widely accepted that the intuitive verdict on this case is that I don't know that my ticket hasn't won (LOSER). Its ability to deliver this verdict was one of the main selling points of Nozick's original truth tracking account of knowledge. My belief that my ticket hasn't won doesn't satisfy Nozick's sensitivity counterfactual, since if my ticket had won I would believe that it hasn't. It follows that according to Nozick I don't know that my ticket has won, even if my belief is true.

---

[12] Roush offers an interesting sociological explanation of the difference between our intuitions on this case: 'In conversation I have found that feelings about whether this is right are highly correlated with one's self-identification as a philosopher of science or an analytic philosopher, with the latter tending to be quite convinced that the verdict that the subject knows "very probably—" is not good enough' (Roush 2005: 66).

My account of truth tracking replicates Nozick's result, since the probability that I believe that my ticket hasn't won doesn't seem to be affected by whether it has or not. On my account of truth tracking my belief that my ticket hasn't won doesn't track the truth either. Notice, however, that unlike Nozick's account, on my proposal a belief that doesn't track the truth may still qualify for the status of knowledge, as I can know inferentially a proposition even if my belief in it doesn't track the truth. Does my account dictate that I know inferentially that I haven't won the lottery? The problem that I want to consider is that the parallels between this case and Vogel's would seem to suggest that I have to answer this question in the affirmative.

Let me use SETUP to denote the proposition that describes the basic facts about the lottery—that it is a fair lottery with ten million tickets. And let's assume that I know SETUP. The worry is that the argument that I used to show that I know MELT on the basis of the evidence provided by LAW might have a legitimate analogue establishing that I know LOSER on the basis of the evidence provided by SETUP.

It is easy to see, however, that this worry is unfounded. Let's concentrate on LR (LOSER, SETUP). It is clear that the probability of SETUP is unaffected by the truth value of LOSER, that is, by whether the winning ticket is the one I hold. It follows from this that LR(LOSER, SETUP) equals one, and hence that SETUP doesn't confirm (or disconfirm) LOSER. It is interesting to see where the disanalogy with Vogel's case arises. I argued in that case that p(LAW | ~MELT) can be assumed to be very low, since this follows from the idea that laws are confuted by their counter-instances. This is the point where the analogy with the lottery case breaks down. We cannot use this line of reasoning to argue that p(SETUP | ~LOSER) is very low since the hypothesis that the lottery is fair and has ten million tickets is not disconfirmed to any degree by the circumstance that the winning ticket happens to be the one I hold. SETUP and LOSER are stochastically independent. Hence p(SETUP | LOSER) = p(SETUP | ~LOSER) = p(SETUP). It follows that on my account I don't know that I haven't won the lottery, either inferentially or non-inferentially, just as intuition would have it.

## 6.7 Adherence

In Chapter 3 I argued for the existence of a fundamental asymmetry in the relative importance of sensitivity and adherence in the concept of knowledge. I argued that whereas sensitivity should in principle be treated as a necessary condition for knowledge, it would be wrong to ascribe this status to adherence. I argued for the irrelevance of adherence with the help of an example: Gladys's belief that the winner of the talent show is from Scotland, based on her disposition to form the belief that someone is from Scotland just in case they speak with a Glaswegian accent. I argued that Gladys's belief should be treated as knowledge, even though it is inadherent: there are nearby worlds in which the belief is true but Gladys doesn't have it—those in which the contest is won by a Scot who speaks, say, in an Edinburgh accent. Then I argued that refusing to treat adherence as a necessary condition for knowledge enabled us to deal with the problem that Nozick faced with the Jesse James case: the fact that the bystander's belief that Jesse James robbed the bank is inadherent poses no obstacle to the intuitive verdict that her belief is knowledge.

However, as we have seen, adherence still plays a role in my account of truth tracking, since it figures in the numerator of the tracking ratio. I have argued that the role of adherence is less important than the role of sensitivity, since a lower bound on the tracking ratio imposes a lower bound on sensitivity but not on adherence. Low levels of adherence can always be compensated for by high levels of sensitivity, but the converse only holds up to a certain point.

Nevertheless the fact remains that on the account of truth tracking that I have put forward, adherence plays some role and it might determine whether a belief counts as knowledge. For a given level of sensitivity, there will be adherence values that make the tracking ratio meet the threshold and values that fall short of this. In light of this, we need to check that the involvement of adherence in my account of truth tracking doesn't preserve the difficulties that I raised for Nozick's account of the notion. I want to argue that the inadherence of the beliefs formed by Gladys and the bank-robbery bystander will have no influence on their tracking ratio, and hence that it is not an obstacle to treating them as knowledge.

Let's consider first the situation in the Jesse James case. Suppose that the probability that the bystander will believe that the bank is being robbed by Jesse James (JESSE-JAMES) if the robber *is* Jesse James and doesn't have a mask on his face when he sees him (~MASK) is 0.95, and the probability that he believes that the bank is being robbed by Jesse James if the robber is not Jesse James and doesn't have a mask on his face when he sees him is 0.05. If we disregard the possibility that the robber is wearing a mask, we have that the tracking ratio of the bystander's belief is $0.95/0.05 = 19$. Now in the scenario described by Nozick the robber is wearing a mask that slips only briefly. Let's assume that it follows from this that the probability that the robber doesn't have a mask on his face when the bystander sees him is reduced to 0.01. And let's suppose that if the robber is wearing a mask when the bystander sees him he won't form the belief that he is Jesse James, whether he is or not.

Clearly this will reduce the adherence of the belief. The probability that he will form the belief in JESSEJAMES if this proposition is true will be reduced by a factor of 0.01. However, and this is the crucial point, the probability that he will form the belief in JESSEJAMES if the proposition is false will also be reduced by this factor, hence leaving the tracking ratio of the belief unchanged.

We can see this with a trivial variant of distribution. On the one hand we have:

p(Bel(JESSEJAMES) | JESSEJAMES)

=

p(Bel(JESSEJAMES) | JESSEJAMES & MASK) · (MASK | JESSEJAMES)

+

p(Bel(JESSEJAMES) | JESSEJAMES & ~MASK) · (~MASK | JESSEJAMES)

$= 0 + 0.95 \cdot 0.01 = 0.0095$[13]

On the other hand we have:

p(Bel(JESSEJAMES) | ~JESSEJAMES)

=

p(Bel(JESSEJAMES) | ~JESSEJAMES & MASK) · (MASK | ~JESSEJAMES)

+

p(Bel(JESSEJAMES) | ~JESSEJAMES & ~MASK) · (~MASK | ~JESSEJAMES)

$= 0 + 0.05 \cdot 0.01 = 0.0005$

It follows that the tracking ratio of the bystander's belief is 0.0095 divided by 0.0005, that is, 19. I conclude that, although the fact that the robber is wearing a mask reduces the adherence of the belief, it has no effect on its tracking ratio.[14]

Let's consider now Gladys's belief that the winner of the talent show is Scottish (SCOTTISH). We can clarify the situation by comparing the status of Gladys's belief in SCOTTISH with that of Scarlett's belief in the same proposition. Scarlett is disposed to form the belief that someone is Scottish if and only if they speak in a Scottish accent (Glaswegian or otherwise). Making a few assumptions will help us focus the issue. Let's assume that Scarlett is infallible at identifying a Scottish accent, and that Gladys is infallible at identifying a Glaswegian accent.[15] Let's assume that 0.9 of the Scottish population (or the Scottish talent show contestants) speaks in a Scottish accent, and 0.3 in a Glaswegian accent. It follows from these assumptions that the adherence level of Scarlett's belief is 0.9, and that of Gladys's belief 0.3.

The question that we need to consider is whether this difference between their adherence levels can be expected to have an influence on their tracking ratios. Clearly this will depend on their respective sensitivity levels, and on our assumption of infallibility this will depend on the probability that someone who is not Scottish speaks with a Scottish or Glaswegian accent. Clearly the former probability is at least as high as the latter, since a Glaswegian accent is a Scottish accent. The crucial question is how much higher it is.

There are three relevant possibilities, bearing in mind that the probability that a Scot speaks in a Scottish accent is three times greater than the probability that a Scot speaks in a Glaswegian accent: (a) that the probability that a non-Scot speaks in a Scottish

---

[13] I am assuming here that the probability that the robber is wearing a mask when the bystander sees him is not affected by whether the robber is or is not Jesse James.

[14] Roush deals with this case with the strategy that I deployed in the previous section, treating the bystander's belief as a case of inferential knowledge, based on the evidence provided by the proposition: 'There was a man with a gun in his hand whose face looked like that of Jesse James from the "WANTED" posters running out of the bank in front of me at such-and-such a time' (Roush 2005: 68). I am arguing that the manoeuvre is unnecessary in this case. Notice that, since Roush's recursive clause applies only to deductive inferences, once again she can only ascribe to the bystander knowledge of the proposition that the robber was *very probably* Jesse James.

[15] Our results won't depend on this simplifying assumption. All that we require is that they both have the same rate of false-positives and the same rate of false-negatives.

accent is also three times greater than the probability that a non-Scot speaks in a Glaswegian accent; (b) that the probability that a non-Scot speaks in a Scottish accent is less than three times greater than the probability that a non-Scot speaks in a Glaswegian accent; (c) that the probability that a non-Scot speaks in a Scottish accent is more than three times greater than the probability that a non-Scot speaks in a Glaswegian accent.

In (a), we have that the denominators of the tracking ratios of Scarlett's and Gladys's belief differ by the same factor as their numerators, and hence that their tracking ratios are identical. In (b) we have that the denominators differ by a smaller factor than their numerators, and hence that the tracking ratio of Gladys's belief is smaller than that of Scarlett's. In (c) we have that the denominators differ by a greater factor than their numerators, and hence that the tracking ratio of Gladys's belief is greater than that of Scarlett's.

What this shows is that the difference between the tracking ratios of Scarlett's and Gladys's beliefs is not determined by the difference in their levels of adherence. What it depends on is how the ratio of Scottish-speaking 'fakes' to Glaswegian-speaking fakes compares to the ratio of Scottish-speaking Scots to Glaswegian-speaking Scots. If the former is smaller than the latter (suppose, e.g., that lots of foreigners speak in a Glaswegian accent, but virtually no foreigner speaks in any other Scottish accent), then the tracking ratio of Gladys's belief will be lower than that of Scarlett's. But if the former is greater than the latter (suppose, e.g., that lots of foreigners speak in Scottish accents, but no one outside Scotland gets the Glaswegian accent quite right), then Gladys's belief will have a higher tracking ratio than Scarlett's. Finally, if both ratios coincide, both beliefs will have the same tracking ratio. In sum, the fact that Gladys's belief has a lower adherence level than Scarlett's has no bearing on how the tracking ratios of the two beliefs compare.

My goal in this section was to determine whether the involvement of adherence in my account of truth tracking leads to the problems that I highlighted for its involvement in Nozick's account. We have found that this is not so. In the cases I have considered, low levels of adherence don't interfere with truth tracking.

## 6.8  Knowledge by default

There are in principle two ways in which a designer could ensure that a cognitive system has correct representations of its environment. One is to endow it with devices that produce a correlation between states of affairs and representations—between how things are and how the system represents them as being. The second is to endow the system directly with correct representations. In terms of design efficacy, which of the two approaches will be more advantageous will depend on the states of affairs in question. On the one hand, for states of affairs that may or may not obtain in the environment that the system is likely to inhabit, trying to endow the system directly with true representations is not a viable approach. It would be much more practical to endow the system with the means to detect whether the relevant states of affairs obtain or fail to obtain. On the other hand, for standing features of the environment that are highly unlikely to change, it wouldn't make much sense to equip the system with devices for determining whether the relevant features are present or not. It would be more economical to endow it directly with the relevant representations.

If we think of ourselves as cognitive systems designed by evolution to have correct representations of our environment, it seems clear that our designer has combined both approaches. We have, on the one hand, an array of devices for detecting the obtaining and non-obtaining of a wide variety of states of affairs. On the other hand, we have strong inclinations to form certain representations whose truth value we are not equipped to detect.

This combination of design approaches can be illustrated with the case of herring gulls (Tinbergen 1951: 145–6). By the time their chicks are five days old, parents can recognize them individually and will look after them, while neglecting or even killing any other young forced upon them. With respect to their eggs, the situation is very different. Parents seem incapable of discriminating between their own eggs and other eggs, even if they look quite different, and they will display the same brooding reactions to any eggs that are placed where they would have expected to find theirs.

This contrast can be explained in terms of the ideas that I have presented. The proposition 'the chicks in my nest are mine' is much more likely to be false, on a given occasion, than the proposition 'the eggs in my nest are mine', for the very simple reason that chicks can move about and eggs can't. This means that, with respect to the former, hardwiring a doxastic representation of the proposition in the gull would often lead to false representations. Endowing the gull with a chick-discriminating device is the only way to ensure consistently true representation in this case. An egg-discriminating device would be, by comparison, a waste of resources. If in the circumstances in which the gulls evolved foreign eggs were rarely found in their nests, a hardwired representation of the proposition 'the eggs in my nest are mine' would be an efficient approach to the production of true representations.

Let me say that a belief is a *standing belief* when we have an innate predisposition to form it that is largely independent of input, but we are not equipped to detect its truth value. Sceptics have always found a rich source of materials among our standing beliefs. It isn't hard to see why. If the designer of our cognitive systems actually intended them to produce true beliefs, if the design was reasonably competent, and if we actually inhabit the environment for which we were designed, then our standing beliefs will be extremely unlikely to be false. However it is in their nature that we are not in a position to detect the obtaining or non-obtaining of the states of affairs that would make them true. Hence, when challenged by the sceptic, we have very little to say in their defence. We are pre-programmed to believe that our sense experiences are produced by the kind of physical world that we take ourselves to inhabit, and not by any of the standard sceptical alternatives, that objects continue to exist when we are not perceiving them, that the future will continue to resemble the past, and so on. But we struggle when we try to offer adequate reasons in support of these beliefs. And the difficulty has a tendency to spread in familiar ways, since the reasons that we can offer in support of adventitious beliefs ultimately seem to depend for their adequacy on the truth of some standing belief.

The account of knowledge that we have reached so far entirely bypasses standing beliefs. In order for a belief to track the truth, the subject has to have the means to detect its falsehood, at least in the situations that are most likely to obtain if the belief is false. It follows that standing beliefs cannot track the truth. Whether standing beliefs can be instances of inferential knowledge is a much more complicated question, that some of the central debates in epistemology aim to answer.[16] I think that the attempt to vindicate the epistemic status of our standing beliefs in this way is unlikely to succeed, but I don't want to pre-judge the question here. I only want to point out that if we think of ourselves, as I am proposing, as cognitive systems designed to form true beliefs, it would be somewhat surprising if the project succeeded. Our designer would simply have implanted these beliefs, without wasting precious resources to provide us with the means to vindicate them if challenged.

All this suggests that on the account that I have presented so far, standing beliefs don't stand much of a chance of qualifying for the status of knowledge. I find this unsatisfactory. It amounts to holding standing beliefs to epistemic standards that are clearly modelled on the form of excellence that we would want our adventitious beliefs to exhibit. Standing beliefs don't meet these standards, but it is not clear why they should. Epistemic excellence for them means something else. It doesn't require that we have the ability to determine whether things are as they represent them as being. All it requires is that the states of affairs they represent actually obtain. For standing beliefs, truth is the only form of epistemic excellence that we can sensibly demand.

I want to suggest that standing beliefs that are true have as much of a claim to count as instances of knowledge as adventitious beliefs that exhibit their own form of epistemic excellence: true standing beliefs should count as knowledge. In order to accommodate this thought, we need to introduce one final component of our account of knowledge. We shall say that a standing belief will have the status of knowledge if it is true, even if it doesn't track the truth and even if we don't have adequate evidence in its support.[17] It follows that my standing belief that I am not a brain in a vat will have the status of knowledge so long as it is true. And the same goes for other standing beliefs

---

[16] Showing that this question can be answered in the affirmative is the main goal of the approaches to scepticism that Thomas Nagel labelled *heroic* (Nagel 1986).

[17] Notice that this line is not incompatible with Nozick's explanation of the value of beliefs that track the truth over and above merely true beliefs (Nozick 1981: 283–6). He writes: 'The evolutionary process can give organisms true beliefs (in a changing world) only by giving them the capability to have true beliefs: so, it will give them more than (merely) true beliefs. In giving them a capability for true beliefs, it makes their beliefs (sometimes) vary somehow with the truth of what is believed; it makes their beliefs somehow sensitive to the facts' (Nozick 1981: 285). Clearly, the argument applies only to changing aspects of the world. For aspects of the world that are relatively unlikely to change, the evolutionary process can give organisms true beliefs without making them sensitive to the facts.

that have attracted the attention of sceptics. I can know in the same way, for example, that the world didn't start five minutes ago, complete with memories, fossil remains, and so on, that objects continue to exist when unperceived, and that the future will continue to resemble the past.[18]

I think that this acknowledgement of the special status of standing beliefs is faithful to our concept of knowledge, and I am offering it as a (final) step in this analytic enterprise. If I had offered it instead as a step in the project of refuting sceptical arguments, it would probably require a much more powerful defence, since the sceptic might simply insist that standing beliefs should not receive any exemptions. However, as we'll see in the next chapter, this is not the dialectical situation. The goal of my discussion of scepticism is not to show that the sceptical problem is an illusion resulting from a mistaken conception of knowledge. My goal is to show that the sceptical problem is real and disturbing, even if we adopt the account of knowledge that I have put forward over the last three chapters. My suggestion that it would be wrong for sceptics to launch their challenge by targeting standing beliefs should be taken as a piece of sympathetic advice.

## 6.9 Closure

I have now finished specifying the conditions under which a true belief counts as knowledge. A true belief is knowledge if it tracks the truth, or if the subject is in possession of adequate evidence in its support, or if it is a standing belief. My next goal will be to consider whether this account of knowledge leaves room for a cogent challenge to our knowledge claims. But before I move on to that, I'd like to finish the chapter by considering briefly the status assigned to the principle of Closure under known entailment by the account of knowledge that I am recommending.

It will help to present the situation in the context of previous accounts of knowledge based on truth tracking. On Nozick's account, the scope of the principle is severely restricted. Truth tracking is treated as both necessary and sufficient for knowledge, and there are many cases in which a subject knows that p entails q and her belief that

---

[18] My proposal here bears some resemblance to ideas developed by Crispin Wright. Wright has explored the possibility of 'a type of rational warrant whose possession does not require the existence of evidence [ . . . ] for the truth of the warranted proposition' (Wright 2004: 174–5). He uses for this type of warrant the label *entitlement*. Wright discusses our entitlement not to belief, but to another form of acceptance to which he refers as trust. He takes this line in recognition of the thought that 'it can seem impossible to understand how it can be rational to believe a proposition for which one has *absolutely no evidence*, whether empirical or *a priori*' (Wright 2004: 176), although he distances himself from this thought ('I do not myself know whether the notion of belief is actually so tightly evidentially controlled as to underwrite that impression' (Wright 2004: 176)). However, even putting this difference to one side, I suspect that Wright would not recognize the form of knowledge that I am discussing as a species of entitlement. Entitlements, he tells us, 'are essentially recognisable by means of traditionally internalist resources—a priori reflection and self-knowledge—and are generally independent of the character of our actual cognitive situation in the wider world—indeed, are designed to be so' (Wright 2004: 209–10). What I'm calling default knowledge clearly violates this requirement. See also (Wright 1985).

p tracks the truth but her belief that q doesn't. This feature of Nozick's account underwrites his trademark treatment of sceptical arguments based on sceptical hypotheses. It enables him to concede to the sceptic that I don't know that sceptical hypotheses don't obtain while maintaining that I know many everyday propositions that are incompatible with them. I don't track the truth of the proposition that I'm not a brain in a vat, so I don't know this, but I do track the truth of the proposition that I have hands, so I do know this, even though I know that it logically entails that I'm not a brain in a vat. However, the fact that Nozick's account licenses widespread violations of the Closure principle is widely seen as one of its weakest points, since this outcome doesn't sit well with our intuitions about knowledge.

Roush's recursive-tracking account is deliberately designed to overcome this problem. On this account, I know not only the propositions whose truth I track, but also those that I know to be logically entailed by (non-equivalent) propositions I know. This move immediately reinstates the universal validity of the Closure principle. The recursive clause of the account ensures that whenever I know p and I know that p entails q I will also know q.

My account reverses some of the gains of Roush's account on this point. In most cases, if I know p and I know that p entails q, it will follow from my account that I also know q, inferentially, on the basis of the (deductive) evidence provided by p. However, my account makes room for counterexamples to this general principle. PI is the culprit.[19] If I know p and I know that p entails q, I still won't know q inferentially on the basis of the evidence provided by p if q is not confirmed by my belief in p. As we have seen, propositions to the effect that sceptical hypotheses don't obtain fall squarely in this category. I can't know that I am not a brain in a vat inferentially on the basis of the evidence provided by the proposition that I have hands because I'm no less likely to believe the latter if the former is false than if it's true.

This means that my account of inferential knowledge, unlike Roush's, does not guarantee the universal applicability of the Closure principle. It does *not* mean, however, that every case in which inferential knowledge of a proposition is thwarted by PI will be a counterexample to Closure. If I know p and I know that p entails q, but inferential knowledge of q on the basis of p is not possible because PI is violated, it clearly doesn't follow that I don't know q. I might still know q in some other way.

This is precisely how my account characterizes the situation concerning sceptical hypotheses. I don't know that I'm not a brain in a vat inferentially on the basis of evidence provided by the proposition that I have hands, since PI is violated. However, this doesn't result in a counterexample to Closure, since I know that I'm not a brain in a vat. I know it because my belief in this proposition is a true standing belief.

I want to argue that this outcome provides a better match for our intuitions than Roush's. I accept that intuition provides substantial support for the Closure principle

---

[19] Notice that Gettier cases will not provide counterexamples to Closure. If E is true and provides deductive evidence for one of the states of affairs that would make H true, then the state of affairs will obtain.

and hence for the verdict that I wouldn't know that I have hands if I didn't know I'm not a brain in a vat. However, when it comes to the explanation of my knowledge that I'm not a brain in a vat, intuition is firmly against the possibility of knowing this inferentially on the basis of the evidence provided by the proposition that I have hands. The strategy deployed by Roush and others to vindicate the Closure intuition achieves this at the expense of our intuition against Moorean inferences.[20] On my account, both intuitions are simultaneously preserved.

We can use this line to save Closure from PI in cases in which the issue concerns the epistemic status of a true standing belief. However, not every case in which Closure if threatened by PI can be handled in this way. The literature on these issues provides numerous cases that don't involve a standing belief. Take, for example, Dretske's zebra case, considered in the previous chapter (Dretske 1970). On my account, Molly will count as knowing that the animals in the enclosure are zebras (ZEBRAS) because her belief to this effect tracks the truth. We can assume that Molly knows that their being zebras entails that they are not mules and in particular that they are not mules cleverly disguised by the zoo authorities to look like zebras (~MULES). As we saw, Molly won't count as knowing ~MULES on the basis of the evidence provided by ZEBRAS, because PI is violated. However, we can't deploy here the strategy that we used for sceptical hypotheses, since Molly's belief in ~MULES is not a standing belief.

It's been argued, however, that this and similar cases do not really provide counter-examples to Closure. The point has been clearly made by Vogel:

> The reason why you know that an animal in the pen is not a disguised mule (if you know it's a zebra) is that you have a true belief to that effect backed up by good evidence. That evidence includes background information about the nature and function of zoos. You know that zoos generally exhibit genuine specimens, and that it would be a great deal of trouble to disguise a mule and to substitute it for a zebra. Only under the most unlikely and bizarre circumstances, if at all, would such a substitution be made, and there is no reason whatsoever to think that any such circumstances obtain. (Vogel 1990: 14)

I think that this is by far the most plausible explanation of how Molly knows ~MULES. She doesn't know it as a result of an inference from ZEBRAS. If she knows it at all, she knows it as a result of independent general evidence to the effect that such an occurrence would be extremely rare.

This raises the question, whether my account of inferential knowledge can under-write this story. Notice that the situation is very similar to Vogel's own case of the melting ice cubes: in both cases we want to say that someone knows that something hasn't happened (~MELT, MULES), which is rendered extremely unlikely by general information at her disposal. And the argument that I presented in the ice cube case can be easily adapted to this case. Let ZOOS denote the widely available general informa-tion about the nature and function of zoos to which Vogel alludes. If my account of

---

[20] See also (Pryor 2000: 546).

inferential knowledge is going to support Vogel's proposal, it will have to be the case that p(~MULES | ZOOS) is very high and that p(ZOOS | MULES) is much lower than p(ZOOS | ~MULES). I take it that the former doesn't pose a problem. The latter is rendered plausible by the thought that a low value for p(ZOOS | MULES) is a straightforward consequence of the claim that MULES is a counterexample to the generalizations expressed by ZOOS, and generalizations are confuted by their counter-instances. Furthermore, since the relatively low value of p(ZOOS | ~MULES) will be a consequence of the low prior probability of ZOOS, we can expect the value of p(ZOOS | MULES) to be affected in equal measure.

This suggests that ZOOS provides adequate support for ~MULES. Treating Molly's belief in ~MULES as a case of inferential knowledge would only require that she knows ZOOS, that she knows that ZOOS supports ~MULES, and that her belief in ZOOS confirms ~MULES. I propose to assume that the first two of these conditions hold. In support of the third, we can argue that, as we have seen, MULES decreases the probability of ZOOS, which in turn decreases the probability of the evidence on which Molly's belief in ZOOS is based. I conclude that Molly knows ~MULES inferentially on the basis of the evidence provided by ZOOS. Dretske's case is not a counterexample to Closure.

As Vogel himself noted, other cases can't be handled in this way. Take, for example, a case that John Hawthorne uses to introduce his discussion of the phenomenon (Hawthorne 2004). Suppose that I believe that I won't have enough money to go on a safari next year (~SAFARI), and that my lottery ticket won't win (LOSER). In this case, intuition supports the verdict that I know ~SAFARI (if true) but not LOSER (even if true). However, I know that ~SAFARI entails LOSER, since if I won the lottery I would have enough money for my safari.

Notice that I won't be able to avoid the situation by saying that I know LOSER inferentially on the basis of evidence provided by ~SAFARI. PI blocks this route, since the truth value of LOSER does not affect the probability that I believe ~SAFARI. And the strategies that we have deployed so far for saving Closure from PI won't work in this case. My belief in LOSER is not a standing belief, and, as we saw earlier on, I don't know LOSER inferentially on the basis of statistical evidence regarding the lottery set-up.

This consequence of my view should not, in principle, count against it, since it is widely accepted that our intuition regarding LOSER is that I don't know it. The problem is that by saving this intuition, together with the intuition that I know ~SAFARI, I seem forced to give up Closure.

I want to suggest that we have here a genuine clash in our intuitions (Vogel 1990: 23). Intuition supports the following three claims:

a. I know ~SAFARI.
b. I don't know LOSER.
c. Knowledge is closed under known entailment.

But given that I know the entailment from ~SAFARI to LOSER, these claims can't be simultaneously true. Furthermore, as Vogel and Hawthorne have shown, the problem generalizes to a wide variety of cases.

One well-known strategy for avoiding the conflict is to invoke the context-relative nature of the verb *to know* to argue that there are contexts in which I count as knowing both ~SAFARI and LOSER and contexts in which I count as knowing neither proposition, but no contexts in which I know the former but not the latter. It follows from this approach that there aren't any contexts in which Closure fails (DeRose 1995). I am not going to undertake here the task of assessing the contextualist position.[21] I only want to register my conviction that each of the sentences 'I know ~SAFARI' and 'I don't know LOSER' expresses the same proposition in every context of assertion and should be interpreted as expressing the same proposition in every context of attribution, and that both propositions are true. We do have an intuitive reluctance to assert them simultaneously. However, this is not due to the context-relativity of the verb *to know*, but to the intuitive appeal of the Closure principle.

If the contextualist approach is not adopted, the clash between the intuitions supporting a, b, and c, has to be treated as genuine, and an account of knowledge will have to reject one in order to preserve the other two. It follows from the account of knowledge that I am putting forward that the conflict should be resolved by rejecting Closure, and it seems to me that this is a less unappealing outcome than either of the alternatives, since the intuitions that support Closure are not as strong as our intuitions concerning the epistemic status of my beliefs in ~SAFARI and LOSER.[22]

Nevertheless, I'd like to end this discussion with a reminder that my account of knowledge sanctions violations of Closure only in a limited range of cases—those in which PI gets in the way of inferential knowledge and we don't have at our disposal other explanations of how we know the controversial proposition. As we have seen, this range does not include cases that Nozick and Dretske presented as counterexamples to the principle.

---

[21] For some objections, see (Schiffer 1996; Conee 2005a, 2005b; Feldman 2001; Sosa 2000; Hofweber 1999; Cappelen and Lepore 2003).

[22] Hawthorne has provided a comprehensive assessment of the other two alternatives (Hawthorne 2004).

# 7

# Sceptical Arguments

In Chapter 1 I presented three main lines of sceptical reasoning against our knowledge claims and I discussed how the adoption of a reliabilist account of knowledge could be expected to affect the prospects of these sceptical arguments. We reached the preliminary conclusion that reliabilism posed formidable obstacles to each of these lines of reasoning, but we postponed our final verdict until we had on the table the precise version of reliabilism that I want to defend. Developing this account has been my goal in the last three chapters. My goal in the present chapter is to consider how the sceptical challenges to our knowledge claims fare with respect to the account of knowledge that I have developed.

## 7.1 The regress argument

Of the three lines of reasoning that we considered in Chapter 1, the regress argument holds the least promise. As we saw there, the argument cannot get off the ground without invoking the evidential constraint, according to which knowledge requires that the subject is in possession of adequate evidence in support of her belief. Like other reliabilist accounts of knowledge, the view that I have presented licenses widespread violations of the evidential constraint. These arise with true beliefs that track the truth and true standing beliefs. In both kinds of case a belief can have the status of knowledge even if the subject doesn't have adequate evidence in its support. It follows that the evidential constraint is false. Hence the regress argument breaks down, as it is deprived of a crucial premise.

There are several ways in which the sceptic might try to overcome this point. One possibility would be to challenge my claim that truth tracking and the truth of a standing belief are sufficient conditions for knowledge. This is certainly a legitimate line to take, as my challenge to the regress argument relies on this claim. However, it is important to appreciate the direction in which the debate would be taken by this move. Let's concentrate on truth tracking. I have argued that an account of knowledge that takes truth tracking as sufficient for knowledge provides a very accurate match for our intuitions concerning the concept and its application, assuming that this match constitutes, at the very least, adequate evidence for the claim. It follows that contesting the claim that truth tracking is sufficient for knowledge would require arguing either that this claim doesn't provide an accurate match for our intuitions or that providing a match for our intuitions doesn't lend support to an account of knowledge. Both lines can certainly be pursued, but I suspect that doing so would take us away from the domain of sceptical challenges towards the kind of constructive epistemological reflection in which I have engaged over the last three chapters.

The second possibility would be to observe that treating truth tracking and the truth of standing beliefs as sufficient for knowledge will vindicate my knowledge claims only if I have, as a matter of fact, a sufficient range of beliefs in these categories. This observation is certainly correct, but it is not clear that it reinstates the sceptical threat. It amounts to replacing the original argument against my knowledge claims based on the evidential constraint with a new sceptical argument. The new argument concedes that there are sufficient conditions for knowledge that don't require the subject to be in possession of adequate evidence, adding, however, that I don't have sufficient beliefs satisfying these conditions.

The new argument would pose a powerful challenge, provided that its central premise could receive adequate support. However, providing support for this premise would take us once more away from the realm of sceptical argumentation, this time towards the kind of empirical investigation of my cognitive devices and their relationship to the environment that could determine the extent to which my beliefs track the truth, or the kind of empirical investigation of the world that would enable us to determine whether my standing beliefs are true.

It is important to distinguish in this connection between two different goals that we might have with respect to a sceptical challenge to our knowledge claims. First, we might aim to show that the argument deployed by the sceptic is unsound. Second, we might aim to show that its conclusion is false—that the knowledge claims challenged by the argument are actually true. Following Robert Audi, I shall refer to the first goal as *rebutting* the sceptic and to the second as *refuting* the sceptic (Audi 1993). My account of knowledge can be invoked for both enterprises, but failing to keep them apart leads to a distorted picture of the dialectical situation.

The characterization I've just provided of the dialectical situation concerning the regress argument corresponds to the enterprise of rebutting the sceptic. I have provided a strategy for showing that the argument is unsound because it rests on a false premise. Let's suppose for the sake of the argument that we have achieved rebuttal, not only with respect to the regress argument, but with respect to every argument deployed by the sceptic against my knowledge claims. We can then move on to the more ambitious goal of refuting the sceptic—of showing that we actually know the things that we claim to know. Here we can deploy once more the account of knowledge that I have defended, arguing that the sceptic's conclusion is incorrect whenever it concerns beliefs that track the truth, true standing beliefs, or beliefs in propositions that we know inferentially on the basis of evidence provided by propositions known in the first two ways.

The sceptic could complain once more that these are not sufficient conditions for knowledge, or that my beliefs don't satisfy them, but this would take us once more either towards philosophical analysis or towards empirical investigation, in any case, away from the regions in which we can expect sceptical reasoning to be effective. Alternatively, the sceptic might target, not my claim that these are sufficient conditions for knowledge or that my beliefs satisfy them, but my claim to know that this is so. However, this move doesn't hold much promise. We are assuming at this stage that the rebuttal task has been accomplished. Hence the sceptic has been left without a workable line of reasoning against these knowledge claims. Furthermore, if truth tracking and so on are sufficient conditions for knowledge, and my beliefs satisfy them, then my beliefs will have the status of knowledge, even if I don't know that the conditions are satisfied or that they are sufficient for knowledge. Whether I know these things is relevant to the second-order question, whether I know that I have knowledge, not to the question of whether I have knowledge of matters other than the epistemic status of my beliefs (Alston 1980).

## 7.2 Sceptical hypotheses

The second line of sceptical reasoning that we considered in Chapter 1 comprises a family of arguments that use sceptical hypotheses to undermine our knowledge claims. As we saw, sceptical hypotheses give rise to two forms of sceptical reasoning. According to the first, sceptical hypotheses invalidate my evidence for many propositions that I claim to know. The second challenges my everyday knowledge claims with the contention that I don't know that sceptical hypotheses don't obtain.

It should be clear that the first approach suffers from the same weakness as the regress argument. Even if we concede that sceptical hypotheses somehow invalidate my evidence for p, advancing from this claim to the conclusion that I don't know p would require invoking the evidential constraint. If my account of knowledge is correct, then the evidential constraint is not universally valid, and the argument is deprived of a crucial premise.

Furthermore, we can now use the account of inferential knowledge provided in Chapters 4 and 5 to cast doubt on the claim that sceptical hypotheses undermine my evidence for everyday propositions. Suppose that I take my son's temperature with a thermometer. The thermometer says that he has a temperature (FEVER) and I come to believe this. My son does have a temperature, and the thermometer works correctly. Do I have inferential knowledge of FEVER based on the evidence provided by the thermometer reading (READING)?

The first question that we need to consider is whether READING provides adequate support for FEVER, that is, whether LR(FEVER, READING) and p(FEVER | READING) are sufficiently high. The possibility described by a sceptical hypothesis will undermine the claim that READING provides adequate evidence for FEVER only if it reduces these values significantly. For the purpose of this question, sceptical hypotheses fall in two relevantly different categories. On the one hand, we have hypotheses like the brain-in-a-vat hypothesis, whose obtaining or otherwise has no effect on the nomological links between thermometers and body temperature. It is clear that these sceptical possibilities do not affect the values of LR(FEVER, READING) and p(FEVER | READING), since p(READING | FEVER & ~BIV), p(READING | ~FEVER & ~BIV), and p(FEVER | READING & ~BIV) are identical to p(READING | FEVER & BIV), p(READING | ~FEVER & BIV), and p(FEVER | READING & BIV), respectively.

The situation is slightly different if we consider sceptical hypotheses whose obtaining would cancel the nomological links from which conditional probabilities arise. Thus let BIV* denote a proposition describing a situation identical to Putnam's brain-in-a-vat hypothesis, except that the laws of nature are radically different from what I take them to be. In this situation, in particular, there is no correlation between thermometer readings and body temperature. Let's assume that in this situation there is no probabilistic link between READING and FEVER. It follows that p(READING | FEVER & BIV*) will be lower than p(READING | FEVER & ~BIV*), p(READING | ~FEVER & BIV*) higher than p(READING | ~FEVER & ~BIV*), and p(FEVER | READING & BIV*) lower than p(FEVER | READING & ~BIV*). This is bound to drag down the values of LR(FEVER, READING) and p(FEVER | READING), but only by a small margin. We can see the point if we concentrate on p(FEVER | READING). By an application of Theorem 28, we have that:

p(FEVER | READING)
=
p(FEVER | READING & ~BIV*) · p(~BIV* | READING)
+
p(FEVER | READING & BIV*) · p(BIV* | READING)

Given the extremely low probability of BIV*, p(FEVER | READING) will be almost identical to p(FEVER | READING & ~BIV*). The same point can be made with respect to p(READING | FEVER) and p(READING | ~FEVER). It follows that the possibility of BIV* won't have a significant effect on the level of support that READING provides for FEVER.

The next question that we need to consider is whether sceptical hypotheses can be expected to interfere with the subjective conditions for inferential knowledge. In order to have inferential knowledge of FEVER based on the evidence provided by READING, I will have to know the latter and that the latter provides adequate support for the former. I want to concentrate on considering the effect of sceptical hypotheses on my ability to track the truth of these propositions.

Consider first my belief in READING. Clearly, the obtaining of BIV would disturb the probabilistic links between READING and Bel(READING). If I am a brain in a vat, there won't be a substantial correlation between the readings of thermometers and my beliefs to this effect. Nevertheless, given the low probability of BIV, this won't have a significant effect on the tracking ratio or the safety level of my belief. Concerning the safety level, one more application of Theorem 28 tells us that:

p(READING | Bel(READING))

=

p(READING | Bel(READING) & ~BIV) · p(~BIV | Bel(READING))

+

p(READING | Bel(READING) & BIV) · p(BIV | Bel(READING))

Given the extremely low probability of BIV, p(READING | Bel(READING)) will be very close to p(READING | Bel(READING) & ~BIV). A parallel point can be made with respect to the tracking ratio of the belief.

Concerning my belief in the connection between READING and FEVER a similar situation obtains. Once again we need to take into account the difference between BIV and BIV*. BIV, on the one hand, has no effect on the ability of my belief to track the truth. As before, BIV* will drag down the tracking ratio and safety level of my belief, but given the improbability of BIV*, the reduction will be insignificant.

Finally, we need to consider the effect of sceptical possibilities on the question, whether my belief in READING confirms FEVER. Here we can see that, even if we assume that p(Bel(READING) | FEVER & BIV) is identical to p(Bel(READING) | ~FEVER & BIV), the difference between p(Bel(READING) | FEVER & ~BIV) and (Bel(READING) | ~FEVER & ~BIV) will ensure that p(Bel(READING) | FEVER) is greater than (Bel(READING) | ~FEVER), and hence that PI is satisfied.

It follows that the line of sceptical reasoning under consideration faces two insurmountable obstacles. On the one hand, even if we assume that sceptical possibilities prevent me from having adequate evidence for the propositions I claim to know, inferring from this that I don't know these propositions would require invoking the evidential constraint, which is rendered false by my account of knowledge. On the other hand, this assumption is incorrect. Sceptical possibilities do not interfere with my ability to have adequate evidence for the propositions I claim to know.

Let's turn now to the attempt to challenge my everyday knowledge claims invoking the contention that I don't know that sceptical hypotheses don't obtain. Nowadays there are two dominant strategies for blocking this argument. The first, due to Nozick, is to treat it as a failure of Closure. According to this line, the major premise of the argument is true: I don't know ~BIV, but the conclusion is false: I do know HANDS. And this is so even though I know that HANDS entails ~BIV. The second strategy is to contend that I can know ~BIV inferentially on the basis of evidence provided by HANDS.

As I argued in Chapter 5, both these strategies do considerable violence to our intuitions. On the one hand, even if we are prepared to countenance counterexamples to Closure, there is a strong intuitive presumption in its favour in any given case, and the features that characterize the counterexamples that we have encountered so far are not present in this case. On the other hand, an inference from HANDS is not an intuitively legitimate method for acquiring knowledge of ~BIV. My proposal differs from both these options. Contrary to Nozick's strategy, my account of knowledge dictates that I know ~BIV, but contrary to the neo-Moorean strategy, this knowledge does not result from an inference from HANDS.

Once again it will clarify matters to see the situation from the point of view of the contrast between rebutting and refuting the sceptic. My strategy for rebutting the argument can be best appreciated by taking the sceptical argument to start from the premises that are offered in support of the claim that I don't know ~BIV. As we have seen, there are two ways in which one might try to support it. The first (Nozick's) is to argue that my belief in ~BIV doesn't track the truth. The second is to argue that I don't have adequate evidence in support of ~BIV.[1] This results in two similar arguments that differ only in the premise that is offered in support of the claim that I don't know ~BIV:

1A My belief in ~BIV doesn't track the truth (Premise).
1B I don't have adequate evidence in support of ~BIV (Premise).
  2 I don't know ~BIV (Either from 1A or from 1B).
  3 If I don't know ~BIV, I don't know HANDS (Premise).
  4 I don't know HANDS (From 2 and 3).

My account of knowledge validates the first premise of this line of reasoning in both versions. My belief in ~BIV doesn't track the truth, and I don't have adequate evidence for ~BIV. The point at which rebuttal is effected is the step from either 1A or 1B to 2. Since my belief in ~BIV is a standing belief, it can acquire the status of knowledge without evidence or truth tracking, as a standing belief will have this status so long as it has a true proposition as its content. Therefore, the argument is unsound. It fails to establish that I don't know HANDS because it derives this conclusion from the lemma that I don't know ~BIV, which is derived, in turn, from premises from which it doesn't follow.

Having rebutted the argument in this way, we can move on once more to refutation. My claim to know that I have hands is easily vindicated. This is one of the many cases in which knowledge is overdetermined. My belief in HANDS tracks the truth, and as we've just seen in connection with the other line of reasoning based on sceptical possibilities, my claim to have adequate evidence for HANDS can withstand the sceptic's challenge.

We can also achieve refutation with respect to the sceptic's claim that I don't know that I'm not a brain in a vat. I know this because my belief in ~BIV is a standing belief, and ~BIV is a true proposition. My appeal in this context to the truth of ~BIV is likely to attract a suspicion of circularity. However, there is nothing improper in this move. The crucial point here is that I am not claiming to have inferential knowledge of ~BIV based on the evidence provided by the proposition that ~BIV is true. That would require that I know that ~BIV is true, and since this would involve knowing ~BIV, a charge of circularity against this line would be perfectly legitimate. What I am claiming is that I have non-inferential knowledge of ~BIV, arising from the fact that this is a true

---

[1] This is the line taken by Fred Dretske (1970) to argue that, in his example, the child doesn't know that the animals in the enclosure are not cleverly disguised mules.

proposition in which I have a standing belief. So long as this condition is as a matter of fact satisfied, I will know ~BIV. Knowledge of ~BIV doesn't require, on this account, that I know that the condition is satisfied. I believe that it is satisfied, and I conclude from this that I know ~BIV. I am saying, if you will, that I know ~BIV because ~BIV is true, but, as I have explained, this account of how I know ~BIV doesn't beg any questions.

The sceptic could only block my conclusion with an argument against the claim that ~BIV is a true proposition or against the claim that having a standing belief in a true proposition is a sufficient condition for knowledge. The former is unlikely to be available, since these are matters on which, by the sceptic's own account, evidence is not to be had. The latter is certainly possible, although it wouldn't be a piece of sceptical reasoning, but an exercise in philosophical analysis. Failing this, my claim to know ~BIV can be upheld.

## 7.3 The criterion

I want to turn next to the third line of sceptical reasoning that I presented in Chapter 1. It is based on the contention that the otherwise adequate evidence that we can adduce in support of the reliability of our basic belief-forming mechanisms has to include propositions whose epistemic status derives from the operation of these same mechanisms.

Let's consider in some detail how the argument goes in the case of sense perception, on which I'm going to focus. Let's say that S's belief that p is *experiential* when the evidence in support of p at S's disposal has to include the proposition that p is sanctioned by sense perception. I'm not going to provide a precise characterization of the form that this sanction can take, but what I have in mind is cases in which your evidence for p is that you have seen/heard/. . . p occur—for example, your evidence for the proposition that John was at the meeting is that you saw him there, and your evidence for the proposition that there is a roast in the oven is that you can smell it.

The sceptical argument that I want to consider starts from the contention that the otherwise adequate evidence that I can adduce in support of the reliability of sense perception has to include propositions such that my beliefs in them are experiential. On the assumption that my knowledge of the reliability of sense perception has to be inferential, it follows that there is a proposition p, where my belief that p is experiential, such that my knowledge of the reliability of sense perception presupposes that I know p. If we now assume that my knowledge of p has to be inferential, we have that my knowledge of p presupposes that I know that p is sanctioned by sense perception and, crucially, that the sanction of sense perception provides adequate support for p. But one could argue that the proposition that the sanction of sense perception provides adequate support for p can only be known, in turn, by inference from the general claim that sense perception is reliable. It follows that the evidence from which we could hope to obtain knowledge of the reliability of sense perception is unavoidably circular. Therefore knowledge of the reliability of sense perception is impossible.

This result can then be used to challenge the ascription of the status of knowledge to any experiential belief. If my belief that p is experiential, my evidence for p consists, by definition, in the sanction of sense perception. Since inferential knowledge requires that I know that the evidence supports the conclusion, knowing p will require knowing that the sanction of sense perception provides adequate support for p, and this would seem to require, in turn, knowing that sense perception is reliable. Since I cannot know this, I cannot know p either. None of my experiential beliefs have the status of knowledge. Sense perception cannot provide me with knowledge of the world.

There are several points where this line of reasoning makes assumptions about knowledge that would be falsified by the account that I have defended. Let's consider first the inference from the lemma that I don't know that sense perception is reliable to the conclusion that no experiential belief has the status of knowledge. The argument at this point clearly relies on the assumption that an experiential belief can only acquire the status of knowledge along the lines of the inferential model. Once this assumption is made, the inference from the impossibility of knowing that sense perception is reliable to the impossibility of experiential knowledge is unstoppable.

But if my account of knowledge is correct, this assumption will have to be rejected. An experiential belief can acquire the status of knowledge not only inferentially, but also by tracking the truth. Clearly an experiential belief can track the truth even if I don't know that sense perception is reliable. Therefore experiential knowledge doesn't require knowing that sense perception is reliable.

Notice that this approach puts forward a different account of how sense perception can produce knowledge. On this account, sense perception doesn't bestow the status of knowledge on experiential beliefs by giving the subject adequate evidence in their support. It achieves this instead by ensuring that experiential beliefs track the truth. Sense perception regulates my experiential beliefs, and the reliability of sense perception ensures that experiential beliefs track the truth and hence that if they are true they'll have the status of knowledge. On this model of how sense perception produces knowledge, sense perception will have to be reliable in order for knowledge to ensue. However, crucially, it is not required that the subject knows that sense perception is reliable. All that's required is that it is in fact so.

We can now move on to consider the line of reasoning offered in support of the claim that I can't know that sense perception is reliable. Here the inferential model of knowledge is assumed at two crucial points. It is assumed, first, in the claim that my experiential evidence for the reliability of sense perception will acquire the status of knowledge inferentially. It is the nature of my evidence for these experiential beliefs that gives rise to a vicious circle. However, as we have seen, my position offers an alternative construal of experiential knowledge, as non-inferential knowledge arising from the fact that my experiential beliefs track the truth. If, as I am suggesting, experiential knowledge is non-inferential, using it as evidence for the reliability of sense perception will no longer involve any obvious circularity.

This is a very influential approach to the problem nowadays (Van Cleve 2003; Alston 1986). According to this proposal, the impression that knowledge of the reliability of sense perception can't be based on experiential evidence is based on the mistaken assumption that experiential knowledge is inferential. Once this mistake is removed, the threat of circularity disappears, and inferential knowledge of the reliability of sense perception based on experiential evidence is no longer problematic.

I find this approach extremely counterintuitive. It seems to me that basing knowledge of the reliability of sense perception on evidence provided by perceptual beliefs is an illegitimate procedure, even if experiential knowledge is construed non-inferentially. The procedure is just as objectionable as Roxanne's bootstrapping argument for the reliability of the petrol gauge, considered in Chapter 5. Licensing this form of knowledge acquisition should be counted as a serious shortcoming of an account of knowledge.

But my account of knowledge doesn't suffer from this problem. Although inferring the reliability of sense perception from experiential knowledge doesn't involve a vicious circularity, it is nevertheless inadmissible. As with Roxanne's inference, the move is blocked by PI. The problem is that the probability that I have my experiential beliefs is not affected by whether or not sense perception is reliable. As the sceptic points out, I am not equipped to detect (systematic) unreliability in my sensory devices. Hence, if they were unreliable, they would be just as likely to produce the experiential beliefs that they actually produce. It follows that I cannot have inferential knowledge of the proposition that sense perception is reliable based on evidence provided by experiential beliefs. On my account, the sceptic is right in treating this inference as illegitimate, although she is mistaken in her diagnosis of what's wrong with it.

Notice that there is a clear parallel between this approach and the neo-Moorean line concerning sceptical hypotheses (Cohen 2002; Zalabardo 2005). In both cases an intuitively illegitimate inference is used to explain knowledge of a problematic proposition (∼BIV, the reliability of sense perception). And in both cases my diagnosis is the same: inferential knowledge is not possible because it would involve a violation of PI.

The parallels between the two cases do not end here, since my account of how I know ∼BIV can also be used to explain how I know that sense perception is reliable. My belief that sense perception is reliable is a standing belief. Hence, so long as it is true it will have the status of knowledge. Once again, my contention that I know that sense perception is reliable because it is reliable is likely to attract suspicion, but as I explained in the case of ∼BIV, the move is perfectly legitimate.

Once we have vindicated my claim to know that sense perception is reliable, we can also restore the ability of sense perception to provide evidence for my experiential beliefs. Sense perception doesn't only regulate my experiential beliefs to ensure that they track the truth. It also provides me with evidence in their support. Knowing, as I do, that sense perception is reliable, makes this evidential role of sense perception possible: I can be in possession of sensory evidence for my experiential beliefs because I know that the sanction of sense perception provides adequate support for a proposition, and I know this because I know that sense perception is reliable.

## 7.4 Reflective knowledge

So far in this chapter I have argued that the account of knowledge that I am putting forward has the resources for rebutting the three main lines of sceptical reasoning, and, after achieving this, for refuting the sceptical conclusion, vindicating our knowledge claims. In the remainder of the chapter I want to present a line of sceptical reasoning for which my account of knowledge doesn't seem to have an obvious response.

Clearly, a sceptic who wanted to adapt her challenge to my account of knowledge would need to be looking for this: an important class of non-standing beliefs that don't track the truth for which I cannot provide adequate evidence. This is, on the face of it, a tall order. We have encountered, of course, many standing beliefs that don't track the truth for which I cannot provide adequate evidence, but non-standing beliefs that satisfy the other two requirements are harder to come by. Notice that what matters here is not so much our actual epistemic situation, but our assessment of it. The sceptic's goal is to mount a cogent argument to undermine my knowledge claims. But cogency is an audience-relative notion. A cogent argument against my knowledge claims that works for me would have to derive its conclusion using premises and inferential steps that I accept, or that the sceptic can make me accept.

As a rule, we believe that our non-standing beliefs track the truth. This is a manifestation of the epistemic optimism that I mentioned in Chapter 1. We accept, of course that there will be cases where we believe we are tracking the truth but as a matter of fact we are not. What is harder to find is cases where we accept that we don't track the truth. With respect to evidence the situation is not dissimilar. Some of us are happy to accept that we believe propositions for which we don't have adequate evidence, but this is always the exception, not the rule, and we think of many of these cases as cases of sensitive belief.[2]

One salient source of cases satisfying the sceptic's requirements are beliefs whose regulation has been affected by non-cognitive factors, as, for example, in Armstrong's case of the father who believes that his son is innocent even before evidence becomes available in court (Armstrong 1973: 209). If he remains convinced of his son's innocence after acknowledging the role of paternal feelings in the regulation of his beliefs about his son, we should expect him to accept that his belief that his son is innocent is a case of non-standing, insensitive belief for which he lacks adequate evidence. These cases are certainly real, but not a very promising source of material for a wide-ranging sceptical challenge.

There is, however, another potential source of cases of this kind that might hold more promise for the sceptic. I have in mind reflective beliefs about the truth value of our (first-order) beliefs. The relevance of these beliefs for truth-tracking accounts was first pointed out by Jonathan Vogel, who based on them an objection to Nozick's proposal. Here's Vogel's presentation of the phenomenon:

---

[2] But see (Adler 2002).

On Nozick's analysis, it appears that it is impossible for anyone to know that he is not deceived about anything in particular. Imagine that I am looking at the statement I just received from the bank, and I believe my balance to be as it appears on the statement. I also believe that the bank is not deceiving me about how much money is in my account. Do I know that the bank isn't tricking me? If it were, I would be none the wiser, since by assumption I would be taken in. [ ... ] it is not true that if the bank were deceiving me, I would not believe that the bank was not deceiving me (on the basis of my actual evidence). The same line of thought can be applied to any claim by someone to know that he is not deceived in some way or other. (Vogel 1987: 203)[3]

Vogel is focusing on the belief that the bank is not (successfully) tricking me. His claim is that this belief violates Nozick's sensitivity counterfactual, since if the bank were (successfully) tricking me I would believe that the bank was not tricking me. On Nozick's account, the belief doesn't track the truth, and hence can't have the status of knowledge.

My account yields the same verdict concerning truth tracking. The probability that I believe that the bank is not successfully tricking me is not lower if the bank is successfully tricking me than if it isn't. Hence the tracking ratio of the belief is at most one, and my belief doesn't track the truth.

However, unlike on Nozick's account, on my account we cannot move directly from the result that my belief doesn't track the truth to the conclusion that it doesn't have the status of knowledge. In order to establish this conclusion we would need to show, in addition, that I don't have adequate evidence in support of the proposition that the bank is not successfully tricking me, and whether I do or not will depend on the specific details of the case. Nevertheless, we have identified a rich source of insensitive beliefs on which the sceptic might focus her efforts.

I want to argue that the phenomenon exhibited by Vogel's case afflicts the form of reflective knowledge that we considered in Chapter 5, that is, beliefs in propositions of the form V ɿx Bx, where V is the truth predicate and B is the predicate ... *is a belief of mine with p as its content*. Let me represent this proposition as $V(Bel_{Me}[p])$, where V is the truth predicate and $Bel_{Me}[p]$ denotes my belief that p.[4] We shall restrict our attention to cases in which $Bel_{Me}[p]$ is non-standing. Thus, for example, if p is the proposition that snow is white, $V(Bel_{Me}[p])$ is the proposition that my belief that snow is white is true. I shall refer to beliefs of this form as *cognitive self-approvals (CSAs)*.

I am suggesting that every CSA fails to track the truth, for the reasons presented by Vogel in the bank statement case. To see this, notice that in order for a CSA to track the truth, $p(Bel(V(Bel_{Me}[p])) \mid V(Bel_{Me}[p]))$ would have to be substantially higher than $p(Bel(V(Bel_{Me}[p])) \mid \sim V(Bel_{Me}[p]))$. As I argued in Chapter 5, $V(Bel_{Me}[p])$ has to be analysed as involving a definite description that has a wide scope when embedded

---

[3] Vogel presents this case as a generalization of a point made by Robert Shope (Shope 1984: 41). The problem has also been highlighted by Ernest Sosa (Sosa 1999: 145). See also (DeRose 1995: 22–3)

[4] Notice that on this symbolism $Bel_S(p)$ is the proposition that S believes that p, while $Bel_S[p]$ is a singular term referring to S's belief that p.

in negation. In this way $p(\mathrm{Bel}(V(\mathrm{Bel}_{Me}[p])) \mid \sim V(\mathrm{Bel}_{Me}[p]))$ will depend on the probability that I believe that my belief that p is true if I believe that p but this belief is not true. It will be unaffected by the probability that I believe that my belief that p is true if I don't believe that p, that is, if '$\mathrm{Bel}_{Me}[p]$' doesn't refer. Notice that, when the description is taken as having wide scope, $\sim V(\mathrm{Bel}_{Me}[p])$ can be rendered as *I falsely believe that p*. This makes it natural to render $V(\mathrm{Bel}_{Me}[p])$ as *I don't falsely believe that p*. This is the form in which CSAs have figured in recent discussions of these issues.

Now, it is clear that, so long as I believe that p, the probability that I believe that this belief is true will be unaffected by whether it is actually true. So long as I have the first-order belief, the probability that I have the second-order belief will be the same independently of whether the beliefs are true or false. It follows that, even if my belief that p tracks the truth, my reflective belief that this belief is true does not, since, no matter how high the tracking ratio of the first-order belief might be, the tracking ratio of the reflective belief is guaranteed to be one.[5]

## 7.5 Evidence for cognitive self-assessments

CSAs don't track the truth, and they are not, in general, standing beliefs. Hence, on the account of knowledge that I have defended, whether they can have this status will depend on whether I can obtain adequate evidence in their support. In this section I am going to argue that this is not a possibility: adequate evidence for CSAs is not to be had. It will follow that, on my account of knowledge, CSAs cannot have this status.

Notice that two tempting accounts of where this evidence might come from have been ruled out by what we have already said. The first would be to treat as evidence in support of a CSA the proposition that provides the content of the belief being assessed. Pursuing this line would involve using p as my evidence for $V(\mathrm{Bel}_{Me}[p])$. This proposal need not detain us, since we already dismissed the idea in Section 5.8. As we saw there, p cannot provide me with adequate support for $V(\mathrm{Bel}_{Me}[p])$ even if I know p, since this evidential link would violate PI: I am no more likely to believe p if I believe p veridically than if I believe p non-veridically.

Another simple proposal that we can dismiss fairly quickly is using as my evidence in support of my CSAs my standing belief to the effect that my beliefs are usually true. Let's assume that I have a standing belief to this effect. Then, if it is true, this belief will have the status of knowledge. I also know that the proposition that my beliefs are usually true provides adequate support for the proposition that my belief in H is true. However, once again PI blocks the inference. The problem is that standing beliefs are not very good sources of evidence. If my belief that my beliefs are generally true is a standing belief, then whether I have it or not does not depend on whether any one of

---

[5] The independence of the epistemic status of a CSA from the epistemic status of the relevant first-order belief shouldn't come as a surprise to readers familiar with the ideas in the area of metacognition. See, e.g., (Yates 1990: esp. chs. 3,4, and 7).

my first-order beliefs is true. I would be just as likely to believe that my beliefs are generally true if my (first-order, non-standing) belief in p were true than if it were false.

In cases where I have inferential knowledge of H, we seem to have at our disposal an obvious source of evidence for $V(\text{Bel}_{\text{Me}}[H])$. Suppose that I know H inferentially on the basis of evidence provided by E. Shouldn't E provide me also with adequate evidence for $V(\text{Bel}_{\text{Me}}[H])$, thus conferring on my CSA the status of knowledge? I am going to argue, first, that it is perfectly possible for E to provide support for H but not for the proposition that someone's belief in H is true. Then I am going to consider the consequences of this situation for the first-person case. I shall argue that my evidence for H will not normally provide me with evidence for the proposition that my belief in H is true.

Let me start by considering a very simple situation in which E will not provide adequate support for $V(\text{Bel}_S[H])$ even if it provides adequate support for H. We will have this situation whenever E is a necessary condition for the existence of $\text{Bel}_S[H]$, that is, when $p(E \mid \text{Bel}_S[H])) = 1$. Since both $V(\text{Bel}_S[H])$ and $\sim V(\text{Bel}_S[H])$ entail $\text{Bel}_S(H)$, it follows that $p(E \mid V(\text{Bel}_S[H])) = p(E \mid \sim V(\text{Bel}_S[H])) = 1$ (Theorem 32). Therefore $LR(V(\text{Bel}_S[H]), E)$ will be 1, no matter how high $LR(H, E)$ might be. This result is what we would expect, so long as we construe $V(\text{Bel}_S[H])$ as a proposition that ascribes a contingent property (truth) to an object (S's belief in H). A necessary condition for the existence of an object cannot provide adequate support for the presence in the object of a contingent property.

Notice that this result will rule out using the fact that S believes H as my evidence for the truth of S's belief, even if this fact provides me with adequate evidence for H. Thus suppose that S believes that the post office is closed today (PO). If S is reliable on these matters, the tracking ratio of S's will be high, and if I know that S believes this, and that she is reliable, I can in principle know inferentially that the post office is closed today, on the basis of the evidence provided by S's belief. What I can't do is use S's belief as evidence for the proposition that S's belief is true, since it follows from the facts we've just presented that $LR(V(\text{Bel}_S[PO]), \text{Bel}_S(PO))$ is only 1.

When $p(\text{Bel}_S(H)\ \&\ \sim E)$ is greater than 0, the situation is slightly more complicated, but it's still perfectly possible that E provides adequate support for H but not for the truth of S's belief that H. Notice that the numerator of $LR(V(\text{Bel}_S[H]), E)$, that is, $p(E \mid H\ \&\ \text{Bel}_S[H])$, can be smaller than the numerator of $LR(H, E)$, that is, $p(E \mid H)$, so long as E is more probable if H is true and S doesn't believe it than if H is true and S believes it (Theorem 33). Likewise, the denominator of $LR(V(\text{Bel}_S[H]), E)$, that is, $p(E \mid \sim H\ \&\ \text{Bel}_S[H])$, according to our wide-scope reading of $\sim V(\text{Bel}_S[H])$, can be larger than the denominator of $LR(H, E)$, that is, $p(E \mid \sim H)$, so long as E is more probable if H is false but S believes it than if H is false and S doesn't believe it. Hence we might find that even if E is much more likely to be true if H is true than if H is false, E is not much more likely to be true if S believes H truly than if S believes H falsely.[6]

---

[6] Similar points apply to $p(H \mid E)$ and $p(V(\text{Bel}_S[H]) \mid E)$. Even if the truth of E makes the truth of H very probable, it might fail to have this effect on S truly believing H. We will continue to focus our discussion on LR.

## 7.6 Using S's evidence in support of assessments of her beliefs

I want to turn next to considering how these ideas bear on the possibility of using S's evidence for H as evidence for the truth of her belief in H. Assume that S knows H inferentially on the basis of evidence provided by E, which S knows non-inferentially. Suppose that E is also my evidence for the truth of S's belief in H.

I want to consider first the case in which S would not believe H unless she had evidence E, that is, $p(Bel_S(H) \& \sim Bel_S(E)) = 0$. I want to argue that in these circumstances, $LR(V(Bel_S[H]), E)$ will be very low. Clearly this scenario is very similar to the case that we considered in the previous section in which E was a necessary condition for the existence of $Bel_S[H]$. Now we are treating as a necessary condition for the existence of $Bel_S[H]$, not E, but S's belief in E: if S didn't believe E she wouldn't believe H either. However, in spite of this difference, the situation is sufficiently similar for E to fail to provide the requisite support here as well.

To show this, it will suffice to establish that

$$p(E \mid \sim V(Bel_S[H])), \tag{1}$$

that is, the denominator of $LR(V(Bel_S[H]), E)$, is very close to 1. We establish this claim with the following argument.

First, since E is logically equivalent to $(E \& Be_S(E)) \vee (E \& \sim Bel_S(E))$, we have that (1) is the same as:

$$p((E \& Bel_S(E)) \vee (E \& \sim Bel_S(E)) \mid \sim V(Bel_S[H])). \tag{2}$$

This, in turn, by Theorem 8, is identical to

$$p(E \& Bel_S(E) \mid \sim V(Bel_S[H])) + p(E \& \sim Bel_S(E) \mid \sim V(Bel_S[H])). \tag{3}$$

Now from the assumption that $p(Bel_S(H) \& \sim Bel_S(E)) = 0$, it follows that (3) is identical to

$$p(E \& Bel_S(E) \mid \sim V(Bel_S[H])). \tag{4}$$

Notice, next, that since S's belief in E tracks the truth, $p(\sim E \& Bel_S(E) \mid \sim V(Bel_S[H]))$ won't be much higher than 0. Hence (4) won't be much lower than

$$p(E \& Bel_S(E) \mid \sim V(Bel_S[H])) + p(\sim E \& Bel_S(E) \mid \sim V(Bel_S[H])), \tag{5}$$

which is identical, again by Theorem 8, to

$$p((E \ \& \ Bel_S(E)) \lor (\sim E \ \& \ Bel_S(E))) \mid \sim V(Bel_S[H])) \tag{6}$$

and to

$$p(Bel_S(E) \mid \sim V(Bel_S[H])). \tag{7}$$

Finally, our assumption that $p(Bel_S(H) \ \& \ \sim Bel_S(E)) = 0$ entails that (7) equals 1.

Summing up, I have argued that (1) is identical to (4), that (4) isn't much lower than (5), and that (5) equals one. I conclude that (1) is very close to one, and hence that LR $(V(Bel_S[H]), E)$ must have a low value, no matter how high the value of LR$(H, E)$ might be.

This result shouldn't come as a surprise in light of our earlier discussion. I argued that a necessary condition for the existence of a belief cannot provide adequate evidence for the truth of the belief. Now the assumption that S would only believe H on the basis of evidence E does not entail that E is a necessary condition for the existence of E's belief in H. The belief would still exist if S believed E falsely. But if S knows E non-inferentially, her belief will track the truth, and she will be very unlikely to believe E falsely. It follows that E is very close to being a necessary condition for the existence of S's belief in E. This is the reason why E cannot be expected to provide me with substantial support for the truth of S's belief in H.

Let's consider now the situation that results when we remove the assumption that S would believe H only on the basis of evidence E. We assume, as before, that S knows H inferentially on the basis of evidence provided by E, which she knows non-inferentially. But now there is a significant probability that S would still believe H in the absence of evidence E. I want to argue that E will not provide adequate support for $V(Bel_S[H])$ if E doesn't increase the gap between the probabilities of $V(Bel_S[H])$ and $\sim V(Bel_S[H])$ much more than it would be increased by S believing H in the absence of evidence E.

Let's say that the support for H that E provides S with is *exceptional* if (a) there is a significant probability of S believing H but not believing E, that is, $p(Bel_S(H) \ \& \ \sim Bel_S(E))$ is reasonably high, and (b) E increases the gap between the probabilities of $V(Bel_S[H])$ and $\sim V(Bel_S[H])$ much more than it would be increased by S believing H in the absence of evidence E, that is:

$$\frac{p(V(Bel_S[H]) \mid Bel_S(H) \ \& \ \sim Bel_S(E))}{p(\sim V(Bel_S[H]) \mid Bel_S(H) \ \& \ \sim Bel_S(E))}$$

is much lower than

$$\frac{p(V(Bel_S[H]) \mid E)}{p(\sim V(Bel_S[H]) \mid E)}$$

When the support for H that E provides S with is not *exceptional*, we say that it is *unexceptional*.

I want to argue that from the assumption that E provides S with unexceptional support for H it follows that $LR(V(Bel_S[H]), E)$ has a low value.

Using Theorem 34, we can express $LR(V(Bel_S[H]), E)$ as:

$$\frac{\left(\dfrac{p(V(Bel_S[H]) \mid E)}{p(\sim V(Bel_S[H]) \mid E)}\right)}{\left(\dfrac{p(V(Bel_S[H]))}{p(\sim V(Bel_S[H]))}\right)}.$$

And this, by the Mixing Principle, can be rewritten as:

$$\frac{\left(\dfrac{p(V(Bel_S[H]) \mid E)}{p(\sim V(Bel_S[H]) \mid E)}\right)}{\left(\dfrac{p(V(Bel_S[H]) \mid Bel_S(E) \& Bel_S(H)) \cdot p(Bel_S(E) \& Bel_S(H)) + p(V(Bel_S[H]) \mid \sim Bel_S(E) \& Bel_S(H)) \cdot p(\sim Bel_S(E) \& Bel_S(H))}{p(\sim V(Bel_S[H]) \mid Bel_S(E) \& Bel_S(H)) \cdot p(Bel_S(E) \& Bel_S(H)) + p(\sim V(Bel_S[H]) \mid \sim Bel_S(E) \& Bel_S(H)) \cdot p(\sim Bel_S(E) \& Bel_S(H))}\right)}. \tag{8}$$

Notice now that we shouldn't expect

$$\frac{p(V(Bel_S[H]) \mid Bel_S(H) \& Bel_S(E))}{p(\sim V(Bel_S[H]) \mid Bel_S(H) \& Bel_S(E))}$$

to be much higher than

$$\frac{p(V(Bel_S[H]) \mid E)}{p(\sim V(Bel_S[H]) \mid E)},$$

since the effect of S believing E and H on the probability that her belief in H is true is in principle entirely due to the effect of E on this gap and to the fact that her belief in E tracks the truth.

It follows from this that (8) is not much higher than

$$\frac{\left(\dfrac{p(V(Bel_S[H]) \mid E)}{p(\sim V(Bel_S[H]) \mid E)}\right)}{\left(\dfrac{p(V(Bel_S[H]) \mid E) \cdot n \cdot p(Bel_S(E) \& Bel_S(H)) + p(V(Bel_S[H]) \mid \sim Bel_S(E) \& Bel_S(H)) \cdot p(\sim Bel_S(E) \& Bel_S(H))}{p(\sim V(Bel_S[H]) \mid E) \cdot n \cdot p(Bel_S(E) \& Bel_S(H)) + p(\sim V(Bel_S[H]) \mid \sim Bel_S(E) \& Bel_S(H)) \cdot p(\sim Bel_S(E) \& Bel_S(H))}\right)}, \tag{9}$$

for some n.

Now, if E provides S with unexceptional support for H, it follows that either (a) $p(Bel_S(H) \& \sim Bel_S(E))$ is very low, or (b) E doesn't increase the gap between the probabilities of $V(Bel_S[H])$ and $\sim V(Bel_S[H])$ much more than $Bel_S(H)$ & $\sim Bel_S(E)$ does.

Notice, first that if (a) obtains, then the denominator of (9) is very close to its numerator. Hence, the value of $LR(V(Bel_S[H]), E)$ is very low.

If (b) holds, it follows that (9) is not much higher than:

$$\frac{\left( \dfrac{p(V(Bel_S[H]) \mid E)}{p(\sim V(Bel_S[H]) \mid E)} \right)}{\left( \begin{array}{c} p(V(Bel_S[H]) \mid E) \cdot n \cdot p\big(Bel_S(E) \,\&\, Bel_S(H)\big) \\ + p(V(Bel_S[H]) \mid E) \cdot m \cdot p(\sim Bel_S(E) \,\&\, Bel_S(H)) \\ \hline p(\sim V(Bel_S[H]) \mid E) \cdot n \cdot p\big(Bel_S(E) \,\&\, Bel_S(H)\big) \\ + p(\sim V(Bel_S[H]) \mid E) \cdot m \cdot p(\sim Bel_S(E) \,\&\, Bel_S(H)) \end{array} \right)}, \tag{10}$$

for some $m$.

Now (10) can be rewritten as:

$$\frac{\left( \dfrac{p(V(Bel_S[H]) \mid E)}{p(\sim V(Bel_S[H]) \mid E)} \right)}{\left( \dfrac{p(V(Bel_S[H]) \mid E) \cdot (n \cdot p(Bel_S(E) \,\&\, Bel_S(H)) + m \cdot p(\sim Bel_S(E) \,\&\, Bel_S(H)))}{p(\sim V(Bel_S[H]) \mid E) \cdot (n \cdot p(Bel_S(E) \,\&\, Bel_S(H)) + m \cdot p(\sim Bel_S(E) \,\&\, Bel_S(H)))} \right)}, \tag{11}$$

and the value of (11) is one. Hence, if E doesn't increase the gap between the probabilities of $V(Bel_S[H])$ and $\sim V(Bel_S[H])$ much more than $Bel_S(H)$ & $\sim Bel_S(E)$ does, it follows that the value of $LR(V(Bel_S[H]), E)$ is very low. In conclusion, if the evidence for H that E provides S with is unexceptional, then the value of $LR(V(Bel_S[H]), E)$ is very low, and E doesn't provide adequate support for $V(Bel_S[H])$.

## 7.7  Evidence for CSAs

We can now turn to the first-person case and consider the bearing of these results on the possibility of obtaining adequate evidence for my CSAs. What we have found is that E will provide me with adequate evidence for $V(Bel_{Me}[H])$ only if it provides me with exceptional evidence for H.

There is in principle no reason why someone's evidence for a proposition shouldn't be exceptional. This will happen, as we know, when there is a substantial probability that S will believe H without believing E and the probability that S's belief in H will be true if it is held in these circumstances is much lower than the probability that it will be true if it is supported by S's belief in E.

Suppose, for example, that I have two thermometers in the house, the one I use by default and another one I keep as back-up. Suppose that the default thermometer is highly reliable, but, unbeknownst to me, the back-up thermometer is defective and produces random readings. Suppose that I believe that my son has a temperature based on the evidence provided by the default thermometer. In this situation, the default-thermometer reading will provide me with adequate evidence for the proposition that my son has a temperature, and my belief can be knowledge as a result. Furthermore, the evidence provided by the default thermometer will be exceptional. There is a substantial probability that I will form the belief that my son has a temperature without using the default thermometer, say because I can't find it or because it is broken. In that case I will use the back-up thermometer, and the probability that my belief is true will then be no better than random. In this situation, the default-thermometer reading provides me with exceptional evidence for the proposition that my son has a temperature. Hence it will be possible to use this evidence to produce inferential knowledge of the proposition that my belief is true.

Notice, however, that the use of this evidence by me, in support of my CSA, is problematic. What poses the difficulty is that in the situation I have described I don't realize that the back-up thermometer is defective. Hence, I believe (wrongly) that my evidence is unexceptional. The relevance of this circumstance will depend on whether or not I realize that my evidence for H can provide adequate support for my CSA only if it is exceptional. If, on the one hand, I realize that this is the case, I won't believe that the default-thermometer reading provides adequate support for my CSA. If I don't believe this, then I don't know it either, and one condition for inferential knowledge will be violated.[7] Hence my CSA won't obtain the status of knowledge inferentially on the basis of the evidence provided by the thermometer reading. If, on the other hand, I don't realize that adequate evidence has to be exceptional, I might believe that the default-thermometer reading provides adequate evidence for my CSA. One might question whether this true belief could qualify for the status of knowledge, but if it did, it would sustain inferential knowledge of my CSA. However, this knowledge could be easily destroyed by the sceptic. All she would need to do is show that my evidence for H can provide adequate support for my CSA only if it is exceptional. If she succeeded in making me accept this conclusion, I would no longer believe that I have adequate evidence for my CSA, which would, as a result, lose the status of knowledge.

Clearly these difficulties arise from the fact that in the case I described I believe that my evidence for the proposition that my son has a temperature is unexceptional. Hence in cases that don't share this feature the difficulties will not arise. This point is correct, but it doesn't offer a workable strategy for resisting the sceptical outcome. We can see why the move won't work if we consider how our case would have to be modified in order to avoid the problem. What is needed is a case in which (a) I realize that the back-up thermometer is defective, but (b) in spite of this realization I believe

---

[7] This argument invokes the assumption that inferential knowledge requires knowledge that the support relation obtains. However, this assumption can be replaced with a substantially weaker alternative—that inferential knowledge is not possible when the subject believes that the support relation doesn't obtain.

that there are probable circumstances in which I would use the back-up thermometer to form my opinion on my son's temperature.

I want to argue that I am not likely to have this combination of beliefs. The reason is that they are in conflict with epistemic optimism. Epistemic optimism has a certain counterfactual depth. I don't merely believe that in the precise conditions that actually obtain the procedures that I use for forming beliefs are generally truth conducive. I endorse a similarly favourable assessment of the procedures that I would use in fairly likely alternative scenarios. I believe that, so long as no radical changes are introduced in my epistemic situation, I would form my beliefs with procedures that tend to produce true beliefs.

If epistemic optimism is understood in this way, it is clearly in conflict with believing (a) and (b). Epistemic optimism dictates that there are no probable situations in which I would form my opinion on my son's temperature with an unreliable procedure. Hence I cannot simultaneously believe that the thermometer is defective and that I am likely to use it.[8]

The same situation obtains generally. There is a conflict between epistemic optimism and the claim that my evidence for the propositions that I believe is exceptional. Hence, so long as I endorse epistemic optimism I am likely to believe that my evidence is unexceptional. This is the irremediable source of the vulnerability to sceptical reasoning of our evidence for CSAs. We usually believe that our evidence for our beliefs is unexceptional. Hence, as soon as the sceptic convinces us that unexceptional evidence cannot support CSAs, we cease to believe that we have adequate evidence for our CSAs. Hence, once we are exposed to sceptical reasoning, if not before, most of our CSAs are prevented from acquiring the status of knowledge inferentially.

## 7.8  The sceptical argument

Over the last four sections I have presented a sceptical argument that doesn't seem to beg any questions against the account of knowledge that I have defended in earlier chapters. It will be useful at this point to survey the overall shape of the argument:

(A) A non-standing belief has the status of knowledge only if it tracks the truth or if the subject has adequate evidence in its support (Premise).

(B) A CSA of a non-standing belief is itself a non-standing belief (Premise).

(C) CSAs don't track the truth (Premise).

---

[8]  There are specific circumstances in which I can believe that my evidence for a proposition is exceptional. Suppose, e.g., that the only way I could determine that the back-up thermometer is defective was by comparing its readings with those of the default thermometer. Then I might believe that if the default thermometer weren't available I would form my opinion on my son's temperature with the back-up thermometer, as I wouldn't realize that it is defective. Epistemic optimism doesn't require that I consider myself actually or counterfactually infallible. It doesn't require believing that this kind of situation can never arise—only that it is sufficiently rare.

(D) In most cases it is not possible to identify adequate evidence in support of a CSA (Premise).

(E) Most CSAs of non-standing beliefs are not knowledge (from (A)–(D)).

I want to suggest that this argument produces a novel situation in the discussion of scepticism. As I mentioned in Chapter 1, it is widely assumed that reliabilist accounts of knowledge provide a powerful antidote against scepticism, since they deprive the sceptic of the premises that she needs in order to generate her conclusions. I think that the account of knowledge that I have defended has unquestionable reliabilist credentials. And yet the sceptical argument that I have presented doesn't rest on any assumptions that wouldn't be licensed by this account of knowledge. If my account of knowledge is the best version of reliabilism, reliabilism doesn't have the power to defuse the sceptical threat. And if my account of knowledge is the right account, then the theory of knowledge doesn't have this power: we will have a sceptical argument that makes no epistemological mistakes.

Someone who accepts that on my account of knowledge CSAs can't have this status (i.e. that premises (B), (C), and (D) are correct, with truth tracking and evidence defined as I propose) might treat this outcome as showing, not that CSAs can't be knowledge, but that my account of knowledge has to be wrong. CSAs *can* be knowledge, the argument would go. Since my account of knowledge is incompatible with this tenet, it can't be the right account of the concept.

This is the line taken by Ernest Sosa on the fact that sensitivity-based accounts can't bestow on CSAs the status of knowledge. He presents the issue in the following terms:

Suppose [. . .] we have two propositions as follows: (a) that p, and (b) that I do not believe incorrectly (falsely) that p. Surely no-one minimally rational and attentive who believes both of these will normally know either without knowing the other. Yet even in cases where one's belief of (a) is sensitive, one's belief of (b) could never be sensitive. After all, even if (b) were false, one would still believe it anyhow. Still it is quite implausible that the assertion that I know (b) could never be true, not even in the many situations where the assertion that I know (a) *would* be true. (Sosa 1999: 145)

In a footnote to this paragraph he adds: 'This sort of counterexample [. . .] strikes me as conclusive' (Sosa 1999: 152).

Sosa might be adducing three related but distinct reasons for rejecting this outcome. The first, suggested by his appeal to minimal rationality and attentiveness, is that someone who knows that p should be able to base on this knowledge inferential knowledge of the proposition that she doesn't believe falsely that p, and vice versa. The second is the general intuitive presumption in favour of Closure, which dictates that someone who knows that p logically entails that she doesn't falsely believe p cannot know the former without knowing the latter. Finally we have a general intuition to the effect that CSAs can be knowledge—that it has to be possible for me to know that

I don't falsely believe the things I believe. Let's consider each of the points in turn in connection with the account of knowledge that I am defending.

The first point was already discussed in Chapter 5. As I argued there, it would be wrong to treat the inference from p to the conclusion that I don't falsely believe p as a legitimate case of inferential knowledge. My account underwrites this verdict and provides what I regard as a plausible explanation of what's wrong with this method of knowledge acquisition. The reason why p doesn't provide me with adequate evidence for the proposition that I don't believe p falsely is that PI is not satisfied. The probability that I believe the former is unaffected by the truth value of the latter. That is, my belief in the former doesn't confirm the latter, contrary to what PI demands.

As I argued in Chapter 5, the second point is in principle independent of the first. Suppose that we accept, as I am suggesting, that I cannot know that I don't falsely believe that p inferentially on the basis of the evidence provided by p. One could still maintain that if I know that p logically entails q, I cannot know p without knowing q. Since I know that p logically entails that I don't falsely believe that p, it follows that I cannot know the former without knowing the latter. This point would raise a separate problem for my account of knowledge, since it entails that there are many cases in which I know p but I don't know that my belief that p is true, even if I know that p logically entails that my belief that p is true. Concerning this point, I argued in Chapter 6 that there is a general presumption in favour of instances of Closure, but we also saw that there are cases in which accepting a counterexample to the principle is the least disruptive option. Hence Closure should be seen as putting some pressure on my account of knowledge on this front, but this pressure is not irresistible. Providing the best possible match for our intuitions might require accepting these counterexamples to Closure.

Let's consider now the final point—that we have a general intuition to the effect that CSAs can be knowledge—that we are capable of knowing that our beliefs are true. This intuition is unquestionably real. Hence, my account would be put under some pressure if it entailed that CSAs can't be knowledge. However, I want to argue that we might be able to deflect this pressure. We could achieve this if we rejected the need to accommodate intuitions or if we could argue that a conflict with this particular intuition is required for securing the best overall match with our intuitions as a whole. I don't want to take either of these lines. Intuitions provide an irreplaceable guide in philosophical analysis, and the intuition that CSAs can be knowledge seems to be as central as any in this area. What I want to argue is that it might not be the job of the theory of knowledge to save this intuition.

As we saw in Chapter 1, on the anti-realist conception of the sceptical problem, sceptical arguments put pressure on realism—on some version of the thought that the reality that our beliefs purport to represent is fundamentally independent of the procedures that we employ for forming and assessing these beliefs. If the anti-realist conception were correct, we would expect to find some argument against epistemic optimism with no objectionable epistemological premises—just what we have found, if my account of knowledge is correct. This wouldn't force us to accept the sceptical outcome if we could show that, in addition to its unobjectionable epistemological premises, the argument rests on a version of realism. Then we would face the situation predicted by the anti-realist conception: our sceptical argument would show that, if the sceptical outcome is to be avoided, realism needs to be abandoned.

It follows that treating the conflict with epistemic optimism as a refutation of my account of knowledge begs the question against the anti-realist conception of the problem. I am going to argue that the point is not merely academic—that the sceptical argument that my account of knowledge underwrites puts genuine pressure on realism. It exposes the unacceptable epistemological consequences of an incorrect metaphysical picture. Now, I'm not claiming that it is obvious at this point that this conception of the problem is correct. This would require that the sceptical argument can only succeed when the objectionable metaphysical picture is in place, and it might not be easy to see how the argument that I have presented is supposed to rest on realist assumptions. Vindicating the anti-realist conception would require identifying the realist assumptions underpinning the argument, and showing that the rejection of these assumptions can in principle result in a viable metaphysical picture. Exploring these issues will be my goal in the next chapter.

# 8

# Scepticism and Realism

## 8.1 The anti-realist conception

In Chapters 4 to 6 I put forward an account of knowledge along broadly reliabilist lines. Then, in Chapter 7, I presented a sceptical argument that doesn't rest on any epistemological assumptions that my account of knowledge would render illegitimate. I have suggested that this outcome generates a novel situation in the discussion of scepticism. Reliabilist accounts of knowledge are generally assumed to have the power to block sceptical arguments. The version of reliabilism that I am putting forward shares with other versions the power to block the standard lines of sceptical reasoning. However, against the sceptical argument presented in Chapter 7 my account of knowledge offers no defence.

One natural reaction to this situation is to take the sceptical consequences of my account of knowledge as a refutation of the account, arguing that the intuition that CSAs can be knowledge is stronger than the intuitions that I have invoked in support of the account. However, as I argued in Chapter 7, there might be an alternative diagnosis of the situation. Sceptical difficulties might result, not from an incorrect analysis of knowledge, but from a mistaken construal of cognition. On this diagnosis, sceptical arguments would bring to the surface the inadequacy of a realist construal of reality and the cognitive enterprise of representing it in thought and language. If this diagnosis is correct, the way to avoid the sceptical outcome is not to reject the analysis of knowledge that makes it possible, but to abandon the metaphysical picture from which the problem ultimately arises. This is what I called in Chapter 1 *the anti-realist conception* of the sceptical problem. In the present chapter I want to explore the prospects for this diagnosis of the sceptical problem. I want to start by trying to identify the involvement of realism in the generation of the sceptical problem. Then I will consider the standard alternatives to the realist view, and argue that they face considerable problems. I'll end by briefly sketching what I regard as the most promising way forward—a position that overcomes the difficulties faced by realism and the standard anti-realist alternatives by challenging an assumption shared by both approaches.

## 8.2 Realism and cognition

A central aspect of the construal of cognition that we have presupposed in generating the sceptical outcome has unmistakeable realist credentials. The problem concerns how successful we are at forming true beliefs. But treating this as a problem presupposes a conception of cognition as an activity whose goal is the formation of true beliefs. Furthermore, it would seem that in order for the problem to arise, truth has to be construed as a property whose presence in or absence from a belief is in principle independent of the procedures at our disposal for detecting its presence or absence. It seems, then, that the sceptical problem presupposes a conception of cognition based on the following thesis:

R.    Cognition is an activity whose goal is the formation of true beliefs, with truth construed as independent of the procedures we employ in its pursuit.

Since, according to R, a belief is cognitively successful just in case it is true, $V(Bel_S[H])$ acquires the status of a cognitive assessment—it asserts that $Bel_S[H]$ attains the goal of cognition. This enables us to see the result that CSAs can't be knowledge as a challenge to epistemic optimism: our cognitive efforts may meet with some success, but we won't be able to know this, as we won't be able to know that our beliefs have attained the goal of cognition.

I am putting R forward as a first approximation to the characterization of the metaphysical picture that gives rise to the sceptical problem. We are about to see that this characterization will need to be refined. We'll see, on the one hand, that some construals of cognition that ascribe to it a different goal will also give rise to the problem. On the other hand, a construal of cognition for which the problem doesn't seem to arise might not be incompatible with endorsing R. I want to argue that the source of the problem is not R itself, but an approach to the task of construing cognition for which R can serve as an adequate slogan. My goal in this section is to outline this approach.

The approach that I have in mind can be motivated by highlighting the parallels between cognition and a family of activities to which I shall refer as *target activities*. Target activities are those in which a subject produces behavioural sequences of a certain type (call them *shots*) that may or may not be of a desired type (call them *hits* and *misses*, respectively). Target activities include all activities in which the subject literally seeks to hit a target (including archery, with which cognition has been compared since antiquity), as well as other activities with the same structure, as, for example, door-to-door canvassing, orienteering, or roulette. The structural parallels between target activities and cognition are perfectly obvious. In cognition, a subject produces outputs of a certain type (beliefs) that may or may not be of the desired type (i.e. true beliefs). Beliefs are cognitive shots: true beliefs cognitive hits and false beliefs cognitive misses.

Target activities have built into them a contrast between success and failure, based on the subject's intention to produce behavioural sequences (shots) of a certain kind (hits).

This circumstance enables us to raise questions about the subject's performance or competence in the activity. It will be useful to distinguish between particular and general assessments. Particular assessments concern whether a specific shot is a hit, whereas general assessments concern the probability of being a hit of a shot in general, or of a shot of a certain kind.

Let's focus on particular assessments. If S is a predicate that uniquely identifies a shot in a given target activity, and H is the predicate that represents a shot as a hit, a favourable assessment of a shot will be a proposition of the form H $\imath$x Sx. Notice that, if we want an unfavourable assessment to be expressed by ~H $\imath$x Sx, we need to take the description to have a wide scope. Then the proposition will be true just in case the shot is not a hit, and not also when the shot doesn't happen.

We can now extend the parallel between target activities and cognition to a parallel between particular assessments of a target activity and assessments of beliefs as true or false. If V is, as before, the truth predicate, and $B_p$ is a predicate describing one of S's beliefs as having p as its content, a favourable particular cognitive assessment of S's performance in cognition will be a proposition of the form V $\imath$x $B_p$x, asserting that S's belief that p is true. Once again, if ~V $\imath$x $B_p$x is to express the proposition that S falsely believes that p, and not the proposition that either S falsely believes that p or S doesn't believe that p, the description will have to be taken as having wide scope. Clearly, a CSA is simply a favourable particular cognitive assessment of S's belief by S herself.

We can explain in these terms the difference in significance between S's belief that p and S's belief that her belief that p is true. The former is to be taken simply as a shot in the activity of cognition, whereas the latter is an assessment of this shot as a hit. S can engage in cognition, as in any other activity, without assessing her performance in it, and when she undertakes this assessment she is engaging in a new, additional activity— assessing her beliefs with respect to a certain criterion. The outcome of the first-order activity is cognition—a representation of the world as being a certain way. The outcome of the reflective activity is an assessment of one's performance in cognition—of the extent to which this representation of the world attains the goal of truth. Successful engagement in the first-order activity will produce true beliefs about the world. Successful engagement in the reflective activity will produce true beliefs about first-order success. CSAs express these reflective assessments.

We can now understand the situation in which we would find ourselves if our first-order beliefs were knowledge but our CSAs were not. In this situation we would know what the world is like, but we would have no knowledge of how good we are at determining what the world is like. Our CSAs express our epistemic optimism—our conviction that things are as our beliefs represent them as being. If they can't have the status of knowledge, then we don't know that things are as our beliefs represent them as being. We may be very good at cognition, and we may believe that we are very good, but if our CSAs can't be knowledge we don't in fact have any knowledge of how good we are.

But if a CSA and the corresponding first-order belief have different contents, how do we explain the unfailing correlation between the two—the fact that particular cognitive self-assessments are always favourable? The parallels between cognition and target activities also supply an answer to this question. Some target activities arise from pre-rational activities in which the subject engages prior to formulating in consciousness the criterion that will distinguish a hit from a miss. We have inclinations to eat certain things and not others before we formulate in consciousness a dietary policy, or inclinations to flee or fight depending on the circumstances before we formulate an explicit policy to this effect. Let's suppose that engagement in the practice continues to be governed by the same sub-personal mechanisms as before the criterion was formulated, while assessment is guided by the subject's beliefs concerning the satisfaction of the criterion. Then assessments will be favourable when there is agreement between the behaviour generated by the sub-personal mechanisms and the subject's beliefs on the satisfaction of the chosen criterion. Suppose, for example, that I continue to eat what I'm inclined to eat, having decided that I should eat only food that is good for me. Then my assessments of my pre-reflective diet choices will be favourable when the things that I am inclined to eat are things that I believe to be good for me.

I want to concentrate on a particular kind of bias that might arise in this situation. Suppose that the subject's beliefs as to whether the criterion is satisfied are actually governed by the same sub-personal mechanisms that generate the behaviour, so that whenever the subject is inclined to behave in a certain way she will believe that this piece of behaviour satisfies the chosen criterion. Thus, in our example, we would have this situation if the inclination to eat a certain food produced in the subject the belief that that food is good for her. Notice that whether this bias exists is in principle independent of whether the sub-personal inclinations track the satisfaction of the criterion. The subject's beliefs as to which foods are good for her might be governed by the same sub-personal mechanisms that generate her inclinations to eat certain things whether or not the things that she is inclined to eat are actually good for her. In any case, when this kind of bias is present, we should expect the subject's self-assessments of her shots to be uniformly favourable, whether or not the shots actually satisfy the criterion.

A similar bias can exist in third-person cognitive assessments. A's favourable cognitive assessment of B's belief that p might be produced by an inclination to believe that what B believes is true, independent of the actual truth-value of p. As before, this bias can be present whether or not p is true and whether or not the things B believes are likely to be true.

We are now in a position to explain the fact that particular cognitive self-assessments are invariably favourable. The phenomenon can be explained as a case of the kind of bias that we have described for self-assessments of shots in target activities and in third-person cognitive assessments. Our engagement in cognition is regulated by sub-personal mechanisms that generate beliefs in us spontaneously, long before we reach the level of intellectual sophistication that enables us to formulate in consciousness a criterion by which we want our cognitive life to be governed. When a criterion is finally formulated, the sub-personal mechanisms that regulated our cognitive activity up to that point continue to be in charge of our cognitive life, spontaneously producing and revising beliefs, with no need for reflective intervention.

Cognitive self-assessment has this spontaneous cognitive activity as its object. We ask ourselves whether the things that we are pre-reflectively inclined to believe satisfy our chosen cognitive criterion. The question can be asked in principle with respect to any criterion.[1] We can ask, for example, whether our pre-reflective beliefs contribute to our happiness, or to the common good, or whether they agree with the teachings of the master. In each case we might find the kind of bias that we have described. Thus, my sub-personal doxastic inclinations as to whether to believe p might regulate my beliefs as to whether believing p promotes my happiness. In this case, if happiness promotion is my chosen cognitive criterion, my cognitive self-assessments will be uniformly favourable, independently of whether or not the beliefs that I am inclined to have actually satisfy the criterion.

With criteria other than truth, this kind of bias may or may not be present, but when we choose truth as our cognitive criterion, bias is inevitable. My belief as to whether my belief that p satisfies this criterion (whether the belief is true or false) is necessarily governed by the same doxastic mechanisms that govern my belief as to whether p. This means that, given that they have produced the belief that p, if they produce a belief on the truth value of this belief, they will produce the belief that my belief that p is true. The fact that this kind of bias is inevitable in cognitive self-assessments with respect to the goal of truth is the reason why they are always favourable.

Clearly this bias can be used to explain why CSAs don't track the truth. $p(Bel_S(V(Bel_S[p])) \mid V(Bel_S[p]))$ is the same as $p(Bel_S(V(Bel_S[p])) \mid \sim V(Bel_S[p]))$ because S's belief in $V(Bel_S[p])$ is governed by the same mechanisms that govern her belief in p. Hence the probability that S believes $V(Bel_S[p])$ won't be affected by the difference between $V(Bel_S[p])$ and $\sim V(Bel_S[p])$, since in both situations she believes that p.

Finally, we can understand from this perspective the importance of evidence for CSAs. Consider once more the case of the subject who is biased towards believing that the things she is inclined to eat are good for her. This bias is clearly an obstacle to her self-assessments of her involvement in the activity qualifying for the status of knowledge. Her bias will make her believe that what she was inclined to have for breakfast this morning is good for her whether or not it is actually good for her. This will be so even if what she felt inclined to eat was actually good for her, and even if she is generally inclined to eat things that are good for her. This handicap is reflected in the fact that her self-assessment doesn't track the truth, as the probability that she believes H ℩x Sx will be unaffected by the difference between H ℩x Sx and ~H ℩x Sx. If she is

---

[1] It has been argued that truth is the intrinsic goal of belief. See, e.g., (Shah 2003, 2006; Shah and Velleman 2005), and my response to Shah and Velleman's arguments in (Zalabardo 2010). Here I shall remain neutral on this issue.

inclined to eat it, she will believe that it is good for her, whether or not it actually is good for her.

Now, this obstacle is not insurmountable, even if the bias is not removed, her self-assessment will attain the status of knowledge if she can acquire adequate evidence in its support. Her belief that the chocolate she was inclined to eat this morning was good for her might have been produced by the same mechanisms that gave rise to the inclination to eat it, but if she managed to acquire adequate evidence in support of the health benefits of eating chocolate, she should still count as knowing that the chocolate was good for her, in spite of the bias.

The same situation obtains concerning CSAs. Here removing the bias is not an option. My belief as to whether my belief that p is true can only be regulated by the same mechanisms as my belief as to whether p. For CSAs, truth tracking is unattainable. We might have thought that the epistemic handicap posed by the bias could be overcome by the acquisition of adequate evidence. But the sceptical argument presented in the previous chapter shows that this option is not available either: adequate evidence in support for CSAs is not to be had.

## 8.3 Anti-realism

The construal of cognition that I have just outlined ascribes to the activity the features that the sceptic needs to invoke in her argument. The question that I want to consider now is whether there are other construals of cognition that deprive the sceptic of what she needs. When realism has been blamed for sceptical difficulties, the aspect of the view that has usually come under attack is its choice of realist truth as the goal of cognition. On this diagnosis, this choice leads ineluctably to the sceptical outcome. We are simply incapable of determining when our beliefs exhibit realist truth. In order to ensure that we can know how successful we are in cognition we need to adopt a different account of cognitive success.

According to this anti-realist approach, the problem will disappear if we replace realist truth with a cognitive goal that is intrinsically connected with the ways in which we engage in cognition. The proposal can be carried out either by abandoning truth in favour of a different cognitive goal or by preserving truth as the goal of cognition while replacing the realist conception of truth with an account in terms of our engagement in the cognitive practice. The alternative cognitive goals/construals of truth that have been put forward in this vein include warranted assertibility, maximally coherent belief systems, beliefs that we would hold under ideal conditions, and beliefs that would secure consensus at the end of enquiry. I am going to argue that this general strategy for vindicating epistemic optimism faces important difficulties.

In the issues that I am going to raise, an important role is played by a principle concerning target activities and its application to cognition when construed along these lines. For target activities, the thought is that engaging in a target activity requires that your performance should be in consonance with your beliefs concerning how likely shots are to be hits. This harmony will be displayed to the highest degree by participants that I shall call *perfectly self-disciplined*:

If the goal of an activity is to produce shots with feature G, then a *perfectly self-disciplined participant* will produce shot X just in case she believes G(X).

We shouldn't expect all participants in a target activity to display this level of self-discipline. However, I want to suggest that a measure of self-discipline is a necessary condition for counting as a participant in a target activity. Someone's actions cannot count as shots in a target activity with G as its goal unless there is a certain level of correlation between the sequences of behaviour that she produces and her beliefs as to whether they have feature G.

When cognition is construed in analogy with target activities, we can define the parallel notion of a *perfectly self-disciplined cognizer*:

If the goal of cognition is to form beliefs with feature F, and S is a *perfectly self-disciplined cognizer*, then S will believe p just in case she believes $F(Bel_{ME}[p])$.

Once again we shouldn't expect all cognizers to display this level of self-discipline. However, a measure of self-discipline is a necessary condition for treating the production of F-beliefs as S's cognitive goal. If there is no connection between whether S believes p and whether she believes $F(Bel_{ME}[p])$, we won't be able to treat F as S's cognitive goal.

Clearly, when cognition is construed as aiming at truth, reflective cognizers automatically display a high-level of self-discipline. In fact, perfect self-discipline will be unavoidable so long as we are prepared to accept that the conditions that warrant ascription of a belief in proposition p also warrant ascription of a belief in the proposition that one's belief in p is true. In the next few sections I am going to assume that any acceptable construal of cognition as aiming at a goal other than truth would have to be compatible with the possibility that cognizers are perfectly self-disciplined, and I am going to consider some difficulties for anti-realism arising from this constraint. Taking account of less-than-perfectly disciplined cognizers would require more complex arguments, but it wouldn't enable the anti-realist to overcome the difficulties that I'm going to consider.

## 8.4  Anti-reductionism

The first issue that I want to raise can be presented more effectively by focusing in the first instance on a specific version of the anti-realist strategy, although, as we shall see in due course, the problems affect other anti-realist proposals. The view on which I want to focus is verificationism. According to verificationism, the meaning of a declarative sentence is given by its method of verification. As I propose to construe the view, it replaces a semantic picture in terms of the contrast between states of affairs that would make the sentence true and those that would make it false with one in terms of the contrast between states of information that would verify the sentence and states of information that wouldn't have this effect. Alternatively, a contrast is invoked between verifying and falsifying states of information, leaving open the possibility of states of information which fall in neither category. States of information, as they figure in the view, are assumed to be unproblematically detectable by the speaker. Although this is in the first instance a proposal about linguistic meaning, it has direct consequences for the content of cognitive states. The same shift from truth conditions to verification conditions would apply to the beliefs expressed by declarative sentences.

It is unquestionable that one of the main selling points of verificationism was its perceived ability to overcome the sceptical problem, and we can easily present the view as the kind of anti-realist construal of the cognitive practice that I have just outlined. The verificationist construal of cognition would simply replace the goal of believing a proposition just in case it is true with the goal of believing a proposition just in case it has been verified, that is, just in case the subject is in one of the states of information that verifies the proposition.

This shift appears to offer a promising strategy for overcoming the sceptical problem presented in Chapter 7. The basic thought is that whereas there might be a problem with determining whether a state of affairs makes a proposition true, there shouldn't be a problem in principle with determining whether a state of information verifies a proposition, since states of information are, by their very nature, identifiable by the subject. Hence, although there is a problem with knowing that I am successful in the enterprise of believing true propositions, there shouldn't be a problem with knowing that I am successful in the enterprise of believing verified propositions.

I want to argue next that self-discipline poses a difficulty for verificationism. In order to generate the problem, we don't need to require that the view should be compatible with perfect self-discipline. The difficulty arises already for what I propose to call *minimal cognitive self-discipline* (MSD):

> If the goal of cognition is to form beliefs with feature F, and S is a *minimally self-disciplined cognizer*, then S won't believe p and $\sim F(Bel_{ME}[p])$ or $F(Bel_{ME}[p])$ and $\sim p$.

Whether or not verificationism is compatible with MSD depends on what account it offers of how each proposition is paired with its verification conditions. If verification conditions were singled out in a way that made it possible for subjects to reject the pairing of a proposition with its verification conditions, violations of MSD would be unavoidable. Then someone who didn't accept that p is verified by the states of information that actually verify it could believe that the relevant states of information obtain but fail to believe p.

Verificationism appears to have the resources for overcoming this difficulty. Conflicts with MSD would be ruled out if the pairings of propositions with their verification conditions were established in terms of the methods of verification actually used by each subject. The proposition expressed by a sentence, as meant by speaker at a time, would then be verified by the states of information that the speaker is inclined to treat as verifying the sentence at that time. This account would rule out cases in which a subject believes that p even though she believes that p hasn't been verified and cases in which a subject believes ~p even though she believes that p has been verified.

This account of how propositions are paired with their verification conditions may succeed in avoiding conflicts with MSD, but it faces other problems. They arise from another plausible constraint on cognition. It is the thought that, in cases that don't involve indexicality or other context-sensitive devices, whether believing a proposition achieves the goal of cognition does not change from subject to subject or from time to time. I am going to refer to this thought as *anti-relativism*:

(AR)    If p is a non-indexical proposition, then for all subjects S1, S2 and times t1, t2, S1 would achieve the goal of cognition by believing p at t1 if and only if S2 would achieve the goal of cognition by believing p at t2.

Now, AR has the following consequence for the verificationist construal of cognition:

(D)    If the conditions under which S1 takes sentence A1 to be verified at t1 are different from the conditions under which S2 takes A2 to be verified at t2, then the proposition expressed by A1, as meant by S1 at t1, is different from the proposition expressed by A2, as meant by S2 at t2.

Unless D is universally valid, verificationism will be incompatible with AR. To see this, notice that if A1 expressed the same proposition for S1 at t1 as A2 does for S2 at t2, and the verification conditions ascribed to A1 by S1 at t1 were satisfied, but those ascribed to A2 by S2 at t2 weren't satisfied, the goal of cognition would be achieved by S1 believing A1 at t1 and by S2 refraining from believing A2 at t2, contrary to what AR requires.

But D is an unacceptable outcome. It imposes a constraint on interpretation that is in open conflict with our intuitions concerning when a sentence expresses the same proposition for different speakers, or for a speaker at different times. The propositions expressed by sentences are more coarsely individuated than the methods employed by speakers to verify them. There are many cases in which speakers who use different methods for verifying a sentence express the same proposition with it, as well as cases in which a speaker changes the method that she uses for verifying a sentence without thereby changing the proposition that she expresses with the sentence.

Perhaps the most prominent instances of this kind of situation concern sentences involving natural-kind terms.[2] The verification methods associated with sentences of the form 'x is made of gold' have changed with the advance of scientific knowledge, and although the methods that have played this role exhibit substantial agreement on when a sentence of this form is verified, there are cases for which they produce conflicting verdicts—cases in which the sentence would be verified according to one method but not according to another. In light of these disagreements, it follows from

---

[2] The general phenomenon was brought to prominence in Hilary Putnam's early criticism of conventionalist and operationalist positions. See, e.g., (Putnam 1962, 1963).

D that speakers at different points in history who used different methods for verifying a sentence of the form 'x is made of gold' would express different propositions by the sentence.

Consider, for example an iron-age subject whose method for verifying these sentences consists in the standard phenomenological tests (colour, shine, hardness) and a medieval subject who takes solubility in aqua regia as her best verification method for these sentences. Suppose that there is a crown made of a metal that passes the phenomenological tests but is not soluble in aqua regia. If both subjects apply their tests to the crown, the iron-age subject will assert 'the crown is made of gold', while the medieval subject will assert 'the crown is not made of gold'.[3] According to D, it would be wrong to take this as expressing a factual disagreement, since the proposition expressed by the medieval subject's assertion is not the negation of the proposition expressed by the utterance of her iron-age counterpart.

But we know that this is not how natural-kind terms work (Putnam 1975; Kripke 1980). The two subjects *are* disagreeing. The proposition expressed by one is the negation of the proposition expressed by the other. The verification methods associated by speakers with sentences involving natural-kind terms may well play a role in determining when these sentences express the same proposition. Even so, the link between verification methods and synonymy is not nearly as tight as D demands. Speakers who associate conflicting verification methods with a sentence often express the same proposition with the sentence. Whether a verification method should be associated with a sentence is in many crucial cases not a matter to be stipulated, as verificationism dictates, but a substantive empirical question on which subjects can disagree without thereby expressing different propositions with the sentence. The verificationist construal of cognition entails an unacceptably inflexible picture of how the verification methods employed by speakers determine when they express the same proposition with a sentence.[4]

The difficulties that verificationism encounters with AR manifest the inadequacy of its strategy for accommodating self-discipline. If success in cognition consists in believing verified propositions, self-discipline requires that the verification conditions of propositions should be singled out by speakers' dispositions. AR forces the verificationist construal to treat differences in verification conditions as differences in proposition expressed, but this, in turn, forces us to treat propositions as different in many cases in which this is clearly the wrong result.

Other anti-realist construals of cognition don't seem to incorporate any resources for accommodating self-discipline. Take, for example, the view that success in cognition consists in believing propositions that would be believed under ideal epistemic conditions. Notice, first of all, that if this is going to provide a genuine alternative to realism,

---

[3] More plausibly, they will assert sentences that are correctly translated by these English sentences. The same point can be made taking account of this complication.

[4] I see this argument as a version of Quine's attack on reductionism (Quine 1980: 37–42).

*ideal epistemic conditions* cannot be understood as conditions that are as a matter of fact conducive to the formation of true belief. Presumably, knowing that I am successful at forming beliefs in propositions that would be believed in conditions that satisfy this description would pose the same problem as knowing that I am successful at forming true beliefs. In an anti-realist construal of cognition aimed at overcoming sceptical difficulties, *ideal epistemic conditions* would have to receive a substantive specification, as, for example, conditions in which the relevant empirical evidence has been carefully considered and so on.

But as soon as ideal conditions are specified in this way, violations of self-discipline seem unavoidable. Believing p is perfectly compatible with believing that p would not be believed, say, if all the relevant empirical evidence had been carefully considered. The connection between careful consideration of the empirical evidence relevant to p, on the one hand, and p, on the other, is an empirical question, and there is no incoherence in believing p while believing that careful consideration of the relevant empirical evidence would not lead to belief in p. If cognition is construed as aiming at believing propositions that would be believed under epistemically ideal conditions, we'll have to accept that cognizers might fall short even of minimal self-discipline.[5] I want to suggest that other anti-realist construals of cognition as aiming at a goal other than truth succumb to the same difficulty. Indeed, the problem seems to afflict any construal of cognition as aiming at a goal other than truth. Construing cognition as aiming at truth is the only way of ensuring that the self-discipline constraint is satisfied.

The difficulty arises also, in a slightly different form, for versions of anti-realism that preserve truth as the goal of cognition but provide a substantive construal of truth in terms of more accessible features of belief. Consider, for example, the view that cognition aims at the formation of true beliefs, but a belief is true just in case it would be believed under ideal epistemic conditions. Now the possibility of believing p while believing that p would not be believed under epistemically ideal conditions doesn't immediately result in a violation of self-discipline. Someone who believes that p would not be believed under epistemically ideal conditions might still believe that p is true, provided that she doesn't subscribe to the account of truth under discussion. The account of truth entails that *p is true* and *p would not be believed under epistemically ideal conditions* can't be simultaneously true, not that they cannot be simultaneously believed. A subject who accepts this account of truth won't be able to believe both propositions, but the account might be true even if it doesn't command universal acceptance.

However, this strategy for avoiding conflicts with self-discipline is clearly unsatisfactory, since it can't be applied to those who accept the account of truth that's being put

---

[5] It would be possible at this point to follow a strategy that mirrors the move that we considered for verificationism, arguing that success in cognition should be defined in terms of what is taken to be ideal epistemic conditions by each subject at each time. However, this move would face the same difficulties that I presented in the case of verificationism.

forward as correct. A subject who subscribes to the anti-realist account of truth can in principle believe both p and that p wouldn't be believed under epistemically ideal conditions, but it follows from her acceptance of the anti-realist account of truth that she will believe both p and the proposition that p is not true, in violation of self-discipline. Since the anti-realist can hardly rule out the possibility that her account of truth is accepted by some cognitive subjects, the strategy for complying with self-discipline is not universally applicable.

## 8.5 Stability[6]

The next difficulty that I want to explore concerns another consequence of self-discipline. If you are a perfectly self-disciplined subject, you engage in a target activity by producing a shot when you *believe* that it attains its goal. In this way, cognition is implicated in your engagement in any target activity. As a result of this connection, your cognitive goals can affect the goals of your target activities. If your nominal goal in an activity is to produce shots with feature G, you will produce a shot just in case you believe that it has feature G. But if your goal in cognition is to form beliefs with feature F, then you will aim at believing that a shot has feature G just in case the belief that it does has feature F. This suggests that even though your nominal goal is to produce shots with feature G, your effective goal in the activity is to produce a shot just in case the belief that the shot has feature G has feature F.

If your goal in cognition is truth, this point has no practical consequences. Then your effective goal in the G-activity is to produce a shot just in case the belief that it has feature G is true, but this goal is equivalent to your nominal goal, since a shot has feature G just in case the belief that it does is true. However, for other cognitive goals, the nominal and effective goals of your target activities cannot be assumed to coincide. Suppose, for example, that you have turned your nourishment into a target activity and you have chosen as your goal to eat things that enhance your longevity. Suppose, in addition, that your goal in cognition is to believe something just in case doing so makes you feel good about yourself. It follows from this that your effective dietary goal is to eat something just in case believing that it enhances your longevity makes you feel good about yourself. Clearly, in this case, your nominal goal and your effective goal cannot be expected to coincide. Whether or not a foodstuff enhances your longevity is in principle independent of whether or not believing that it does makes you feel good about yourself.

Now, just as we have used the dictates of practical self-discipline to map out how cognition is involved in our engagement in target activities, we can use cognitive self-discipline to draw parallel conclusions for our engagement in cognition. Suppose that your goal in cognition with respect to a range of propositions including p is to believe

---

[6] A version of the argument in this section appears in (Zalabardo forthcoming-a).

X just in case your belief in X would have feature F. Then, if you are a perfectly self-disciplined cognizer, you will believe p just in case you believe $F(\text{Bel}_{\text{ME}}[p])$. Suppose, in addition, that your goal in cognition with respect to a range of propositions including $F(\text{Bel}_{\text{ME}}[p])$ is to believe X just in case your belief in X would have feature H. Then your effective cognitive goal with respect to p will be to believe p just in case your belief in $F(\text{Bel}_{\text{ME}}[p])$ would have feature H, that is, just in case $H(\text{Bel}_{\text{ME}}[F(\text{Bel}_{\text{ME}}[p])])$.

As before, if truth is your goal in cognition with respect to $F(\text{Bel}_{\text{ME}}[p])$, this observation won't have any practical consequences. If H is the truth predicate, then $H(\text{Bel}_{\text{ME}}[F(\text{Bel}_{\text{ME}}[p])])$ is equivalent to $F(\text{Bel}_{\text{ME}}[p])$, and your cognitive goal with respect to p won't have to be altered to comply with self-discipline. However, for other cognitive goals, equivalence cannot be guaranteed. Suppose, for example, that your cognitive goal with respect to p is to believe it just in case your belief that p would enhance your career prospects. Suppose, in addition, that your cognitive goal with respect to propositions as to whether a belief would enhance your career prospects is to believe them just in case they make you feel good about yourself. Then your effective goal with respect to p will be to believe p just in case the belief that believing p would enhance your career prospects makes you feel good about yourself. Clearly in this example we cannot assume that your nominal and effective goals will coincide. Whether a belief would enhance your career prospects is in principle independent of whether believing that it would makes you feel good about yourself.

So far we have considered consequences of self-discipline in cases in which a subject has different cognitive goals for different propositions. The difficulty on which I want to concentrate arises when we move from this kind of situation to cases in which subjects have a single goal for all their cognitive activities—where the feature that they seek in their beliefs doesn't change from case to case. In these cases we shall say that cognition has a *global goal*. I want to present a difficulty that arises when cognition is construed as aiming at a global goal other than truth.

The difficulty is very simple. Suppose that your global cognitive goal is to believe a proposition just in case it has feature F. Then, if you are a perfectly self-disciplined cognizer, you will believe p just in case you believe $F(\text{Bel}_{\text{ME}}[p])$. But since having F-beliefs is your global cognitive goal, it follows that you will aim to believe $F(\text{Bel}_{\text{ME}}[p])$ just in case your belief in this proposition would have feature F, that is, just in case $F(\text{Bel}_{\text{ME}}[F(\text{Bel}_{\text{ME}}[p])])$. Hence your effective goal with respect to p would seem to be to believe it just in case $F(\text{Bel}_{\text{ME}}[F(\text{Bel}_{\text{ME}}[p])])$. This is clearly not the end of the story, since the same reasoning can be applied to the new goal. Self-discipline dictates that you will believe p just in case you believe $F(\text{Bel}_{\text{ME}}[F(\text{Bel}_{\text{ME}}[p])])$, but since having F-beliefs is your global cognitive goal, you would aim to believe this just in case $F(\text{Bel}_{\text{ME}}[F(\text{Bel}_{\text{ME}}[F(\text{Bel}_{\text{ME}}[p])])])$. A regress looms.

Is this regress vicious? I want to suggest that the answer to this question depends on the behaviour of F. Let's say that F is *completely stable* just in case, necessarily, for every proposition p and every subject S, $F(\text{Bel}_S[F(\text{Bel}_S[p])])$ if and only if $F(\text{Bel}_S[p])$. If F is completely stable, the infinite regress generated by self-discipline doesn't pose a problem. Then the cognitive goal that is ascribed to you with respect to p at each step of the regress is necessarily identical to the goal ascribed to you at the previous step, and ultimately to your original nominal goal—to believe p just in case $F(Bel_{ME}[p])$. In light of this, it is natural to suppose that this is the goal ascribed to you by the whole infinite chain.

In other cases, however, the regress will be problematic. Let $F^1(Bel_S[p])$ be $F(Bel_S[p])$, and for every n let $F^{n+1}(Bel_S[p])$ be $F(Bel_S[F^n(Bel_S[p])])$. Let's say that F is *ultimately unstable* (with respect to p) just in case, for every n, there is an m greater than n such it is not the case that necessarily $F^m(Bel_S[p])$ just in case $F^{m+1}(Bel_S[p])$.

If F is ultimately unstable, the regress will never settle permanently on a single cognitive goal. No matter how far along the regress we advance, your effective cognitive goal will remain liable to change. In these circumstances, we seem forced to conclude that taking F as a global cognitive goal doesn't result in a coherent ascription of effective cognitive goals, or, indeed, of an effective goal to any target activity, provided that you are also self-disciplined with respect to these. There isn't a feature whose presence in or absence from your belief in p will determine whether success in cognition requires that you believe p or that you refrain from doing so.

Clearly, if we construe cognition as aiming at truth, the problem doesn't arise, since truth is completely stable. Necessarily, your belief that p is true just in case your belief that your belief that p is true is also true. Iterations of the truth predicate necessarily collapse. From this point of view, truth is perfectly suitable as a global cognitive goal.

The challenge for anti-realists is to show that their chosen alternative goal for cognition doesn't succumb to this problem. Thus, for example, verificationists would need to argue that, necessarily, p is verified just in case the proposition that p is verified is verified, and advocates of construals of cognition in terms of epistemically ideal conditions would need to argue that, necessarily, p would be believed in epistemically ideal conditions just in case it would be believed under epistemically ideal conditions that p would be believed under epistemically ideal conditions.[7] Assessing the anti-realist's prospects in this task would require a much more detailed characterization of anti-realist cognitive goals than we can provide here. I have not argued that the anti-realist cannot meet this challenge, only that her proposal will be unacceptable unless the challenge is met.

---

[7] This is, in fact, too strong, some properties that are not completely stable are not ultimately unstable either, and for these the problem doesn't arise either. Let's say that F is *ultimately stable* just in case there is an n such that, for every m greater than n, necessarily $F^m(Bel_S[p])$ just in case $F^{m+1}(Bel_S[p])$. Completely stable properties are ultimately stable for n = 1. Properties that are ultimately stable only for higher values of n are not completely stable, but they enjoy the same immunity to the ravages of the regress as completely stable properties. Hence it would suffice for the anti-realist to show that her chosen cognitive goal is ultimately stable, even if it isn't completely stable.

## 8.6 Anti-realist reductions and the sceptical problem

The challenges to anti-realism that I have presented in the last two sections question the viability of anti-realist construals of cognition, leaving to one side their ability to solve the problem of scepticism. Trying to overcome these challenges would seem to be a worthwhile pursuit, so long as the outcome is a viable construal of cognition for which the sceptical problem doesn't arise. In this section I want to argue that this is not the situation, since anti-realist construals of cognition don't offer any protection against the sceptical argument that I presented in Chapter 7. The reason why anti-realism won't help with the problem is that the sceptical argument that we presented can be run in the same terms for any construal of cognition as analogous to a target activity, so long as the goal of cognition abides by the self-discipline constraint.

Consider first the claim that CSAs don't track the truth. I argued that $p(Bel(V(Bel_{Me}[A])) \mid V(Bel_{Me}[A]))$ is the same as $p(Bel(V(Bel_{Me}[A])) \mid \sim V(Bel_{Me}[A]))$ because, so long as I believe A, the probability that I believe $V(Bel_{Me}[A])$ is unaffected by whether A is true or false. But, clearly, self-discipline will enable us to draw the same conclusion for any account of cognitive success. Thus, if F is a property for which I satisfy the self-discipline constraint, so long as I believe A I will believe $F(Bel_{Me}[A])$. Hence $p(Bel(F(Bel_{Me}[A])) \mid F(Bel_{Me}[A]))$ will be the same as $p(Bel(F(Bel_{Me}[A])) \mid \sim F(Bel_{Me}[A]))$, as both will equal 1. Hence the tracking ratio of my belief in $F(Bel_{Me}[A])$ will also be 1, and the belief won't track the truth.

This means that, for anti-realists no less than for realists, the status of CSAs as knowledge will depend on whether adequate evidence in their support can be identified. Here we find once more that the difficulties that we presented for the realist construal of cognition can be replicated for the anti-realist alternatives. I argued there that if E is S's evidence for H, it can provide adequate support for $V(Bel_S[H])$ only if it provides S with *exceptional* support for H, that is, if there is a significant probability that S believes H but not E and E increases the gap between the probabilities of $V(Bel_S[H])$ and $\sim V(Bel_S[H])$ much more than it would be increased by S believing H in the absence of evidence E. It can be easily seen that we would be able to obtain a parallel result for the support that $F(Bel_S[H])$ receives from S's evidence E for H. The claim now is that E can provide adequate support for $F(Bel_S[H])$ only if E provides S with *F-exceptional* support for H, that is, if there is a significant probability that S believes H but not E and E increases the gap between the probabilities of $F(Bel_S[H])$ and $\sim F(Bel_S[H])$ much more than it would be increased by S believing H in the absence of evidence E.

We saw in Chapter 7 that there is no reason in principle why someone's evidence for a proposition shouldn't be exceptional. What poses a problem is the possibility of a subject believing that her evidence for the propositions that she believes is exceptional, as this belief would be in conflict with epistemic optimism. When cognition is construed as aiming at a goal other than truth, the difficulty doesn't disappear. My belief that I am generally good at forming beliefs with property F will be in conflict with the belief that my evidence for the propositions that I believe is F-exceptional. Optimism will now dictate that, not only in the precise circumstances that actually obtain, but also in fairly probable alternative scenarios, I form beliefs in ways that are likely to secure my goal in cognition. It follows that I believe that my evidence for the propositions I believe is generally F-unexceptional, and hence unsuitable for supporting F-denominated CSAs. I conclude that construing cognition at aiming at a goal other than truth would not sustain a successful strategy for resisting scepticism.

## 8.7 The middle position

Over the last three sections I have argued that the anti-realist strategy of linking the goal of cognition to features of our engagement in the activity has little to recommend it. It produces a deeply counterintuitive account of the activity, while offering no anti-sceptical returns. If realism and anti-realism are the only options at our disposal, realism will have to be embraced as the lesser evil. A wider consequence of this outcome is the collapse of the anti-realist conception of the sceptical problem. If anti-realism is the only credible alternative to the realist account of cognition that we have used to generate the sceptical problem, then the problem cannot be solved by adjustments to our account of cognition. This will force upon us the choice we were trying to avoid, between accepting the sceptical outcome and rejecting the account of knowledge that I have defended.

Avoiding this result would seem to require showing that realism and anti-realism are not the only options at our disposal for an account of cognition—that there is a third position that we can take on this issue, and that this position has the resources for defusing the sceptical threat. On the face of it, it is hard to see how the choice between realism and anti-realism could be avoided. If cognition is analogous to a target activity, if there is a genuine contrast between cognitive success and cognitive failure, then cognitive success will have to be defined either as independent of our engagement in the activity, as realism dictates, or in terms of some aspect of our engagement in the activity, as the various forms of anti-realism propose. It seems to follow from this observation that the only way to avoid the choice between realism and anti-realism is to abandon the construal of cognition as analogous to a target activity—to give up the idea that there is a genuine contrast between cognitive success and cognitive failure. But this move would be highly implausible. If we give up the notion of cognitive success, it is hard to see how we could make sense of questions concerning whether our beliefs represent the world correctly, but these questions have to make sense for any attitudes that deserve to be described as beliefs.

Thus we seem to face a dilemma. Either we construe cognition as analogous to a target activity, and then, if my account of knowledge is along the right lines, we can't have knowledge of the extent to which we achieve the goal of cognition; or we abandon the construal of cognition as a target activity, but then we lose our grip on the idea that our beliefs represent the world as being a certain way. I believe that this is not a genuine dilemma, that it is possible to formulate a coherent account of cognition that avoids both horns. Articulating this middle position at the level of detail that would enable us to assess its plausibility is a formidable task that I cannot hope to discharge in the concluding chapter of a book on knowledge and scepticism. My goal in the remainder is only to give the briefest indication of the main changes in our conception of cognition from which I hope the middle position will emerge.

## 8.8 Two conceptions of cognitive assessment

The disagreement between realism and anti-realism, on the one hand, and the middle position, on the other, concerns in the first instance the question of what needs to be done in order to account for the contrast between cognitive success and failure. For realists and anti-realists alike, accounting for the contrast requires specifying what it consists in—what facts about a belief determine whether it is cognitively successful or cognitively unsuccessful. According to the middle position, accounting for the contrast does not require specifying what it consists in. The middle position proposes to account for the contrast instead with a description of the procedures that we employ for ascribing cognitive success and failure.[8]

In order to get a sense of how the proposal would work, I want to introduce an artificially simplified model of cognition and cognitive assessment—one that abstracts from much of the complexity of the real-life activities. In the simplified model that I want to discuss, cognition is entirely conducted in terms of conscious episodes in which we see ourselves as detecting the presence in, or absence from, a particular of a universal. I shall refer to these episodes as *universal detections*.[9] In this simplified model of cognition, universal detections are assessed as cognitively successful or unsuccessful according to the following procedure. Participants in the cognitive activity sometimes see a universal detection by a fellow participant, or one of their own past universal detections, as involving the same particular and the same universal as one of their current universal detections. Cognitive assessments take place in this situation. If I see you as detecting the presence (absence) of a universal in a particular in which I now detect the absence (presence) of this same universal, I will declare your detection a failure. If, on the contrary, I see you as detecting the presence (absence) of a universal in a particular in which I have also detected the presence (absence) of this same universal, I will declare your detection a success. Similarly, if I see myself as having detected at an

---

[8] I see the middle position as belonging to a loose family of contemporary views including those defended by Donald Davidson (Davidson 1990) and Hilary Putnam (Putnam 1994) in their recent work, John McDowell (McDowell 1981, 1984, 1987), Huw Price (Price 1988), and Arthur Fine (Fine 1984a, 1984b). My previous attempts to articulate a position along these lines were presented in (Zalabardo 1996, 2000b, 2001).

[9] This description of cognition doesn't need to assume the existence of a relation pairing universal detections with universal-particular pairs. Universal detections can be treated as mere phenomenal occurrences, abstracting from any links to universals and particulars.

earlier time the presence (absence) of a universal in a particular in which I now detect the absence (presence) of this same universal, I will declare my past detection a failure. If, on the contrary, I see myself as having detected at an earlier time the presence (absence) of a universal in a particular in which I now detect again the presence (absence) of this same universal, I will declare my past detection a success. This procedure for ascribing cognitive success and failure is also a procedure for using the words 'true' and 'false'. 'True' is used to ascribe success, and 'false' to ascribe failure, according to the procedure I've just described.

According to the middle position, this description of the procedure for ascribing cognitive success and cognitive failure is all that is required for explaining the contrast. 'Cognitively successful', that is, 'true', and 'cognitively unsuccessful', that is, 'false', are terms that acquire their significance from the fact that they are ascribed in this way. Specifically, they don't become significant by being paired with a property whose presence in or absence from a belief is asserted by cognitive assessments.

As we have seen, the middle position rejects an assumption shared by realist and anti-realist construals of cognition—that accounting for cognitive success consists in specifying what it consists in. However, the resulting position is related to realism and anti-realism in ways that justify thinking of it as occupying a middle ground between the two.

Notice, first, that from the point of view of the materials in terms of which cognitive success is construed, the middle position can be regarded as a particularly radical form of anti-realism: the only facts that are invoked in the account are subjects' inclinations to find universals present in particulars and to see their current universal detections as involving the same particular and universal as other universal detections. However, the way in which the middle position uses these materials differs sharply from the use to which they would be put in an anti-realist construal. The anti-realist would seek to formulate in terms of them an account of cognitive success—of the facts that determine whether a belief is cognitively successful or unsuccessful. The advocate of the middle position would not follow the anti-realist in this. She would insist that a description of our procedures for ascribing cognitive success and failure provides a complete explanation of the significance of the contrast even though it doesn't result in a specification of necessary and sufficient conditions for cognitive success. Furthermore, given the open-ended nature of these procedures, they will not sustain a specification of necessary and sufficient conditions for cognitive success. Any ascription of success or failure that they produce at a given time is open to revision in light of further universal detections that their subjects see as involving the same universal and particular as the universal detection being assessed.

This difference between anti-realism and the middle position brings the middle position closer to realism. Like the realist, the advocate of the middle position will reject the idea that we can specify necessary and sufficient conditions for cognitive success in terms of our procedures for assessing the success of cognitive episodes. Since, in addition, the advocate of the middle position will be happy to use the terms 'true' and 'false' to express ascriptions of cognitive success and failure, we can expect her to subscribe to the principle that we employed in our initial characterization of realism:

R.   Cognition is an activity whose goal is the formation of true beliefs, with truth construed as independent of the procedures we employ in its pursuit.

However, although the advocate of the middle position and the realist agree on the truth of this principle, they disagree about the information it conveys. For the realist, R takes truth as independently understood, and characterizes cognition as an activity that has truth as its goal. For the advocate of the middle position, by contrast, R takes the activity of cognition and its associated assessment procedures as given, and tells us that 'true' is what we call a belief when we assess it as cognitively successful.[10]

As we have presented it so far, the middle position is open to the complaint that, far from vindicating the contrast between success and failure, the picture of cognition that it presents is indistinguishable from one according to which the contrast is not real, and cognizers are simply under the illusion that their universal detections (/beliefs) can be meaningfully assessed as cognitively successful or unsuccessful.[11] Overcoming this challenge would require arguing that it follows from the middle position that the conception of cognition endorsed by its participants constitutes the real truth about the activity. They regard the contrast between success and failure as perfectly real, and since this verdict is sanctioned by the procedures that the middle position treats as the ultimate foundation of the contrast, the middle position will treat this verdict as correct. However, this manoeuvre is problematic, as it appears to involve a form of self-referential inconsistency (Fitch 1946): accepting its construal of cognitive success seems to lead to its rejection.

The challenge now is to avoid treating this as a refutation of the middle position and a vindication of realism.[12] One possibility would be to introduce a distinction between two levels of description of cognition: an external or transcendental level, at which our assessment procedures appear as the ultimate reality, and an internal or empirical level, at which the contrast between cognitive success and failure can be seen as fundamental. However, this move faces familiar challenges. It is hard to see how we could avoid treating the way cognition appears at the transcendental level as constituting the real

[10] This aspect of the middle position is reminiscent of the views on the relationship between truth and assertion that Tom Ricketts ascribes to Frege (Ricketts 1986, 1996).

[11] This complaint is germane to the charge of idealism sometimes levelled against Wittgenstein's late philosophy. See (Williams 1974).

[12] For the difficulties that we face when we try to articulate the contrast between realism and views along the lines of the middle position, see (Blackburn 1980).

truth about it, and hence conceding that the middle position is guilty as charged of treating the contrast between cognitive success and failure as illusory.[13]

## 8.9  The middle position and the sceptical problem

I do not claim to have shown in the preceding section that the middle position can be developed into a viable account of cognition. An adequate assessment of the view lies beyond the scope of this book. However, I want to suggest, in closing, that if we could develop a workable account of cognition along the lines of the sketch that I have provided, the resulting view might have the resources for defusing the sceptical argument that I presented in the preceding chapter.

Notice, first of all, that the sceptical argument presupposes that a favourable cognitive assessment of a belief in p is a belief with a different content from the belief it assesses. Only on this assumption can the epistemic status of my favourable cognitive assessment of my belief in p be called into question, as the argument does, while conceding the favourable epistemic status of my belief in p. On the realist construal of cognition, this assumption is inescapable. The realist presupposes that there is a belief-property, truth, whose presence or absence determines cognitive success. Once this assumption is made, it's hard to see how we could avoid construing cognitive assessments as beliefs that assert the presence in, or absence from, the belief they assess of the truth property. And this content will be different in general from the content of the belief in which the truth property is asserted to be present or absent. First-order and second-order beliefs will have the same truth value, but they might have different epistemic statuses even when they are simultaneous beliefs of a single subject. This is the weakness that the sceptical argument exploits. And moving to an anti-realist construal of cognitive success doesn't help matters in this regard. A belief in p and a belief in the presence in a belief in p of the anti-realist success-determining belief-property will still have different contents, allowing the argument to develop once more.

On the middle position, however, things are slightly different. There is still an obvious analogy between the episodes within the scope of cognitive assessment (universal detections, in our simplified model of cognition) and the episodes in which these are assessed. The procedure for assessing universal detections can be easily extended to the assessment of assessments of universal detections: if I see universal detection D as involving the same universal and particular as one of my current universal detections, and I see you as ascribing cognitive success to D, I will ascribe success or failure to your assessment of D in the same way that I ascribe success or failure to D. Following this train of thought, it seems natural to think of cognitive assessments as universal detections, in which a universal (truth) is found present in, or absent from,

---

[13] See in this connection John McDowell's attack on the views on rule-following that Crispin Wright attributes to Wittgenstein (McDowell 1984).

a particular (a universal detection), and this takes us once more to the assumption from which the sceptical argument can be launched.

But this last step is highly questionable. It ignores the crucial fact that the procedure that we have described for assessing an assessment of D connects this assessment inextricably to our assessment of D: a favourable assessment of D will necessarily produce a favourable assessment of a favourable assessment of D and an unfavourable assessment of an unfavourable assessment of D; and an unfavourable assessment of D will necessarily produce an unfavourable assessment of a favourable assessment of D, and a favourable assessment of an unfavourable assessment of D. This link between assessments of D and assessments of assessments of D is a fundamental immutable feature of the assessment procedure from which the notion of cognitive success emerges on the middle position.

This suggests that on the middle position, if we ascribe success conditions to cognitive assessments of D, these will have to be parasitic on the success conditions of D. In particular, a favourable assessment of D will have the same success conditions as D. And if we construe content in terms of success conditions, a favourable assessment of D will have the same content as D. If we translate these ideas to our real-life cognitive practice, the outcome is that if we think of the ascription of truth to a belief B1 as itself a belief B2, we have to ascribe to B2 the same content as to B1: the belief that S's belief that p is true has the same content as S's belief, namely p.[14] This still allows for S's belief that p at t and S⋆'s belief at t⋆ that S's belief that p at t is true to have a different epistemic status, but it rules out the possibility that S's belief that her current belief that p is true could have a different epistemic status from her current belief that p: CSAs must have the same epistemic status as the beliefs they assess. My current belief that V $(Bel_{ME}[p])$ tracks the truth if my current belief that p does, and I have adequate evidence for $V(Bel_{ME}[p])$ just in case I have adequate evidence for p. My belief in p and my belief in $V(Bel_{ME}[p])$ are one and the same belief.

Both the middle position and the anti-sceptical strategy that it generates would need to be developed in much more detail before they could be claimed to provide an adequate solution to the sceptical problem. This is a task for the future. My goal in this brief sketch has been to motivate the suggestion that the sceptical problem might have a metaphysical solution. If the account of knowledge that I have offered in this book is along the right lines, this might be the only solution. This would vindicate the anti-realist conception of the sceptical problem. The problem would be a symptom of the inadequacy of the metaphysical outlook that allows it to develop, and ultimately an argument not against the epistemic optimism, but against this metaphysical outlook, based on the assumption that epistemic optimism is correct.

[14] Hence the middle position would lead to an account of truth according to which ascriptions of truth have the same assertoric content as the propositions, sentences, or beliefs to which they ascribe it. Extant positions that satisfy this description include redundancy theories (Quine 1970), expressive theories (Strawson 1949), and prosentential theories (Grover, Camp, and Belnap 1975).

# Appendix

This appendix contains results in the theory of probability invoked in the main text, together with proofs based on the Kolmogorov axioms. Readers with a background in probability theory won't find anything new here. Readers without this background are encouraged to work through the proofs, which presuppose only basic familiarity with logic and arithmetic.

Let $\Gamma$ be a set of propositions closed under truth-functional composition, and let p be a function from $\Gamma$ to the set of real numbers. The *theory of probability* is the set of logical consequences of the following axioms:

Axiom 1: For every A in $\Gamma$, $p(A) \geq 0$.
Axiom 2: If A is logically true, $p(A) = 1$.
Axiom 3: For all A, B in $\Gamma$ such that A & B is logically false, $p(A \vee B) = p(A) + p(B)$.

**Theorem 1:** $p(A) + p(\sim A) = 1$.

**Proof:** Notice that, by Axiom 2, $p(A \vee \sim A) = 1$. Furthermore, since A & $\sim$A is logically false, by Axiom 3 we have that $p(A \vee \sim A) = p(A) + p(\sim A)$. It follows that $p(A) + p(\sim A) = 1$, as desired.

**Theorem 2:** $p(A \,\&\, \sim A) = 0$.

**Proof:** Notice that $(A \vee \sim A) \vee (A \,\&\, \sim A)$ is logically true. Hence, by Axiom 2, $p((A \vee \sim A) \vee (A \,\&\, \sim A)) = 1$. Now, $(A \vee \sim A) \,\&\, (A \,\&\, \sim A)$ is logically false. Hence, by Axiom 3, we have that $p((A \vee \sim A) \vee (A \,\&\, \sim A)) = p(A \vee \sim A) + p(A \,\&\, \sim A)$. Therefore, $1 = 1 + p(A \,\&\, \sim A)$, and $p(A \,\&\, \sim A) = 0$, as desired.

**Theorem 3:** If B is a logical consequence of A, then $p(A) \leq p(B)$.

**Proof:** Notice that A & $(\sim A \,\&\, B)$ is logically false. Hence, by Axiom 3, $p(A \vee (\sim A \,\&\, B)) = p(A) + p(\sim A \vee B)$. Now, since B is a logical consequence of A, we have that $B = A \vee (\sim A \,\&\, B)$. Hence $p(B) = p(A) + p(\sim A \vee B)$. But, by Axiom 1, $p(\sim A \vee B) \geq 0$. Therefore $p(A) \leq p(B)$, as desired.[1]

**Theorem 4:** $0 \leq p(A) \leq 1$.

**Proof:** $0 \leq p(A)$ follows from Axiom 1. Now, A $\vee \sim$A is a logical consequence of A. It follows by Theorem 3 that $p(A) \leq p(A \vee \sim A)$. By Axiom 2, $p(A \vee \sim A) = 1$. It follows that $p(A) \leq 1$, as desired.

**Theorem 5:** $p(A \vee B) = p(A) + p(B) - p(A \,\&\, B)$.

**Proof:** Notice that A & $(B \,\&\, \sim A)$ is logically false. Hence, by Axiom 3, $p(A \vee (B \,\&\, \sim A)) = p(A) + p(B \,\&\, \sim A)$. Since $A \vee (B \,\&\, \sim A) = A \vee B$, it follows that

---

[1] Here and throughout the Appendix I am relying on the assumption I make in the main text that propositions are individuated semantically, by their truth conditions, so that if two propositions are logically equivalent they are the same proposition.

$$(\star)\quad p(A \lor B) = p(A) + p(B \ \& \ \sim A).$$

Now, we have that B = (B & A) ∨ (B & ~A). Since (B & A) & (B & ~A) is logically false, it follows by Axiom 3 that p(B) = p(B & A) + p(B & ~A), and that p(B & ~A) = p(B) − p(B & A). Substituting in ($\star$) we have that p(A ∨ B) = p(A) + p(B) − p(B & A), as desired.

If p(B) ≠ 0, p(A | B) is defined as follows:

$$(CP)\quad p(A \mid B) = p(A \ \& \ B) \ / \ p(B).$$

All the results involving p(A | B) are subject to the implicit assumption that p(B) ≠ 0.

**Theorem 6:** p(A | B) ≥ 0.

**Proof:** By Axiom 1, p(A & B) and p(B) are non-negative. Hence, by (CP), so is p(A | B).

**Theorem 7:** p(A ∨ ~A | B) = 1.

**Proof:** Notice that (A ∨ ~A) & B = B. Hence p((A ∨ ~A) & B) / p(B) = p(B) / p(B) = 1.

**Theorem 8:** If C entails ~(A & B), then p(A ∨ B | C) = p(A | C) + p(B | C).

**Proof:** Assume that C entails ~(A & B).

p((A ∨ B) | C)
    = (by (CP))
p((A ∨ B) & C) / p(C)
    = (since (A ∨ B) & C = (A & C) ∨ (B & C))
p((A & C) ∨ (B & C)) / p(C)
    = (by Axiom 3, since it follows from our assumption that (A & C) & (B & C) is
       is logically false)
[p(A & C) + p(B & C)] / p(C)
    = (by (CP))
p(A | C) + p(B | C).

**Theorem 9:** p(A | B) + p(~A | B) = 1

**Proof:**

p(A | B) + p(~A | B)
    = (by (CP))
p(A & B) / p(B) + p(~A & B) / p(B)
    =
(p(A & B) + p(~A & B)) / p(B)
    = (by Axiom 3, since (A & B) & (~A & B) is logically false)
p((A & B) ∨ (~A & B)) / p(B)
    = (since (A & B) ∨ (~A & B) = B)
p(B) / p(B) = 1.

**Theorem 10:** $p(A \ \& \sim A \mid B) = 0$.

**Proof:**

$p(A \ \& \sim A \mid B)$
    $= $ (by (CP))
$p((A \ \& \sim A) \ \& \ B) \ / \ p(B)$
    $= $ (by Theorem 2, since $(A \ \& \sim A) \ \& \ B = A \ \& \sim A$)
$0 \ / \ p(B) = 0$.

**Theorem 11:** If $A \ \& \ C$ entails $B$, then $p(A \mid C) \leq p(B \mid C)$.

**Proof:** Assume that $A \ \& \ C$ entails $B$.

$p(A \mid C)$
    $= $ (by (CP))
$p(A \ \& \ C) \ / \ p(C)$
    $\leq$ (from Theorem 3, since from the assumption that $A \ \& \ C$ entails $B$ it follows
         that $A \ \& \ C$ entails $B \ \& \ C$)
$p(B \ \& \ C) \ / \ p(C)$
    $= $ (by (CP))
$p(B \mid C)$.

**Theorem 12:** $0 \leq p(A \mid B) \leq 1$.

**Proof:** By (CP), it will suffice to show that $0 \leq p(A \ \& \ B) \ / \ p(B) \leq 1$. For this it would suffice to show that $p(A \ \& \ B)$ and $p(B)$ are non-negative and that $p(A \ \& \ B) \leq p(B)$. The former follows from Axiom 1, and the latter from Theorem 3, since $B$ is a logical consequence of $A \ \& \ B$.

**Theorem 13:** $p(A \lor B \mid C) = p(A \mid C) + p(B \mid C) - p(A \ \& \ B \mid C)$.

**Proof:**

$p(A \lor B \mid C)$
    $= $ (since $A \lor B = A \lor (B \ \& \sim A)$)
$p(A \lor (B \ \& \sim A) \mid C)$
    $= $ (by Theorem 8, since $C$ entails $\sim(A \ \& \ (B \ \& \sim A))$)
$p(A \mid C) + p(B \ \& \sim A \mid C)$
    $= $ (by (CP))
$p(A \mid C) + (p(B \ \& \sim A \ \& \ C) \ / \ p(C))$
    $= $ (we have that $B \ \& \ C = (B \ \& \ A \ \& \ C) \lor (B \ \& \sim A \ \& \ C)$. Since $(B \ \& \ A \ \& \ C) \ \&$
        $(B \ \& \sim A \ \& \ C)$ is logically false, by Axiom 3, $p(B \ \& \ C) = p(B \ \& \ A \ \& \ C)$
        $+ \ p(B \ \& \sim A \ \& \ C)$, and $p(B \ \& \sim A \ \& \ C) = p(B \ \& \ C) - p(B \ \& \ A \ \& \ C)$)
$p(A \mid C) + (p(B \ \& \ C) - p(B \ \& \ A \ \& \ C) \ / \ p(C))$
    $= $
$p(A \mid C) + (p(B \ \& \ C) \ / \ p(C) - p(B \ \& \ A \ \& \ C) \ / \ p(C))$
    $= $ (by (CP))
$p(A \mid C) + p(B \mid C) - p(A \ \& \ B \mid C)$.

**Theorem 14 (Mixing Principle):** Let $B, A_1, \ldots, A_n$ be propositions such that $B$ entails $A_1 \vee \ldots \vee A_n$ and for all $i, j$ between 1 and n, $B$ entails $\sim(A_i \,\&\, A_j)$. Then $p(B) = p(B \mid A_1) \cdot p(A_1) + \ldots + p(B \mid A_n) \cdot p(A_n)$.

**Proof:** Assume that $A_1, \ldots, A_n$ are propositions such that $B$ entails $A_1 \vee \ldots \vee A_n$ and for all $i, j$ between 1 and n, $B$ entails $\sim(A_i \,\&\, A_j)$.

$p(B)$

$\qquad$ = (since $B = B \,\&\, (A_1 \vee \ldots \vee A_n)$, from the assumption that $B$ entails $A_1$
$\qquad\qquad \vee \ldots \vee A_n$)

$p(B \,\&\, (A_1 \vee \ldots \vee A_n))$

$\qquad$ =

$p((B \,\&\, A_1) \vee \ldots \vee (B \,\&\, A_n))$

$\qquad$ = (by $n - 1$ applications of Axiom 3, from the assumption that for all $i, j$
$\qquad\qquad$ between 1 and n, $B$ entails $\sim(A_i \,\&\, A_j)$)

$p(B \,\&\, A_1) + \ldots + p(B \,\&\, A_n)$

$\qquad$ =

$(p(B \,\&\, A_1) \,/\, p(A_1)) \cdot p(A_1) + \ldots + (p(B \,\&\, A_n) \,/\, p(A_n)) \cdot p(A_n)$

$\qquad$ = (by (CP))

$p(B \mid A_1) \cdot p(A_1) + \ldots + p(B \mid A_n) \cdot p(A_n)$.

**Theorem 15 (Bayes's Theorem):** $p(A \mid B) \,/\, p(A) = p(B \mid A) \,/\, p(B)$.

**Proof:**

$p(A \mid B) \,/\, p(A)$

$\qquad$ = (by (CP))

$p(A \,\&\, B) \,/\, [p(A) \cdot p(B)]$

$\qquad$ = (by (CP))

$p(B \mid A) \,/\, p(B)$.

**Theorem 16:** $p(A \mid B) > p(A)$ if and only if $p(B \mid A) > p(B \mid \sim A)$.

**Proof:**

$p(A \mid B) > p(A)$

$\qquad \updownarrow \qquad$ (by Bayes's Theorem)

$p(B \mid A) \cdot p(A) \,/\, p(B) > p(A)$

$\qquad \updownarrow$

$p(B \mid A) > p(B)$

$\qquad \updownarrow \qquad$ (by the Mixing Principle)

$p(B \mid A) > p(B \mid A) \cdot p(A) + p(B \mid \sim A) \cdot p(\sim A)$

$\qquad \updownarrow$

$p(B \mid A) - p(B \mid A) \cdot p(A) > p(B \mid \sim A) \cdot p(\sim A)$

$\qquad \updownarrow$

$p(B \mid A) \cdot [1 - p(A)] > p(B \mid \sim A) \cdot p(\sim A)$

$\qquad \updownarrow \qquad$ (Theorem 1)

$p(B \mid A) \cdot p(\sim A) > p(B \mid \sim A) \cdot p(\sim A)$

$\qquad \updownarrow$

$p(B \mid A) > p(B \mid \sim A)$.

**Theorem 17:** Let $\Gamma$ be a set of logically independent propositions $A_1, \ldots, A_n$, and let $\Gamma^\star$ be the closure of $\Gamma$ under truth-functional composition. Let $\Delta$ be the set of $(2^n)$ propositions of the form $A_1{}^\star \& \ldots \& A_n{}^\star$, where $A_i{}^\star$ denotes either $A_i$ or $\sim A_i$. Let f be a function from $\Delta$ to the set of non-negative real numbers, such that the sum of the images of all the elements of $\Delta$ equals 1. Then f can be extended to a function p from $\Gamma^\star$ to the set of real numbers that satisfies the axioms of the theory of probability.

**Proof:** We define p as follows:

$p(A \& \sim A) = 0$

For every disjunction of distinct elements of $\Delta$, $C_1 \vee \ldots \vee C_m$, let $p(C_1 \vee \ldots \vee C_m) = f(C_1)$
$+ \ldots + f(C_m)$

Notice first that p is a function, since disjunctions of elements of $\Delta$ with different disjuncts are different propositions.

Also, the domain of p is the whole of $\Delta$, by the familiar logical fact that every element of $\Gamma^\star$ other than $A \& \sim A$ is a disjunction of elements of $\Delta$.[2]

Finally, we can easily verify that p satisfies the axioms of the theory of probability.

Axiom 1 is trivially satisfied, since the image under p of each element of $\Gamma^\star$ is either 0 or the sum of non-negative real numbers.

Axiom 2 is also satisfied, since the disjunction of all the elements of $\Delta$ is logically true, and their images under f add up to one.

Finally, for Axiom 3, let A, B be two elements of $\Gamma^\star$ such that $A \& B$ is logically false. We know that A and B are disjunctions $A_1 \vee \ldots \vee A_p$ and $B_1 \vee \ldots \vee B_q$ of distinct elements of $\Delta$. Then $A \vee B = A_1 \vee \ldots \vee A_p \vee B_1 \vee \ldots \vee B_q$.

All the disjuncts of A are distinct from one another and all the disjuncts of B are distinct from one another. Furthermore, since $A \& B$ is logically false, all the disjuncts of A are distinct from all the disjuncts of B. Hence all the disjuncts of $A_1 \vee \ldots \vee A_p \vee B_1 \vee \ldots \vee B_q$ are distinct.

Then, by the definition of p, we have that

$$p(A_1 \vee \ldots \vee A_p \vee B_1 \vee \ldots \vee B_q) = f(A_1) + \ldots + f(A_p) + f(B_1) + \ldots + f(B_q).$$

But we also have that

$$p(A_1 \vee \ldots \vee A_p) = f(A_1) + \ldots + f(A_p)$$

and

$$p(B_1 \vee \ldots \vee B_q) = f(B_1) + \ldots + f(B_q).$$

It follows that $p(A \vee B) = p(A) + p(B)$, as desired.

**Definitions:**

$$PD(H, E) = p(H \mid E) - p(H)$$
$$PR(H, E) = p(H \mid E) \,/\, p(H)$$
$$LD(H, E) = p(E \mid H) - p(E \mid \sim H)$$
$$LR(H, E) = p(E \mid H) \,/\, p(E \mid \sim H).$$

---

[2] See, e.g., the proof of the Expressive Completeness Theorem in (Zalabardo 2000a: 65–8).

**Theorem 18:** PR(H, E) < PR(H$\star$, E) iff LR(H, E) < LR(H$\star$, E) is not a theorem of the theory of probability.

**Proof (Joyce 2003):** We describe a model of the theory of probability in which, for some propositions H, H$\star$, E, PR(H, E) > PR(H$\star$, E), LR(H, E) < LR(H$\star$, E).

Let H, H$\star$, E be three propositions, and let $\Gamma$ be the closure under truth-functional combination of the set {H, H$\star$, E}. Let p be a function from $\Gamma$ to the set of real numbers that satisfies the axioms of the theory of probability and yields the following values for the conjunctions with E or $\sim$E, H or $\sim$H, and H$\star$ or $\sim$H$\star$ as conjuncts:

|       | H & H$\star$ | H & $\sim$H$\star$ | $\sim$H & H$\star$ | $\sim$H & $\sim$H$\star$ |
|-------|------|-------|-------|-------|
| E     | 0.12  | 0.001 | 0.378 | 0.001 |
| $\sim$E | 0.003 | 0.005 | 0.2   | 0.292 |

By Theorem 17, we know that this function exists (notice that from the fact that all the probabilities ascribed in this table are non-zero it follows that E, H, and H$\star$ are logically independent).

We show first that p(H | E) / p(H) > p(H$\star$ | E) / p(H$\star$).

On the one hand, we have:

p(H | E)/p(H)

=

$$\frac{p(H \ \& \ E)/p(E)}{p(H)}$$

=

$$\frac{p(H \ \& \ E)}{p(E) \cdot p(H)}$$

=

$$\frac{p(E \ \& \ H \ \& \ H\star) + p(E \ \& \ H \ \& \ \sim H\star)}{[p(E \ \& \ H \ \& \ H\star) + p(E \ \& \ H \ \& \ \sim H\star) + p(E \ \& \ \sim H \ \& \ H\star) + p(E \ \& \ \sim H \ \& \ \sim H\star)] \cdot [p(E \ \& \ H \ \& \ H\star) + p(E \ \& \ H \ \& \ \sim H\star) + p(\sim E \ \& \ H \ \& \ H\star) + p(\sim E \ \& \ H \ \& \ \sim H\star)]}$$

$\approx 1.88$

On the other hand we have:

p(H$\star$ | E)/p(H$\star$)

=

$$\frac{p(H\star \ \& \ E)/p(E)}{p(H\star)}$$

=

$$\frac{p(H\star \ \& \ E)}{p(E) \cdot p(H\star)}$$

=

$$\frac{p(E \ \& \ H \ \& \ H\star) + p(E \ \& \ \sim H \ \& \ H\star)}{[p(E \ \& \ H \ \& \ H\star) + p(E \ \& \ H \ \& \ \sim H\star) + p(E \ \& \ \sim H \ \& \ H\star) + p(E \ \& \ \sim H \ \& \ \sim H\star)] \cdot [p(E \ \& \ H \ \& \ H\star) + p(E \ \& \ \sim H \ \& \ H\star) + p(\sim E \ \& \ H \ \& \ H\star) + p(\sim E \ \& \ \sim H \ \& \ H\star)]}$$

$\approx 1.42$

We show now that $p(E \mid H) / p(E \mid \sim H) < p(E \mid H^\star) / p(E \mid \sim H^\star)$.

On the one hand,

$$p(E \mid H)/p(E \mid \sim H)$$

$$=$$

$$\frac{p(E \& H)/p(H)}{p(E \& \sim H)/p(\sim H)}$$

$$=$$

$$\frac{\left(\dfrac{p(E \& H \& H^\star) + p(E \& H \& \sim H^\star)}{p(E \& H \& H^\star) + p(E \& H \& \sim H^\star) + p(\sim E \& H \& H^\star) + p(\sim E \& H \& \sim H^\star)}\right)}{\left(\dfrac{p(E \& \sim H \& H^\star) + p(E \& \sim H \& \sim H^\star)}{p(E \& \sim H \& H^\star) + p(E \& \sim H \& \sim H^\star) + p(\sim E \& \sim H \& H^\star) + p(\sim E \& \sim H \& \sim H^\star)}\right)}$$

$$\approx 2.16$$

On the other hand we have

$$p(E \mid H^\star)/p(E \mid \sim H^\star)$$

$$=$$

$$\frac{p(E \& H^\star)/p(H^\star)}{p(E \& \sim H^\star)/p(\sim H^\star)}$$

$$=$$

$$\frac{\left(\dfrac{p(E \& H \& H^\star) + p(E \& \sim H \& H^\star)}{p(E \& H \& H^\star) + p(E \& \sim H \& H^\star) + p(\sim E \& H \& H^\star) + p(\sim E \& \sim H \& H^\star)}\right)}{\left(\dfrac{p(E \& H \& \sim H^\star) + p(E \& \sim H \& \sim H^\star)}{p(E \& H \& \sim H^\star) + p(E \& \sim H \& \sim H^\star) + p(\sim E \& H \& \sim H^\star) + p(\sim E \& \sim H \& \sim H^\star)}\right)}$$

$$\approx 106.2$$

**Theorem 19:** $PD(H, E) < PD(H^\star, E)$ iff $PR(H, E) < PR(H^\star, E)$ is not a theorem of the theory of probability.

**Proof (Joyce 2003):** We describe a model of the theory of probability such that, for some propositions H, H$^\star$, E, $PD(H, E) < PD(H^\star, E)$, $PR(H, E) > PR(H^\star, E)$.

Let H, H$^\star$, E be three propositions, and let $\Gamma$ be the closure under truth-functional combination of the set {H, H$^\star$, E}. Let p be a function from $\Gamma$ to the set of real numbers that satisfies the axioms of the theory of probability and yields the following values for the conjunctions with E or $\sim$E, H or $\sim$H, and H$^\star$ or $\sim$H$^\star$ as conjuncts:

|          | H & H$^\star$ | H & $\sim$H$^\star$ | $\sim$H & H$^\star$ | $\sim$H & $\sim$H$^\star$ |
|----------|---------------|---------------------|---------------------|--------------------------|
| E        | 0.007         | 0.02                | 0.184               | 0.004                    |
| $\sim$E  | 0.001         | 0.002               | 0.08                | 0.702                    |

By Theorem 17, we know that this function exists.

We show first that $p(H \mid E) - p(H) < p(H^\star \mid E) - p(H^\star)$.

On the one hand we have:

$p(H \mid E) - p(H) = [p(H \& E) / p(E)] - p(H) =$

$$\left( \frac{p(E \& H \& H^\star) + p(E \& H \& {\sim}H^\star)}{p(E \& H \& H^\star) + p(E \& H \& {\sim}H^\star) + p(E \& {\sim}H \& H^\star) + p(E \& {\sim}H \& {\sim}H^\star)} \right)$$

$- [p(E \& H \& H^\star) + p(E \& H \& {\sim}H^\star) + p({\sim}E \& H \& H^\star) + p({\sim}E \& H \& {\sim}H^\star)]$

$\approx 0.09$

On the other hand we have:

$p(H^\star \mid E) - p(H^\star) = [p(H^\star \& E)/p(E)] - p(H^\star) =$

$$\left( \frac{p(E \& H \& H^\star) + p(E \& {\sim}H \& H^\star)}{p(E \& H \& H^\star) + p(E \& H \& {\sim}H^\star) + p(E \& {\sim}H \& H^\star) + p(E \& {\sim}H \& {\sim}H^\star)} \right)$$

$- [p(E \& H \& H^\star) + p(E \& {\sim}H \& H^\star) + p({\sim}E \& H \& H^\star) + p({\sim}E \& {\sim}H \& H^\star)]$

$\approx 0.61$

We now show that $p(H \mid E) / p(H) > p(H^\star \mid E) / p(H^\star)$.

On the one hand we have:

$p(H \mid E) / p(H)$

$=$

$\dfrac{p(H \& E) / p(E)}{p(H)}$

$=$

$\dfrac{p(H \& E)}{p(E) \cdot p(H)}$

$=$

$$\frac{p(E \& H \& H^\star) + p(E \& H \& {\sim}H^\star)}{[p(E \& H \& H^\star) + p(E \& H \& {\sim}H^\star) + p(E \& {\sim}H \& H^\star) + p(E \& {\sim}H \& {\sim}H^\star)] \cdot [p(E \& H \& H^\star) + p(E \& H \& {\sim}H^\star) + p({\sim}E \& H \& H^\star) + p({\sim}E \& H \& {\sim}H^\star)]}$$

$\approx 4.19$

On the other hand we have:

$p(H^\star \mid E) / p(H^\star)$

$=$

$\dfrac{p(H^\star \& E) / p(E)}{p(H^\star)}$

$=$

$\dfrac{p(H^\star \& E)}{p(E) \cdot p(H^\star)}$

$=$

$$\frac{p(E \& H \& H^\star) + p(E \& {\sim}H \& H^\star)}{[p(E \& H \& H^\star) + p(E \& H \& {\sim}H^\star) + p(E \& {\sim}H \& H^\star) + p(E \& {\sim}H \& {\sim}H^\star)] \cdot [p(E \& H \& H^\star) + p(E \& {\sim}H \& H^\star) + p({\sim}E \& H \& H^\star) + p({\sim}E \& {\sim}H \& H^\star)]}$$

$\approx 3.27$

**Theorem 20:** LD(H, E) < LD(H★, E) iff LR(H, E) < LR(H★, E) is not a theorem of the theory of probability.

**Proof:** We describe model of the theory of probability such that, for some propositions H, H★, E, LD(H, E) > LD(H★, E), LR(H, E) < LR(H★, E).

Let H, H★, E be three propositions, and let $\Gamma$ be the closure under truth-functional combination of the set {H, H★, E}. Let p be a function from $\Gamma$ to the set of real numbers that satisfies the axioms of the theory of probability and yields the following values for the conjunctions with E or ~E, H or ~H, and H★ or ~H★ as conjuncts:

|      | H & H★ | H & ~H★ | ~H & H★ | ~H & ~H★ |
|------|--------|---------|---------|----------|
| E    | 0.09   | 0.01    | 0.285   | 0.015    |
| ~E   | 1/35   | 1/70    | 361/840 | 107/840  |

By Theorem 17, we know that this function exists.

We show first that $p(E \mid H) - p(E \mid \sim H) > p(E \mid H★) - p(E \mid \sim H★)$.

On the one hand we have:

$$p(E|H) - p(E|\sim H)$$
$$=$$
$$[p(E \text{ \& } H)/p(H)] - [p(E \text{ \& } \sim H)/p(\sim H)]$$
$$=$$

$$\frac{p(E \text{ \& } H \text{ \& } H★) + p(E \text{ \& } H \text{ \& } \sim H★)}{p(E \text{ \& } H \text{ \& } H★) + p(E \text{ \& } H \text{ \& } \sim H★) + p(\sim E \text{ \& } H \text{ \& } H★) + p(\sim E \text{ \& } H \text{ \& } \sim H★)}$$
$$- \frac{p(E \text{ \& } \sim H \text{ \& } H★) + p(E \text{ \& } \sim H \text{ \& } \sim H★)}{p(E \text{ \& } \sim H \text{ \& } H★) + p(E \text{ \& } \sim H \text{ \& } \sim H★) + p(\sim E \text{ \& } \sim H \text{ \& } H★) + p(\sim E \text{ \& } \sim H \text{ \& } \sim H★)}$$
$$= 0.7 - 0.35 = 0.35$$

On the other hand we have

$$p(E \mid H★) - p(E \mid \sim H★)$$
$$=$$
$$[p(E \text{ \& } H★)/p(H★)] - [p(E \text{ \& } \sim H★)/p(\sim H★)]$$
$$=$$

$$\frac{p(E \text{ \& } H \text{ \& } H★) + p(E \text{ \& } \sim H \text{ \& } H★)}{p(E \text{ \& } H \text{ \& } H★) + p(E \text{ \& } \sim H \text{ \& } H★) + p(\sim E \text{ \& } H \text{ \& } H★) + p(\sim E \text{ \& } \sim H \text{ \& } H★)}$$
$$- \frac{p(E \text{ \& } H \text{ \& } \sim H★) + p(E \text{ \& } \sim H \text{ \& } \sim H★)}{p(E \text{ \& } H \text{ \& } \sim H★) + p(E \text{ \& } \sim H \text{ \& } \sim H★) + p(\sim E \text{ \& } H \text{ \& } \sim H★) + p(\sim E \text{ \& } \sim H \text{ \& } \sim H★)}$$
$$= 0.45 - 0.15 = 0.3$$

We show now that $p(E \mid H) / p(E \mid \sim H) < p(E \mid H★) / p(E \mid \sim H★)$.

On the one hand

$$p(E \mid H) / p(E \mid \sim H)$$

$$=$$

$$\frac{p(E \& H) / p(H)}{p(E \& \sim H) / p(\sim H)}$$

$$=$$

$$\frac{\left( \dfrac{p(E \& H \& H\star) + p(E \& H \& \sim H\star)}{p(E \& H \& H\star) + p(E \& H \& \sim H\star) + p(\sim E \& H \& H\star) + p(\sim E \& H \& \sim H\star)} \right)}{\left( \dfrac{p(E \& \sim H \& H\star) + p(E \& \sim H \& \sim H\star)}{p(E \& \sim H \& H\star) + p(E \& \sim H \& \sim H\star) + p(\sim E \& \sim H \& H\star) + p(\sim E \& \sim H \& \sim H\star)} \right)}$$

$$= 0.7/0.35 = 2$$

On the other hand we have

$$p(E \mid H\star) / p(E \mid \sim H\star)$$

$$=$$

$$\frac{p(E \& H\star) / p(H\star)}{p(E \& \sim H\star) / p(\sim H\star)}$$

$$=$$

$$\frac{\left( \dfrac{p(E \& H \& H\star) + p(E \& \sim H \& H\star)}{p(E \& H \& H\star) + p(E \& \sim H \& H\star) + p(\sim E \& H \& H\star) + p(\sim E \& \sim H \& H\star)} \right)}{\left( \dfrac{p(E \& H \& \sim H\star) + p(E \& \sim H \& \sim H\star)}{p(E \& H \& \sim H\star) + p(E \& \sim H \& \sim H\star) + p(\sim E \& H \& \sim H\star) + p(\sim E \& \sim H \& \sim H\star)} \right)}$$

$$= 0.45/0.15 = 3$$

**Theorem 21:** $PD(H, E) < PD(H, E\star)$ iff $PR(H, E) < PR(H, E\star)$ iff $LR(H, E) < LR(H, E\star)$ iff $p(H \mid E) < p(H \mid E\star)$.

**Proof:** $PD(H, E) < PD(H, E\star)$ iff $PR(H, E) < PR(H, E\star)$ iff $p(H \mid E) < p(H \mid E\star)$ is trivial, since $p(H \mid E) - p(H) < p(H \mid E\star) - p(H)$ iff $p(H \mid E) < p(H \mid E\star)$ iff $p(H \mid E) / p(H) < p(H \mid E\star) / p(H)$.

We show that $LR(H, E) < LR(H, E\star)$ if and only if $p(H \mid E) < p(H \mid E\star)$ with the following argument, adapted from (Iranzo and Martínez de Lejarza 2010):

$$\frac{p(E \mid H)}{p(E \mid \sim H)} < \frac{p(E^\star \mid H)}{p(E^\star \mid \sim H)}$$

$$\updownarrow \qquad \qquad \text{(By Bayes's Theorem)}$$

$$\frac{p(H \mid E) \cdot p(E) / p(H)}{p(\sim H \mid E) \cdot p(E) / p(\sim H)} < \frac{p(H \mid E^\star) \cdot p(E^\star) / p(H)}{p(\sim H \mid E^\star) \cdot p(E^\star) / p(\sim H)}$$

$$\updownarrow \qquad \qquad \text{(Simplifying)}$$

$$\frac{p(H \mid E)}{p(\sim H \mid E)} < \frac{p(H \mid E^\star)}{p(\sim H \mid E^\star)}$$

$$\updownarrow \qquad \qquad \text{(Theorem 9)}$$

$$\frac{p(H \mid E)}{1 - p(H \mid E)} < \frac{p(H \mid E^\star)}{1 - p(H \mid E^\star)}$$

$$\updownarrow$$

$$p(H \mid E) \cdot (1 - p(H \mid E^\star)) < p(H \mid E^\star) \cdot (1 - p(H \mid E))$$

$$\updownarrow$$

$$p(H \mid E) - (p(H \mid E) \cdot p(H \mid E^\star)) < p(H \mid E^\star) - (p(H \mid E^\star) \cdot p(H \mid E))$$

$$\updownarrow$$

$$p(H \mid E) < p(H \mid E^\star).$$

**Theorem 22:** $p(H \mid E) > p(H \mid E^\star)$ iff $p(E \mid H) - p(E \mid \sim H) > p(E^\star \mid H) - p(E^\star \mid \sim H)$ is not a theorem of the theory of probability.

**Proof (Fitelson 2001b: 72–4):** To show this, we describe a model of the theory of probability that doesn't satisfy the principle.

Let E, $E^\star$, and H be three propositions, and let $\Gamma$ be the closure under truth-functional combination of $\{E, E^\star, H\}$. Let p be a function from $\Gamma$ to the set of real numbers that satisfies the axioms of the theory of probability and yields the following values for the conjunctions with H or $\sim$H, E or $\sim$E, and $E^\star$ or $\sim E^\star$ as conjuncts:

| | E & $E^\star$ | E & $\sim E^\star$ | $\sim$E & $E^\star$ | $\sim$E & $\sim E^\star$ |
|---|---|---|---|---|
| H | 1/100 | 1/100 | 1/25 | 1/500 |
| $\sim$H | 1/1000 | 1/1000 | 1/200 | 931/1000 |

By Theorem 17, we know that this function exists.

We show that $p(H \mid E) > p(H \mid E^\star)$, $p(E \mid H) - p(E \mid \sim H) < p(E^\star \mid H) - p(E^\star \mid \sim H)$.

We show first that $p(H \mid E) > p(H \mid E^\star)$.

On the one hand, we have:

$$p(H \mid E)$$
$$=$$
$$p(H \& E) / p(E)$$
$$=$$
$$\frac{p(E \& E^\star \& H) + p(E \& \sim E^\star \& H)}{p(E \& E^\star \& H) + p(E \& \sim E^\star \& H) + p(E \& E^\star \& \sim H) + p(E \& \sim E^\star \& \sim H)}$$
$$= 10 / 11 \approx 0.909.$$

On the other hand we have that:

$p(H \mid E^\star)$

$=$

$p(H \& E^\star) / p(E^\star)$

$=$

$$\frac{p(E \& E^\star \& H) + p(\sim E \& E^\star \& H)}{p(E \& E^\star \& H) + p(\sim E \& E^\star \& H) + p(E \& E^\star \& \sim H) + p(\sim E \& E^\star \& \sim H)}$$

$= 25 / 28 \approx 0.893.$

We show now that $p(E \mid H) - p(E \mid \sim H) < p(E^\star \mid H) - p(E^\star \mid \sim H)$.

On the one hand we have:

$p(E \mid H) - p(E \mid \sim H) = p(E \& H) / p(H) - p(E \& \sim H) / p(\sim H) =$

$$\frac{p(E \& E^\star \& H) + p(E \& \sim E^\star \& H)}{p(E \& E^\star \& H) + p(\sim E \& E^\star \& H) + p(E \& \sim E^\star \& H) + p(\sim E \& \sim E^\star \& H)}$$

$$-\frac{p(E \& E^\star \& \sim H) + p(E \& \sim E^\star \& \sim H)}{p(E \& E^\star \& \sim H) + p(\sim E \& E^\star \& \sim H) + p(E \& \sim E^\star \& \sim H) + p(\sim E \& \sim E^\star \& \sim H)}$$

$= 59/279 \approx 0.21.$

On the other hand we have that:

$p(E^\star \mid H) - p(E^\star \mid \sim H) = p(E^\star \& H) / p(H) - p(E^\star \& \sim H) / p(\sim H) =$

$$\frac{p(E \& E^\star \& H) + p(\sim E \& E^\star \& H)}{p(E \& E^\star \& H) + p(\sim E \& E^\star \& H) + p(E \& \sim E^\star \& H) + p(\sim E \& \sim E^\star \& H)}$$

$$-\frac{p(E \& E^\star \& \sim H) + p(\sim E \& E^\star \& \sim H)}{p(E \& E^\star \& \sim H) + p(\sim E \& E^\star \& \sim H) + p(E \& \sim E^\star \& \sim H) + p(\sim E \& \sim E^\star \& \sim H)}$$

$= 44 / 93 \approx 0.47.$

**Theorem 23:** $PR(H, E) > PR(H^\star, E)$ and $LR(H, E) < LR(H^\star, E)$ if and only if $1 < p(E \mid H) / p(E \mid H^\star) < p(E \mid \sim H) / p(E \mid \sim H^\star)$.

**Proof:** We show first that $PR(H, E) > PR(H^\star, E)$ if and only if $p(E \mid H) / p(E \mid H^\star) > 1$.

$$p(H \mid E) / p(H) > p(H^\star \mid E)/p(H^\star)$$
$$\updownarrow \quad \text{(by Bayes's Theorem)}$$
$$p(E \mid H) / p(E) > p(E \mid H^\star) / p(E)$$
$$\updownarrow$$
$$p(E \mid H) > p(E \mid H^\star)$$
$$\updownarrow$$
$$p(E \mid H) / p(E \mid H^\star) > 1.$$

We show now that $LR(H, E) < LR(H^\star, E)$ if and only if $p(E \mid H) / p(E \mid H^\star) < p(E \mid \sim H) / p(E \mid \sim H^\star)$.

$$p(E \mid H) \,/\, p(E \mid \sim H) \;<\; p(E \mid H\star) \,/\, p(E \mid \sim H\star)$$
$$\updownarrow$$
$$p(E \mid H) \cdot p(E \mid \sim H\star) \;<\; p(E \mid H\star) \cdot p(E \mid \sim H)$$
$$\updownarrow$$
$$p(E \mid H) \,/\, p(E \mid H\star) \;<\; p(E \mid \sim H) \,/\, p(E \mid \sim H\star).$$

**Theorem 24:** If $p(E \mid H) \neq p(E \mid \sim H)$ and $p(E \mid H) = p(E \mid H\star)$, then $p(E \mid \sim H) = p(E \mid \sim H\star)$ if and only if $p(H) = p(H\star)$.

**Proof:** Assume $p(E \mid H) \neq p(E \mid \sim H)$, $p(E \mid H) = p(E \mid H\star)$.

Suppose first $p(H) = p(H\star)$. By the mixing principle we have: $p(E) = p(E \mid H) \cdot p(H) + p(E \mid \sim H) \cdot p(\sim H)$. It follows that $p(E \mid \sim H) = [p(E) - p(E \mid H) \cdot p(H)] \,/\, p(\sim H)$. In the same way we obtain that $p(E \mid \sim H\star) = [p(E) - p(E \mid H\star) \cdot p(H\star)] \,/\, p(\sim H\star)$. From our assumptions it follows that $[p(E) - p(E \mid H) \cdot p(H)] \,/\, p(\sim H) = [p(E) - p(E \mid H\star) \cdot p(H\star)] \,/\, p(\sim H\star)$. Therefore $p(E \mid \sim H) = p(E \mid \sim H\star)$.

Assume now $p(E \mid \sim H) = p(E \mid \sim H\star)$. We argue as follows:

$$p(E \mid H) \cdot p(H) + p(E \mid \sim H) \cdot p(\sim H) = p(E \mid H\star) \cdot p(H\star) + p(E \mid \sim H\star) \cdot p(\sim H\star)$$
$$\downarrow \qquad \text{(Theorem 1)}$$
$$p(E \mid H) \cdot p(H) + p(E \mid \sim H) \cdot (1 - p(\sim H)) = p(E \mid H\star) \cdot p(H\star) + p(E \mid \sim H\star) \cdot (1 - p(\sim H\star))$$
$$\downarrow$$
$$p(E \mid H) \cdot p(H) + p(E \mid \sim H) - p(E \mid \sim H) \cdot p(H) = p(E \mid H\star) \cdot p(H\star) + p(E \mid \sim H\star) - p(E \mid \sim H\star) \cdot p(H\star)$$
$$\downarrow$$
$$[p(E \mid H) - p(E \mid \sim H)] \cdot p(H) + p(E \mid \sim H) = [p(E \mid H\star) - p(E \mid \sim H\star)] \cdot p(H\star) + p(E \mid \sim H\star)$$
$$\downarrow \qquad (\text{Since } p(E \mid \sim H)) = p(E \mid \sim H\star))$$
$$[p(E \mid H) - p(E \mid \sim H)] \cdot p(H) = [p(E \mid H\star) - p(E \mid \sim H\star)] \cdot p(H\star)$$
$$\downarrow \qquad (\text{Since } p(E \mid H) - p(E \mid \sim H) = p(E \mid H\star) - p(E \mid \sim H\star) \neq 0)$$
$$p(H) = p(H\star)$$

**Theorem 25:** If $p(H) < 1$, then for every n, $LR(H, E) > n$ if and only if $p(E \,\&\, \sim H) < [1 - p(H) \,/\, (n \cdot p(H))] \cdot p(E \,\&\, H)$.

**Proof:** Assume $p(H) < 1$. We argue as follows:

$$p(E \mid H) \,/\, p(E \mid \sim H) > n$$
$$\updownarrow$$
$$\frac{\dfrac{p(E \,\&\, H)}{p(H)}}{\dfrac{p(E \,\&\, \sim H)}{p(\sim H)}} > n$$
$$\updownarrow$$
$$\frac{p(E \,\&\, H) \cdot p(\sim H)}{p(E \,\&\, \sim H) \cdot p(H)} > n$$
$$\updownarrow$$
$$\frac{1 - p(H)}{n \cdot p(H)} \cdot p(E \,\&\, H) > p(E \,\&\, \sim H)$$

**Theorem 26:** For all m, n < 1, if p(E) = m, then p(H | E) > n if and only if p(H & E) > m · n.
**Proof:** Assume p(E) = m. We reason as follows:

$$p(H \mid E) > n$$
$$\updownarrow \qquad \text{(by CP)}$$
$$p(H \& E) \ / \ p(E) > n$$
$$\updownarrow$$
$$p(H \& E) > n \cdot p(E)$$
$$\updownarrow$$
$$p(H \& E) > m \cdot n$$

**Theorem 27:** If p(A | B) > p(A | C) and B & C is logically false, then p(A | B) > p(A | C ∨ B).

**Proof:**

$$p(A \mid B) > p(A \mid C)$$
$$\downarrow \qquad\qquad \text{by (CP)}$$
$$\frac{p(A \& B)}{p(B)} > \frac{p(A \& C)}{p(C)}$$
$$\downarrow$$
$$p(A \& B) \cdot p(C) > p(A \& C) \cdot p(B)$$
$$\downarrow$$
$$p(A \& B) \cdot p(C) + p(A \& B) \cdot p(B) > p(A \& C) \cdot p(B) + p(A \& B) \cdot p(B)$$
$$\downarrow$$
$$p(A \& B) \cdot (p(C) + p(B)) > p(B) \cdot (p(A \& C) + p(A \& B))$$
$$\downarrow$$
$$\frac{p(A \& B) \cdot (p(C) + p(B))}{p(B) \cdot (p(C) + p(B))} > \frac{p(B) \cdot (p(A \& C) + p(A \& B))}{p(B) \cdot (p(C) + p(B))}$$
$$\downarrow$$
$$\frac{p(A \& B)}{p(B)} > \frac{p(A \& C) + p(A \& B)}{p(C) + p(B)}$$
$$\downarrow \qquad\qquad \text{(by Axiom 3, since C \& B is logically false)}$$
$$\frac{p(A \& B)}{p(B)} > \frac{p((A \& C) \vee (A \& B))}{p(C) + p(B)}$$
$$\downarrow$$
$$\frac{p(A \& B)}{p(B)} > \frac{p(A \& (C \vee B))}{p(C) + p(B)}$$
$$\downarrow \qquad\qquad \text{(by Axiom 3, since C \& B is logically false)}$$
$$\frac{p(A \& B)}{p(B)} > \frac{p(A \& (C \vee B))}{p(C \vee B)}$$
$$\downarrow \qquad\qquad \text{by (CP)}$$
$$p(A \mid B) > p(A \mid B \vee C).$$

**Theorem 28:** If $C_1 \vee \ldots \vee C_n$ is logically true and $C_1, \ldots, C_n$ are pairwise inconsistent, then
$p(A \mid B) = p(A \mid B \,\&\, C_1) \cdot p(C_1 \mid B) + \ldots + p(A \mid B \,\&\, C_n) \cdot p(C_n \mid B)$.

**Proof:**

$$p(A \mid B)$$

$$= \quad \text{(by CP)}$$

$$\frac{p(A \,\&\, B)}{p(B)}$$

$$= \quad (\text{since } C_1 \vee \ldots \vee C_n \text{ is logically true})$$

$$\frac{p\big(A \,\&\, B \,\&\, (C_1 \vee \ldots \vee C_n)\big)}{p(B)}$$

$$= \quad \text{(propositional logic)}$$

$$\frac{p\big((A \,\&\, B \,\&\, C_1) \vee \ldots \vee (A \,\&\, B \,\&\, C_n)\big)}{p(B)}$$

$$= \quad (\text{by Axiom 3, since } C_1, \ldots, C_n \text{ are pairwise inconsistent})$$

$$\frac{p(A \,\&\, B \,\&\, C_1) + \cdots + p(A \,\&\, B \,\&\, C_n)}{p(B)}$$

$$= \quad \text{(arithmetic)}$$

$$\frac{\dfrac{p(A \,\&\, B \,\&\, C_1)}{p(B \,\&\, C_1)} \cdot p(B \,\&\, C_1) + \cdots + \dfrac{p(A \,\&\, B \,\&\, C_n)}{p(B \,\&\, C_n)} \cdot p(B \,\&\, C_n)}{p(B)}$$

$$= \quad \text{(by CP)}$$

$$\frac{p(A \mid B \,\&\, C_1) \cdot p(B \,\&\, C_1) + \cdots + p(A \mid B \,\&\, C_n) \cdot p(B \,\&\, C_n)}{p(B)}$$

$$= \quad \text{(arithmetic)}$$

$$p(A \mid B \,\&\, C_1) \cdot \frac{p(B \,\&\, C_1)}{p(B)} + \cdots + p(A \mid B \,\&\, C_n) \cdot \frac{p(B \,\&\, C_n)}{p(B)}$$

$$= \quad \text{(by CP)}$$

$$p(A \mid B \,\&\, C_1) \cdot p(C_1 \mid B) + \cdots + p(A \mid B \,\&\, C_n) \cdot p(C_n \mid B).$$

**Theorem 29:** If $p(A_1 \mid B) = n \cdot p(A_2 \mid B)$ and $p(A_1 \mid \sim B) = n \cdot p(A_2 \mid \sim B)$, then $p(A_1) = n \cdot p(A_2)$.

**Proof:** Assume $p(A_1 \mid B) = n \cdot p(A_2 \mid B)$ and $p(A_1 \mid \sim B) = n \cdot p(A_2 \mid \sim B)$. Then we have:

$$p(A_1)$$

$$= \quad \text{(Mixing)}$$

$$p(A_1 \mid B) \cdot p(B) + p(A_1 \mid \sim B) \cdot p(\sim B)$$

$$= \quad \text{(From our assumption)}$$

$$n \cdot p(A_2 \mid B) \cdot p(B) + n \cdot p(A_2 \mid \sim B) \cdot p(\sim B)$$

$$=$$

$$n \cdot [p(A_2 \mid B) \cdot p(B) + p(A_2 \mid \sim B) \cdot p(\sim B)]$$

$$= \quad \text{(Mixing)}$$

$$n \cdot p(A_2).$$

**Theorem 30:** $LR(A, B) = LR(A, B\star)$ if and only if $p(A \mid B) = p(A \mid B\star)$.

**Proof:** (see the proof of Theorem 21)

$$\frac{p(B \mid A)}{p(B \mid \sim A)} = \frac{p(B\star \mid A)}{p(B\star \mid \sim A)}$$

$\updownarrow$           (By Bayes's Theorem)

$$\frac{p(A \mid B) \cdot \dfrac{p(B)}{p(A)}}{p(\sim A \mid B) \cdot \dfrac{p(B)}{p(\sim A)}} = \frac{p(A \mid B^{*}) \cdot \dfrac{p(B^{*})}{p(A)}}{p(\sim A \mid B^{*}) \cdot \dfrac{p(B^{*})}{p(\sim A)}}$$

$\updownarrow$           (Simplifying)

$$\frac{p(A \mid B)}{p(\sim A \mid B)} = \frac{p(A \mid B^{*})}{p(\sim A \mid B^{*})}$$

$\updownarrow$           (Theorem 9)

$$\frac{p(A \mid B)}{1 - p(A \mid B)} = \frac{p(A \mid B^{*})}{1 - p(A \mid B^{*})}$$

$\updownarrow$

$$p(A \mid B) \cdot (1 - p(A \mid B\star)) = p(A \mid B\star) \cdot (1 - p(A \mid B))$$

$\updownarrow$

$$p(A \mid B) - (p(A \mid B) \cdot p(A \mid B\star)) = p(A \mid B\star) - (p(A \mid B\star) \cdot p(A \mid B))$$

$\updownarrow$

$$p(A \mid B) = p(A \mid B\star).$$

**Theorem 31:** If $p(A) = p(A\star)$, then $LR(A, B) = LR(A\star, B\star)$ if and only if $p(A \mid B) = p(A\star \mid B\star)$.

**Proof:** Use the same argument as in the previous theorem.

**Theorem 32:** If $p(A \mid B) = p(B \mid C) = 1$, then $p(A \mid C) = 1$.

**Proof:**

$p(A \mid B) = p(B \mid C) = 1$

   $\downarrow$  (CP)

$p(A \& B) / p(B) = p(B \& C) / p(C) = 1$

   $\downarrow$

$p(A \& B) = p(B)$ and $p(B \& C) = p(C)$

   $\downarrow$  (since $X = X \& (Y \lor \sim Y) = (X \& Y) \lor (X \& \sim Y)$, we have, by Axiom 3, that
         $p(X) = p(X \& Y) + p(X \& \sim Y)$, and $p(X \& \sim Y) = p(X) - p(X \& Y)$)

$p(\sim A \& B) = p(\sim B \& C) = 0$

   $\downarrow$  (by Theorem 3)

$p(\sim A \& C \& B) = p(\sim A \& C \& \sim B) = 0$

   $\downarrow$

$p(\sim A \ \& \ C \ \& \ B) + p(\sim A \ \& \ C \ \& \ \sim B) = 0$

$\quad \downarrow \quad$ (by Axiom 3)

$p((\sim A \ \& \ C \ \& \ B) \lor (\sim A \ \& \ C \ \& \ \sim B)) = 0$

$\quad \downarrow$

$p((\sim A \ \& \ C) \ \& \ (B \lor \sim B)) = 0$

$\quad \downarrow$

$p(\sim A \ \& \ C) = 0$

$\quad \downarrow \quad$ (since $X = X \ \& \ (Y \lor \sim Y) = (X \ \& \ Y) \lor (X \ \& \ \sim Y)$, we have, by Axiom 3, that $p$
$\quad\quad (X) = p(X \ \& \ Y) + p(X \ \& \ \sim Y)$, and $p(X \ \& \ \sim Y) = p(X) - p(X \ \& \ Y)$)

$p(A \ \& \ C) = p(C)$

$\quad \downarrow \quad$ (CP)

$p(A \mid C) = 1.$

**Theorem 33:** $p(A \mid B \ \& \ C) < p(A \mid B)$ if and only if $p(A \mid B \ \& \ C) < p(A \mid B \ \& \ \sim C)$.

**Proof:**

$p(A \mid B \ \& \ C) < p(A \mid B)$

$\quad \updownarrow \quad$ (Theorem 28)

$p(A \mid B \ \& \ C) < p(A \mid B \ \& \ C) \cdot p(C \mid B) + p(A \mid B \ \& \ \sim C) \cdot p(\sim C \mid B)$

$\quad \updownarrow$

$p(A \mid B \ \& \ C) - p(A \mid B \ \& \ C) \cdot p(C \mid B) < p(A \mid B \ \& \ \sim C) \cdot p(\sim C \mid B)$

$\quad \updownarrow$

$p(A \mid B \ \& \ C) \cdot [1 - p(C \mid B)] < p(A \mid B \ \& \ \sim C) \cdot p(\sim C \mid B)$

$\quad \updownarrow \quad$ (Theorem 9)

$p(A \mid B \ \& \ C) \cdot p(\sim C \mid B) < p(A \mid B \ \& \ \sim C) \cdot p(\sim C \mid B)$

$\quad \updownarrow$

$p(A \mid B \ \& \ C) < p(A \mid B \ \& \ \sim C).$

**Theorem 34:**

$$\frac{p(A \mid B)}{p(A \mid \sim B)} = \frac{\dfrac{p(B \mid A)}{p(\sim B \mid A)}}{\dfrac{P(B)}{P(\sim B)}}$$

**Proof:**

$$\frac{p(A \mid B)}{p(A \mid \sim B)}$$

$$= \quad \text{(by Bayes's Theorem)}$$

$$\frac{\left(\dfrac{p(B|A) \cdot p(A)}{p(B)}\right)}{\left(\dfrac{p(\sim B|A) \cdot p(A)}{p(\sim B)}\right)}$$

$$=$$

$$\frac{\left(\dfrac{p(B|A)}{p(B)}\right)}{\left(\dfrac{p(\sim B|A)}{p(\sim B)}\right)}$$

$$=$$

$$\frac{\left(\dfrac{p(B|A)}{p(\sim B|A)}\right)}{\left(\dfrac{p(B)}{p(\sim B)}\right)}$$

# References

Adler, Jonathan Eric. 2002. *Belief's Own Ethics*. Cambridge, Mass.; London: MIT Press.

Alston, William P. 1980. 'Level-Confusions in Epistemology'. In *Midwest Studies in Philosophy, vol. V: Studies in Epistemology*, edited by P. French, T. Uehling Jr, and H. K. Wettstein. Minneapolis: University of Minnesota Press.

———. 1983. 'What's Wrong with Immediate Knowledge?'. *Synthese* 55: 73–95.

———. 1986. 'Epistemic Circularity'. *Philosophical Studies* 47: 1–28.

———. 1993. *The Reliability of Sense Perception*. Ithaca, N.Y.: Cornell University Press.

Aristotle. 1994. *Posterior Analytics*. Translated by J. Barnes. 2nd ed. Oxford: Clarendon.

Armstrong, David M. 1973. *Belief, Truth and Knowledge*. London: Cambridge University Press.

Audi, Robert. 1993. *The Structure of Justification*. Cambridge: Cambridge University Press.

Bergmann, Michael. 2000. 'Externalism and Skepticism'. *Philosophical Review* 109: 159–94.

Bird, Alexander. 2003. 'Nozick's Fourth Condition'. *Facta Philosophica* 5: 141–51.

Blackburn, Simon. 1980. 'Truth, Realism, and the Regulation of Theory'. In *Midwest Studies in Philosophy, Vol. V, Studies in Epistemology*, edited by P. French, T. Uehling Jr, and H. K. Wettstein. Minneapolis: University of Minnesota Press.

Boghossian, Paul. 2000. 'Knowledge of Logic'. In *New Essays on the A Priori*, edited by P. Boghossian and C. Peacocke. Oxford: Oxford University Press.

———. 2001. 'How Are Objective Epistemic Reasons Possible?'. *Philosophical Studies* 106: 340–80.

———. 2003. 'Blind Reasoning'. *Aristotelian Society Supplementary Volume* 77: 225–48.

BonJour, Laurence. 1985. *The Structure of Empirical Knowledge*. Cambridge, Massachusetts: Harvard University Press.

———. 1999. 'The Dialectic of Foundationalism and Coherentism'. In *The Blackwell Guide to Epistemology*, edited by J. Greco and E. Sosa. Malden, Massachusetts and Oxford: Blackwell.

Brown, Jessica. 2003. 'The Reductio Argument and Transmission of Warrant'. In *New Essays on Semantic Externalism and Self-Knowledge*, edited by S. Nuccetelli. Cambridge, Massachusetts: MIT Press.

Brueckner, Anthony. 1994. 'The Structure of the Skeptical Argument'. *Philosophy and Phenomenological Research* 54: 827–35.

Burnyeat, Myles, and Michael Frede, eds. 1997. *The Original Sceptics: A Controversy*. Indianapolis: Hackett.

Byrne, Alex. 2004. 'How Hard Are the Sceptical Paradoxes?'. *Noûs* 38: 299–325.

Cappelen, Herman, and Ernie Lepore. 2003. 'Context Shifting Arguments'. In *Philosophical Perspectives 17: Language and Philosophical Linguistics*, edited by D. Zimmerman and J. Hawthorne.

Carnap, Rudolf. 1962. *Logical Foundations of Probability*. 2nd ed. Chicago and London: University of Chicago Press.

Christiensen, David. 1999. 'Measuring Confirmation'. *Journal of Philosophy* 96: 437–61.

Cohen, Stewart. 2002. 'Basic Knowledge and the Problem of Easy Knowledge'. *Philosophy and Phenomenological Research* 65: 309–29.

Conee, Earl. 2005a. 'Contextualism Contested'. In *Contemporary Debates in Epistemology*, edited by M. Steup and E. Sosa. Oxford: Blackwell.

——. 2005b. 'Contextualism Contested Some More'. In *Contemporary Debates in Epistemology*, edited by M. Steup and E. Sosa. Oxford: Blackwell.

Davidson, Donald. 1990. 'The Structure and Content of Truth'. *Journal of Philosophy* 87: 279–328.

Davies, Martin. 1998. 'Externalism, Architecturalism, and Epistemic Warrant'. In *Knowing Our Own Minds*, edited by C. Wright, B. Smith, and C. Macdonald. Oxford: Oxford University Press.

DeRose, Keith. 1995. 'Solving the Skeptical Problem'. *Philosophical Review* 104: 1–52.

Descartes, René. 1984. 'Meditations on First Philosophy'. In *The Philosophical Writings of Descartes. Volume II*, edited by J. Cottingham, R. Stoothoff, and D. Murdoch. Cambridge: Cambridge University Press.

Dowling, W. Jay. 1999. 'The Development of Music Perception and Cognition'. In *The Pychology of Music*, edited by D. Deutsch. San Diego, California: Academic Press.

Dretske, Fred. 1970. 'Epistemic Operators'. *Journal of Philosophy* 67: 1007–23.

Earman, John. 1992. *Bayes or Bust?: A Critical Examination of Bayesian Confirmation Theory*. Cambridge, Mass.: MIT Press.

Feldman, Richard. 1985. 'Reliability and Justification'. *The Monist* 68: 159–74.

——. 1988. 'Epistemic Obligations'. In *Philosophical Perspectives, 2, Epistemology*, edited by J. E. Tomberlin. Atascadero, California: Ridgeview.

——. 2001. 'Skeptical Problems, Contextualist Solutions'. *Philosophical Studies* 103: 61–85.

Fennell, Damien, and Nancy Cartwright. 2010. 'Does Roush Show that Evidence Should be Probable?'. *Synthese* 175: 289–310.

Fine, Arthur. 1984a. 'And Not Antirealism Either'. *Noûs* 18: 51–65.

——. 1984b. 'The Natural Ontological Attitude'. In *Scientific Realism*, edited by J. Leplin. Berkeley: University of California Press.

Fitch, Frederic B. 1946. 'Self-Reference in Philosophy'. *Mind* 55: 64–73.

Fitelson, Branden. 2001a. 'A Bayesian Account of Independent Evidence with Applications'. *Philosophy of Science* 68: 123–40.

——. 2001b. 'Studies in Bayesian Confirmation Theory'. PhD Dissertation, University of Wisconsin, Madison.

Fogelin, Robert J. 1994. *Pyrrhonian Reflections on Knowledge and Justification*. New York and Oxford: Oxford University Press.

Foley, Richard. 1993. *Working without a Net*. New York: Oxford University Press.

Forbes, Graeme. 1983. 'Nozick on Scepticism'. *Philosophical Quarterly* 34: 43–52.

Forster, Michael N. 2008. *Kant and Skepticism*. Princeton, N.J.: Princeton University Press.

Gettier, Edmund. 1963. 'Is Justified True Belief Knowledge?'. *Analysis* 23: 121–3.

Gillies, Donald. 1986. 'In Defense of the Popper-Miller Argument'. *Philosophy of Science* 53: 110–13.

Glynn, Luke. 2010. 'Deterministic Chance'. *British Journal for the Philosophy of Science* 61: 51–80.

Goldman, Alvin I. 1976. 'Discrimination and Perceptual Knowledge'. *Journal of Philosophy* 73: 771–91.

——. 1983. 'Review of Robert Nozick, Philosophical Explanations'. *Philosophical Review* 92: 81–8.

Goldman, Alvin I. 1986. *Epistemology and Cognition*. Cambridge, Mass.: Harvard University Press.

——. 1988. 'Strong and Weak Justification'. In *Philosophical Perspectives, 2 Epistemology*, edited by J. E. Tomberlin. Atascadero, California: Ridgeview.

——. 1991. 'Epistemic Folkways and Scientific Epistemology'. In *Liaisons: Philosophy Meets the Cognitive and Social Sciences*. Cambridge, Massachusetts and London, England: MIT Press.

——. 2009. 'Recursive Tracking versus Process Reliabilism'. *Philosophy and Phenomenological Research* 79: 223–30.

Grover, D., J. Camp, and N. Belnap. 1975. 'A Prosentential Theory of Truth'. *Philosophical Studies* 27: 73–125.

Haack, Susan. 1997. '"The Ethics of Belief" Reconsidered'. In *The Philosophy of Roderick M. Chisholm*, edited by L. E. Hahn. Chicago and La Salle, Illinois: Open Court.

Hájek, Alan. 2003. 'What Conditional Probability Could Not Be'. *Synthese* 137: 273–323.

Hankinson, R. J. 1995. *The Sceptics*. London: Routledge.

Harman, Gilbert. 1973. *Thought*. Princeton, N.J.: Princeton University Press.

Hawthorne, John. 2004. *Knowledge and Lotteries*. Oxford: Oxford University Press.

——. 2005. 'The Case for Closure'. In *Contemporary Debates in Epistemology*, edited by M. Steup and E. Sosa. Malden, Massachusetts and Oxford: Blackwell.

Hoefer, Carl. 2007. 'The Third Way on Objective Probability: A Sceptic's Guide to Objective Chance'. *Mind* 116: 549–996.

Hofweber, Thomas. 1999. 'Contextualism and the Meaning-Intention Problem'. In *Cognition, Agency and Rationality*, edited by K. Korta, E. Sosa and X. Arrazola. Dortrecht: Kluwer Academic Publishers.

Huber, Franz. 2008. 'Milne's Argument for the Log-Ratio Measure'. *Philosophy of Science* 75: 413–20.

Iranzo, Valeriano, and Ignacio Martínez de Lejarza. 2010. 'Medidas de confirmación incremental. Un análisis comparativo'. *Teorema* 29.

Jeffrey, Richard. 1992. *Probability and the Art of Judgment*. Cambridge: Cambridge University Press.

Joyce, James. 1999. *The Foundations of Causal Decision Theory*. Cambridge: Cambridge University Press.

——. 2003. 'Bayes' Theorem', *The Stanford Encyclopedia of Philosophy (Fall 2008 Edition)*, edited by Edward N. Zalta. URL = <http://plato.stanford.edu/ archives/fall2008/entries/bayes-theorem/>

Klein, Peter. 1998. 'Foundationalism and the Infinite Regress of Reasons'. *Philosophy and Phenomenological Research* 58: 919–25.

——. 1999. 'Human Knowledge and the Infinite Regress of Reasons'. *Philosophical Perspectives* 13: 297–325.

Kolmogorov, A. N. 1933. *Grundbegriffe der Wahrscheinlichkeitsrechnung*. Berlin: Springer.

Kripke, Saul. 1980. *Naming and Necessity*. Oxford: Blackwell.

Kvanvig, Jonathan L. 2006. 'Closure Principles'. *Philosophy Compass* 1/3: 256–67.

Lehrer, Keith. 1965. 'Knowledge, Truth and Evidence'. *Analysis* 25: 168–75.

——. 1974. 'The Gettier Problem and the Analysis of Knowledge'. In *Justification and Knowledge*, edited by G. S. Pappas. Dordrecht: Reidel.

Lehrer, Keith. and Thomas Paxson Jr 1969. 'Knowledge: Undefeated Justified True Belief'. *Journal of Philosophy* 66: 225–37.

Lewis, David. 1973. *Counterfactuals*. Oxford: Blackwell.

——. 1986. 'A Subjectivist's Guide to Objective Chance'. In *Philosophical Papers, Volume II*. Oxford: Oxford University Press.

——. 1994. 'Humean Supervenience Debugged'. *Mind* 103: 473–90.

Luper-Foy, Steven. 1984. 'The Epistemic Predicament: Knowledge, Nozickian Tracking, and Scepticism'. *Australasian Journal of Philosophy* 62: 26–49.

Luzzi, Federico. 2010. 'Counter-Closure'. *Australasian Journal of Philosophy* 88: 673–83.

Lycan, William G. 1977. 'Evidence One Does Not Possess'. *Australasian Journal of Philosophy* 55: 114–26.

McDowell, John. 1981. 'Anti-realism and the Epistemology of Understanding'. In *Meaning and Understanding*, edited by H. Parret and J. Bourveresse. Berlin: de Gruyter.

——. 1984. 'Wittgenstein on Following a Rule'. *Synthese* 58: 325–63.

——. 1987. 'In Defence of Modesty'. In *Michael Dummett: Contributions to Philosophy*, edited by B. Taylor. Dordrecht: Martinus Nijhoff.

Martin, Raymond. 1983. 'Tracking Nozick's Sceptic: A Better Method'. *Analysis* 43: 28–33.

Milne, Peter. 1996. 'log[p(h/eb)/p(h/b)] is the One True Measure of Confirmation'. *Philosophy of Science* 63: 21–6.

Moore, G. E. 1939. 'Proof of an External World'. *Proceedings of the British Academy* 25: 273–300.

Nagel, Thomas. 1986. *The View from Nowhere*. Oxford: Oxford University Press.

Nozick, Robert. 1981. *Philosophical Explanations*. Cambridge, Massachusetts: Harvard University Press.

Papineau, David. 1992. 'Reliabilism, Induction and Scepticism'. *Philosophical Quarterly* 42: 1–20.

Plantinga, Alvin. 1993. *Warrant: The Current Debate*. New York and Oxford: Oxford University Press.

Plato. 1963. 'Theaetetus'. In *The Collected Dialogues of Plato*, edited by E. Hamilton and H. Cairns. Princeton, N.J.: Princeton University Press.

Popkin, Richard H. 1951–2. 'Berkeley and Pyrrhonism'. *Review of Metaphysics* 5: 223–46.

——. 2003. *The History of Scepticism: From Savonarola to Bayle*. Oxford: Oxford University Press.

Popper, Karl. 2002. *The Logic of Scientific Discovery*. London: Routledge.

Price, H. H. 1932. *Perception*. London: Methuen.

Price, Huw. 1988. *Facts and the Function of Truth*. Oxford: Blackwell.

Pryor, James. 2000. 'The Skeptic and the Dogmatist'. *Noûs* 34: 517–49.

——. 2004. 'What's Wrong With Moore's Argument?'. *Philosophical Issues* 14: 349–78.

Putnam, Hilary. 1962. 'The Analytic and the Synthetic'. In *Scientific Explanation, Space, and Time, Minnesota Studies in the Philosophy of Science, vol. 111*, edited by H. Feigl and G. Maxwell. Minneapolis: University of Minnesota Press.

——. 1963. 'An Examination of Grünbaum's Philosophy of Geometry'. In *Philosophy of Science, the Delaware Seminar, vol. 2. 1962–1963*, edited by B. Baumrin. New York: John Wiley & Sons.

——. 1975. 'The Meaning of "Meaning"'. In *Mind, Language and Reality. Philosophical Papers, Volume 2*. Cambridge: Cambridge University Press.

——. 1981. *Reason, Truth and History*. Cambridge: Cambridge University Press.

Putnam, Hilary. 1994. 'Sense, Nonsense and the Senses: An Inquiry into the Powers of the Human Mind'. *Journal of Philosophy* 91: 445–517.

Quine, Willard Van Orman. 1970. *Philosophy of Logic.* Englewood Cliffs: Prentice Hall.

———. 1980. 'Two Dogmas of Empiricism'. In *From a Logical Point of View.* Cambridge, Mass.: Harvard University Press. Original edition, 1953.

Ricketts, Thomas G. 1986. 'Objectivity & Objecthood: Frege's Metaphysics of Judgment'. In *Frege Synthesized: Essays on the Philosophical and Foundational Work of Gottlob Frege*, edited by L. Haaparanta and J. Hintikka. Dordrecht: Reidel.

———. 1996. 'Logic and Truth in Frege'. *Aristotelian Society Supplementary Volume* 70: 121–40.

Roush, Sherrilyn. 2005. *Tracking Truth.* Oxford: Oxford University Press.

Russell, Bruce. 2001. 'Epistemic and Moral Duty'. In *Knowledge, Truth, and Duty*, edited by M. Steup. Oxford and New York: Oxford University Press.

Schaffer, J. 2007. 'Deterministic Chance?'. *British Journal for the Philosophy of Science* 58: 113–40.

Schiffer, Stephen. 1996. 'Contextualist Solutions to Scepticism'. *Proceedings of the Aristotelian Society* 96: 317–33.

Schlesinger, George N. 1995. 'Measuring Degrees of Confirmation'. *Analysis* 55: 208–12.

Sextus Empiricus. 1990. *Outlines of Pyrrhonism.* Translated by R. G. Bury. Buffalo, New York: Prometheus Books.

Shah, Nishi. 2003. 'How Truth Governs Belief'. *Philosophical Review* 112: 447–82.

———. 2006. 'A New Argument for Evidentialism'. *Philosophical Quarterly* 56: 481–98.

——— and J. David Velleman. 2005. 'Doxastic Deliberation'. *Philosophical Review* 114: 497–534.

Shope, Robert. 1978. 'The Conditional Fallacy in Contemporary Philosophy'. *Journal of Philosophy* 75: 397–413.

———. 1984. 'Cognitive Abilities, Conditionals, and Knowledge'. *Journal of Philosophy* 81: 29–48.

Sosa, Ernest. 1970. 'Two Conceptions of Knowledge'. *Journal of Philosophy* 67: 59–66.

———. 1994. 'Philosophical Scepticism and Epistemic Circularity'. *Aristotelian Society Supplementary Volume* 68: 263–90.

———. 1999. 'How to Defeat Opposition to Moore'. In *Philosophical Perspectives, 13, Epistemology*, edited by J. E. Tomberlin. Malden, Massachusetts and Oxford: Blackwell.

———. 2000. 'Skepticism and Contextualism'. *Philosophical Issues* 10: 1–18.

Stalnaker, Robert C. 1968. 'A Theory of Conditionals'. In *Studies in Logical Theory*, edited by N. Rescher. Oxford: Blackwell.

Steup, Matthias. 1996. *An Introduction to Contemporary Epistemology.* Upper Saddle River, N.J.: Prentice Hall.

Strawson, Peter F. 1949. 'Truth'. *Analysis* 9: 83–97.

Stroud, Barry. 1984. *The Significance of Philosophical Scepticism.* Oxford: Clarendon Press.

———. 1989. 'Understanding Human Knowledge in General'. In *Knowledge and Scepticism*, edited by M. Clay and K. Lehrer. Boulder, Colorado: Westview Press.

———. 1994. 'Scepticism, "Externalism", and the Goal of Epistemology'. *Aristotelian Society Supplementary Volume* 68: 291–307.

Swain, Marshall 1974. 'Epistemic Defeasibility'. *American Philosophical Quarterly* 11: 15–25.

Tinbergen, N. 1951. *The Study of Instinct.* Oxford: Clarendon.

Van Cleve, James. 1979. 'Foundationalism, Epistemic Principles and the Cartesian Circle'. *Philosophical Review* 88: 55–91.

Van Cleve, James. 1984. 'Reliability, Justification, and the Problem of Induction'. In *Midwest Studies in Philosophy, Vol. 9: Causation annd Causal Theories*, edited by P. French, T. Uehling Jr and H. K. Wettstein. Minneapolis: University of Minnesota Press.

——. 2003. 'Is Knowledge Easy—or Impossible? Externalism as the Only Alternative to Skepticism'. In *The Skeptics. Contemporary Essays*, edited by S. Luper. Aldershot, Hampshire: Ashgate.

van Fraasen, Bas. 1995. 'Fine-Grained Opinion, Conditional Probability and the Logic of Belief'. *Journal of Philosophical Logic* 24: 349–77.

Vogel, Jonathan. 1987. 'Tracking, Closure, and Inductive Knowledge'. In *The Possibility of Knowledge: Nozick and His Critics*, edited by S. Luper-Foy. Totowa, New Jersey: Rowman & Littlefield.

——. 1990. 'Are There Counterexamples to the Closure Principle?'. In *Doubting. Contemporary Perspectives on Skepticism*, edited by M. D. Roth and G. Ross. Dordrecht: Kluwer Academic Publishers.

——. 2000. 'Reliabilism Leveled'. *Journal of Philosophy* 97: 602–23.

——. 2004. 'Skeptical Arguments'. *Philosophical Issues* 14: 426–55.

Ward, W. Dixon. 1999. 'Absolute Pitch'. In *The Psychology of Music*, edited by D. Deutsch. San Diego, California: Academic Press.

Warfield, Ted A. 2005. 'Knowledge from Falsehood'. *Philosophical Perspectives* 19: 405–16.

Williams, Bernard. 1974. 'Wittgenstein and Idealism'. In *Understanding Wittgenstein, Royal Institute of Philosophy Lectures, vol. 7, 1972–73*, edited by G. Vesey. London: Macmillan.

Williamson, Tim. 2000. *Knowledge and Its Limits*. Oxford: Oxford University Press.

Wright, Crispin. 1985. 'Facts and Certainty'. *Proceedings of the British Academy* 71: 429–72.

——. 2000. 'Cogency and Question-Begging: Some Reflections on McKinsey's Paradox and Putnam's Proof'. *Philosophical Issues* 10: 140–63.

——. 2002. '(Anti-)Sceptics Simple and Subtle: G. E. Moore and John McDowell'. *Philosophy and Phenomenological Research* 65: 330–48.

——. 2004. 'Warrant for Nothing (and Foundations for Free)?'. *Proceedings of the Aristotelian Society Supp. Vol.* 78: 167–212.

Yates, J. Frank. 1990. *Judgement and Decision Making*. Englewood Cliffs: Prentice Hall; London: Prentice-Hall International (UK).

Zalabardo, José L. 1996. 'Predicates, Properties and the Goal of a Theory of Reference'. *Grazer Philosophische Studien* 51: 121–62.

——. 2000a. *Introduction to the Theory of Logic*. Boulder, Colorado: Westview Press.

——. 2000b. 'Realism Detranscendentalized'. *European Journal of Philosophy* 8 (1): 63–88.

——. 2001. 'Towards a Nominalist Empiricism'. *Proceedings of the Aristotelian Society* 101: 29–52.

——. 2005. 'Externalism, Skepticism and the Problem of Easy Knowledge'. *Philosophical Review* 114: 33–61.

——. 2006. 'BonJour, Externalism and the Regress Problem'. *Synthese* 148: 135–68.

——. 2008. 'Internalist Foundationalism and the Problem of the Epistemic Regress'. *Philosophy and Phenomenological Research* 77: 34–58.

——. 2009a. 'An Argument for the Likelihood-Ratio Measure of Confirmation'. *Analysis* 69: 630–5.

——. 2009b. 'How I Know I'm Not a Brain in a Vat'. *Royal Institute of Philosophy Supplement* 64: 65–88.

Zalabardo, José L. 2010. 'Why Believe the Truth? Shah and Velleman on the Aim of Belief'. *Philosophical Explorations* 13: 1–21.

——. 2011. 'Boghossian on Inferential Knowledge'. *Analytic Philosophy* 52: 124–39.

——. forthcoming-a. 'Semantic Normativity and Naturalism'. In *Continuum Companion to Philosophy of Language*, edited by M. García Carpintero and M. Kölbel. London: Continuum.

——. forthcoming-b. 'Wright on Moore'. In *Wittgenstein, Epistemology and Mind. Themes from the Philosophy of Crispin Wright*, edited by A. Coliva. Oxford: Oxford University Press.

# Index